AF778427

Attorney's Guide *to* Document Examination

Attorney's Guide *to* Document Examination

Katherine M. Koppenhaver

QUORUM BOOKS
Westport, Connecticut • London

Library of Congress Cataloging-in-Publication Data

Koppenhaver, Katherine.
Attorney's guide to document examination / Katherine M. Koppenhaver.
p. cm.
Includes bibliographical references and index.
ISBN 1-56720-470-8 (alk. paper)
1. Legal documents—Identification. 2. Writing—Identification. 3. Forgery—Prevention. 4. Criminal investigation. I. Title.
HV8074.K66 2002
363.25'65—dc21 2001041801

British Library Cataloguing in Publication Data is available.

Copyright © 2002 by Katherine M. Koppenhaver

All rights reserved. No portion of this book may be reproduced, by any process or technique, without the express written consent of publisher.

Library of Congress Catalog Card Number: 2001041801
ISBN: 1-56720-470-8

First published in 2002

Quorum Books, 88 Post Road West, Westport, CT 06881
An imprint of Greenwood Publishing Group, Inc.
www.quorumbooks.com

Printed in the United States of America

The paper used in this book complies with the Permanent Paper Standard issued by the National Information Standards Organization (Z39.48-1984).

P

Copyright Acknowledgments

The author and publisher gratefully acknowledge permission for use of the following material:

Figures 3.1, 3.2, 3.3, 3.4, 4.1, 4.2, 6.1, 7.1, 9.1, 9.2, 11.1, 11.2, 11.3, 11.4 by William A. Koppenhaver

In order to keep this title in print and available to the academic community, this edition was produced using digital reprint technology in a relatively short print run. This would not have been attainable using traditional methods. Although the cover has been changed from its original appearance, the text remains the same and all materials and methods used still conform to the highest book-making standards.

This book is dedicated to David Preller, Jr.
who personifies what a good lawyer should be

Contents

Figures and Tables

FIGURES

TABLES

Acknowledgments

Thanks to Marcel Matley, who has a Master's degree in Library Science, for his research in the field of document examination and his assistance with Chapter 18. Also thanks to Emily Will, and Lee Kilty, for their assistance in editing the book; and to Susan Abbey, Phyllis Cook, Terry Davenport, Barbara Downer, Heidi Harralson, Reed Hayes, Gertrude Lawrence, David Liebman, Rita Lord, Sheila Lowe, Joe Lucas, Jacqueline Joseph, and my secretary, Claire Strozyk, for their assistance in proof-reading; and to my daughter, Carol Vitek, and Jim Hunter who assisted with the typing.

A special thanks goes to my husband, Bill, who photographed the exhibits used throughout this book and assisted me with the chapters dealing with technical material.

Introduction

Forensic document examiners study questioned documents in order to draw conclusions about the authenticity or spuriousness of the documents. This includes comparing and identifying handwriting and signatures, detecting alterations such as erasures and overwrites, deciphering indented writing, and determining the sequence of writing and similar problems that concern suspect documents and their content. Forensic document examination includes documents created on typewriters and printers as well as counterfeit documents.

The most common problems in forensic document examination revolve around signature identification on negotiable instruments such as checks, contracts, deeds, and credit charges. Other types of cases include embezzlement, industrial espionage, threats, extortion, and blackmail. Who is the rightful heir in a contested will case? Who has made threats through an anonymous letter? Have medical records been altered? Any type of financial or legal document can be questioned.

The process of examination involves a thorough and detailed study of the questioned documents. In most cases, questioned documents are compared with known genuine writing to determine their status. Attorneys need to know how to select appropriate documents for forensic document examiners and what forensic document examiners can and cannot determine about the evidence.

In the age of junk science, attorneys need to know the basic principles of handwriting identification in order to challenge incorrect statements or conclusions.

Many attorneys have asked for basic information about document examination. This book has been written for all the attorneys who find themselves dealing with questioned document cases.

Part I

The Document Examiner

1

Choosing a Forensic Document Examiner

WHAT IS A FORENSIC DOCUMENT EXAMINER?

The field of forensic document examination offers services related to the study of documents or other materials containing handwriting, typewriting, or printing. A forensic document examiner draws conclusions about documents including verification of the authenticity of documents, signature comparison and identification, alterations of documents such as erasures, indented writing, the sequence of writing, and any other problem that arises concerning the writing on documents. Forensic document examiners are also known as handwriting experts or handwriting analysts.

Some forensic document examiners specialize in a particular aspect of forensic document examination. There are ink experts and experts on typewriters, rare books, stamps of all kinds, baseball cards and autographs of the rich and famous. A few document examiners are involved in the chemical analysis of paper and ink while others study only the characteristics of handwriting in order to identify the executor of a document.

Forensic document examiners work with any substance that can impart a written message. While documents most frequently consist of paper and pen or pencil, forensic document examiners study typewritten materials, spray painted graffiti on walls or locker doors, lipstick on mirrors, chalk on blackboards and many other substances.

Forensic document examiners can act as consultants to attorneys. This involves doing research, conducting experiments, checking credentials of an opposing expert, teaching a lawyer about handwriting identification, and helping prepare cross-examination questions for deposition and court. Examiners may be asked to review the deposition of an opposing document examiner in order to prepare questions for cross-examination in court. They may provide resource material, and assist the attorney during a deposition or court appearance in evaluating the answers of opposing examiners.

QUALIFICATIONS NEEDED BY DOCUMENT EXAMINERS

An expert is a person qualified by knowledge, experience, special training, or skill who is capable of forming accurate opinions of his own that represent a division of science, branch of art, or department of trade in matters not generally known without specialized education or training.

One who has made a specialized study of technical subjects is usually regarded as competent to testify as an expert concerning these subjects. There are some document examiners who claim that there is only one method of learning to be a forensic document examiner and it is usually the method in which they learned the subject. There is always more than one way to learn any subject and this is also true for document examination, however, anyone can claim to be a handwriting expert. It is in everyone's best interest to carefully screen the credentials of anyone claiming to be a forensic document examiner.

EDUCATIONAL BACKGROUND

Unlike other professions, there isn't a college or graduate degree in forensic document examination. A college degree can be of value to a document examiner, but it is not an essential qualification since students cannot learn how to examine documents in college. For a college degree to be relevant, it should relate to criminal justice or forensic science.

There are a few college courses in forensic document examination. George Washington University, in Washington, D.C., offers a course as part of its Master's degree in forensic science. Other courses are offered as part of a criminal justice or forensic science curriculum at other colleges. These courses are introductory courses that cover basic information in the field of questioned documents.

Expert witnesses have varied backgrounds that qualify them to be experts in their fields. This is especially true in the field of document examination. Most forensic document examiners obtain their credentials independently through reading as well as observing, studying, comparing, and experimenting. They generally apprentice to other document examiners because there is no standard training program for document examiners.

Some correspondence courses are now on the market for anyone interested in learning how to analyze documents. At present there are courses being offered by Andrew Bradley, the Institute of Applied Science (IAS), and the National Questioned Document Association (NQDA) through the Institute of Graphological Science (TIGS). Andrew Bradley's course offers an introduction to document examination. He also markets an advanced course for document examiners who wish to continue their education. The American Institute of Applied Science's course is an introductory course consisting of eight lessons on various aspects of questioned documents.

The Basic Forensic Document Examination Course offered by the National Questioned Document Association has been written by Katherine Koppenhaver and Judith Housley, both Certified Document Examiners (CDE). This course provides detailed information that document examiners need to know in order to analyze questioned document cases. In addition to the principles of document examination, the course includes over 50 actual cases that each student must solve. Many of the document examiners who have completed this course are working actively in the field of questioned document examination.

AFFILIATION IN A NATIONAL DOCUMENT ORGANIZATION

Affiliation in an organization of forensic document examiners is important. Professionals need to continually update their knowledge in their area of expertise. Membership in a professional association gives document examiners access to new information in their field and enables them to broaden their perspective and share new ideas with others in their profession.

There are several organizations for document examiners in the United States. These fall into two categories: government trained examiners and privately trained examiners. The government trained examiners belong to the:

- American Society of Questioned Document Examiners (ASQDE),
- Questioned Document Section of the American Academy of Forensic Science (AAFS),
- International Association for Identification, Questioned Document Section, (IAI).

Regional chapters in the field of forensic science include the:

- Southwest Association of Forensic Scientists,
- Southern Association of Forensic Scientists,
- Northeast Association of Forensic Scientists,
- Mid-Atlantic Association of Forensic Scientists,
- Mid-Western Association of Forensic Scientists.

The associations for document examiners in private practice consist of the:

- National Association of Document Examiners (NADE),
- World Association of Document Examiners (WADE),
- Independent Association of Questioned Document Examiners (IAQDE),
- Association of Forensic Document Examiners (AFDE), and
- National Questioned Document Association (NQDA).

Some pseudo-experts have created document organizations in which they are the only member in order to enhance their credentials.

CERTIFICATION

One of the purposes of the associations for document examiners is certification of its qualified members. The American Academy of Forensic Sciences and the American Society of Questioned Document Examiners formed the American Board of Forensic Document Examiners. According to a pamphlet published by the ABFDE, the purpose of the board was "to identify forensic scientists qualified to provide essential professional services for the nation's judicial and executive branches of government, by means of structured Certifying Boards whose objective is to establish, enhance, and maintain as necessary, standards of qualification for those who practice forensic science and to certify as qualified specialists those voluntary applicants who comply with the requirements of the Board."

All of the organizations of document examiners in the private sector provide certification for their members. Certification requirements vary for each organization, but they all require testing before a member can be certified and some have a requirement that members be recertified periodically. Some members are required to participate in proficiency testing.

Certification is not required in order for a document examiner to qualify in court as an expert, but it does assist in identifying experts who have been tested and found to be knowledgeable in the field. Most certifying organizations require written and/or oral testing. The organizations that certify their members include NADE, WADE, NQDA, IAQDE, AFDE, and ABFDE. Some experts have been certified without undergoing testing. The American Board of Forensic Document Examiners grandfathered in a majority of their original members.

The American Board of Forensic Document Examiners calls their members Fellows. Other organizations call their members diplomates. Diplomate is generally reserved for experts who are more experienced document examiners.

SEMINARS

The document examiners' associations generally conduct annual seminars. Many organizations require their certified members to update their training by attending conferences. Most conferences are open to all document examiners and provide an opportunity for them to keep abreast of new developments in the field.

Some seminars consist of the presentation of papers that cover research projects or experiments. Other seminars provide training workshops and lectures to reinforce standard procedures and to introduce advances in the detection of fraudulent documents.

GRAPHOLOGISTS

A graphologist studies handwriting to determine the personality of writers from their handwriting characteristics. Training in graphology will not prepare an individual to testify as a document examiner, but it can be a valuable supplement to document examination training. The graphologist is trained to recognize the subtle similarities and differences in handwriting. She learns to distinguish class and individual characteristics and to recognize the frequency with which a particular characteristic in handwriting is likely to occur. If the expert is a graphologist, make sure that she has sufficient additional training in document examination.

GOVERNMENT DOCUMENT EXAMINERS

Forensic document examiners employed by various government agencies attend formal classes in all aspects of questioned document work. Trainees are required to read relevant books on the subject during their apprenticeship to certified document examiners in an approved laboratory. They are allowed to testify as experts only after they have worked under supervision for several years. Forensic document examiners who work for police departments often do not have as much training as federally employed document examiners.

The Secret Service offers training in two-to-three-week increments to members of their organization and to police officers. The training is only an introduction to document examination and is not sufficient to establish anyone as a document examiner. The Federal Bureau of Investigation offers a similar program and both organizations have published letters indicating that their two-week training course does not make one proficient in document examination.

Some retired government agents have taken the Secret Service course or the FBI course and claim it as their only credential for establishing themselves as forensic document examiners. Always check with an examiner to verify that she has had sufficient training in the field of questioned documents.

EXPERIENCE

A forensic document examiner must base her conclusions in part on the frequency that a particular characteristic of handwriting is likely to show up in a writing sample, therefore, she must know how frequently a particular characteristic will appear in handwriting. She must be able to distinguish between class characteristics (those traits shared by a large number of people) and individual characteristics (those not shared) as well as the frequency with which the individual characteristics occur in the general population. This information is based on the examination of thousands of handwriting samples over a period of time.

The amount of actual experience in handling cases both in and out of court is important.

- Does the document examiner work fulltime in the field of document examination?
- How many cases does she handle a year?

- How long has she been a document examiner?
- How many times has she testified in court?
- What percentage of cases are brought to court?
- How many cases has the examiner handled in her career?

PROFICIENCY TESTING

Proficiency testing is a method used to measure the capabilities of technicians in their chosen field. Proficiency testing is available to forensic scientists who want to validate their competency.

Document examiners can participate in proficiency testing through Collaborative Testing Services which offers two tests per year to document examiners. One test is designed for handwriting experts, the other test is geared toward all areas of document examination. Some document examiners' associations also offer proficiency testing to their members.

Dr. Bryan Found and Dr. Doug Rogers of the Forensic Profiling Laboratory at LaTrobe University in Bundoora, Victoria, Australia, are offering proficiency testing to document examiners on a more extensive level. They also offer two tests to document examiners, but their tests are much more comprehensive since they involve a comparison of 250 questioned signatures of handwriting samples for each test. These tests also provide feedback enabling document examiners to review their performance and take corrective action in areas of difficulty.

REFERENCE BOOKS

Every document examiner needs to maintain reference books in her library for easy access. These books need to be read and referenced. Albert Osborn is recognized as the father of document examination and his book, *Questioned Documents*, is considered the bible in the field. *Questioned Documents* was originally published in 1910 with a second edition published in 1929. The principles of handwriting identification have not changed, but other books contain more updated information in other areas of questioned document work, especially modern office equipment.

Ordway Hilton authored the book, *Scientific Examination of Questioned Documents* in 1982. His book, considered a companion to Osborn's *Questioned Documents*, contains information on typewriters and other office equipment. Hilton's book is becoming outdated due to the proliferation of modern communication systems including computers and their peripherals, such as scanners and printers.

Suspect Documents written by Wilson Harrison, is considered the leading authoritative text in England. Russell R. Bradford and Ralph B. Bradford have written *Introduction to Handwriting Examination and Identification,* which complements the information in other textbooks related to the field of questioned documents. Roy A. Huber and A. M. Headrick have published *Handwriting*

Identification: Facts and Fundamentals, which collates information from the leading books in the field of questioned documents. For a more complete listing of books related to the field of questioned documents, see the Appendixes.

Serious document examiners subscribe to trade journals to keep their knowledge up-to-date. Most of the organizations that cater to forensic document examiners produce trade journals and newsletters. The *International Journal of Forensic Document Examiners* published scholarly articles on questioned documents from 1995 to 2000.

Document examiners should have access to a reference library. Marcel Matley compiled *QDE Index* which contains a listing of all articles published in the United States in the past hundred years that pertain to document examination. The book also contains a list of the periodicals where these articles can be found, as well as a list of the authors. This book is ideal for locating articles written by experts in the field of questioned document examination.

Patricia Wellingham-Jones authored *Drugs and Handwriting,* which lists the side effects of various families of drugs, to assist document examiners who study handwriting written under many different conditions. Many document examiners find the *Physician's Desk Reference* also useful for listing the side effects of various medications.

RESEARCH

Research conducted by a document examiner shows a serious interest in one's work. Research projects revolve around the effects of various factors on handwriting, including pathological factors, emotional disturbances, and various physical conditions such as drugs and medication, illnesses, and the affect of the aging process on handwriting.

AUTHORITY

An expert is an authority in the field if she writes books and articles and lectures frequently to her peers on document examination. Authorities are also consulted by other document examiners to give second opinions on cases.

CURRICULUM VITAE

Most experts have a curriculum vitae (CV) available for potential clients. The curriculum vitae should be detailed enough to cover the background of the expert and her history without describing every case that the document examiner has handled.

The information on the curriculum vitae usually covers training and education, membership in a professional association, and the accomplishments of the expert. Accomplishments include articles and books written, lectures and seminars presented, and research projects completed. Awards and special titles may be listed on the curriculum vitae. Court and deposition appearances should also appear on the CV.

The curriculum vitae should be kept up-to-date to accurately reflect the achievements of the expert. Experts revise their curriculum vitae as needed.

Experts should maintain a detailed list of court appearances covering the last four years since this is needed in federal court cases. Publications for the past ten years must also be presented in federal cases.

HOW TO FIND A COMPETENT FORENSIC DOCUMENT EXAMINER

The most important factor in determining competency is the skill of the expert. Does the expert have the necessary skill and experience to do the job? Reputation and referrals are excellent methods of finding a suitable expert. Check the credentials of an expert carefully. What experience does she have? Has she testified in court as an expert witness? Is she certified by a professional organization? Reputable document examiners will provide a list of references and welcome an investigation of their credentials.

A document examiner can usually be located through a state lawyer's manual, law journals (both national and state), legal papers, business newspapers, the yellow pages, and expert witness referrals. There are organizations that maintain lists of experts both in book form, on disk, and on the internet.

Check out the background of a document examiner carefully before engaging her services. Some document examiners have made claims in their curriculum vitae that cannot be substantiated because they do not expect to have their credentials challenged. They may claim to have completed an apprenticeship or state that they are certified when they are not. Some experts have worked for government agencies and imply that they held the position of document examiner for the government when they have never worked in a forensic document laboratory.

Ask specific questions about a document examiner's background and training. One document examiner said, "No," when asked if he had learned anything on his own. Ordway Hilton writes in *Scientific Examination of Questioned Documents*, "The most important qualification of a witness is his ability to do the work. There is no school at which a document examiner, unlike an engineer or a doctor, can study to prepare himself. Self study is the chief means of gaining this special knowledge, and some men have been able to supplement this study by apprenticeship or association with a recognized document examiner or in a recognized laboratory" (p. 405).

Some document examiners always find in favor of their clients. You will get an impartial opinion from such experts only if the document examiner does not know which side you represent in a particular case.

Some forensic document examiners work as parttime examiners, others are retired government employees who enter the field as a means of supplementing their retirement income.

A document examiner should be able to give you specific information about her credentials. If she is vague, she may be trying to cover up a lack of background or experience.

The most important criteria is the ability to do the job. M. K. Mehta in his book, *Identification of Handwriting and Cross-Examination of Experts*, writes, "Identification of handwriting depends mostly on two factors: keen observations and correct interpretation of the writing characteristics" (p. 51). The ability to present evidence convincingly in court is also an essential requirement of a forensic document examiner. All the knowledge and experience that a document examiner possesses is of no use if she cannot communicate that information to the trier-of-fact in a courtroom.

EQUIPMENT FOUND IN A DOCUMENT EXAMINER'S LABORATORY

A forensic document examiner needs instruments to examine documents and determine facts that may not be visible without proper scientific aids.

The microscope is the document examiner's most useful piece of equipment. Most examiners prefer a stereoscopic microscope. A document examiner should have a stereoscopic microscope between ten and fifty power that includes both incident and transmitted illumination. Most stereoscopic microscopes offer a combination of two different powers such as ten and thirty power or fifteen and forty-five power. A more expensive version of a stereoscopic microscope, known as a zoom microscope, offers variable magnification of any power between ten and forty-five power.

A stereoscopic microscope gives the viewer a magnified three-dimensional view. This depth assists in the study of pressure patterns, line intersections, erasures, indentations, writing over folds, and similar queries.

Good nondistorting magnifiers coupled with powerful light sources are part of the document examiner's basic equipment. Various strength magnifiers in the two to eight power range complement a microscope by filling in the gap between what can be seen with the unaided eye and the low power setting of the microscope.

Accurate measuring devices such as rulers, gauges, and grids are necessary for obtaining precise measurements. A twelve-inch steel machinist's ruler with both inch and metric scales is needed as a standard to check other rulers or templates. Plastic grids and transparent evidence rulers are lightweight and nonbreakable but may not be as accurate as steel grids because the plastic may stretch or shrink.

Document examiners use typewriter grids for pica and elite type, that is ten characters per inch (cpi) or twelve cpi. These gauges should be accurate because even a very badly aligned typewritten document will seldom vary more than a 1/25 of an inch. Modern fonts may require additional size grids.

A protractor simplifies the measuring of angles. A micrometer measures the thickness of paper. Digital or dial calipers can be used to make precise size comparisons. Drafting tools, such as a compass or dividers, are also useful for comparing measurements.

A light box simplifies the comparison of documents by the use of transmitted light. One document is superimposed over the other on the light box for quick and easy comparisons. A light box also reveals erasures and alterations to documents. Watermarks can be examined more easily on a light box.

Forensic document examiners use camera equipment for microphotography. Document examiners need to take good close-up pictures of the original documents. A good photograph can be studied in place of the original and can also assist document examiners when they make detailed analyses. Since the handling of an original document can damage it, photographs and photocopies are often used for extended examinations by forensic document examiners. Special effects in photography enable the examiner to study details that cannot be examined otherwise. This includes sidelighting for indented writing and infrared photography for material outside the range of normal light.

SPECIALIZED EQUIPMENT

Specialized equipment is occasionally needed by the document examiner to handle specific technical problems. An Electrostatic Detection Apparatus (ESDA) is an instrument that enables the document examiner to create a visual image of indented writing and make a permanent record of the indentations. It is typically used in the detection of indentations on successive pages of a multipage document such as the pages of a notepad found at a crime scene. An ESDA also reveals indentations left on a document that has been erased. The ESDA is an expensive piece of equipment that is frequently found in federal and state crime labs and some private laboratories (private examiners usually have access to one if needed). Photographing a document using sidelighting generally produces the same results as using the ESDA. Kinderprint also markets a similar device to the ESDA called a Vacu-box.

Infrared and ultraviolet illumination can be used for deciphering and restoring erased or altered material by revealing changes in ink or paper that may not be visible to the naked eye. This enables the document examiner to determine if the same pen was used throughout an entire document or if a page has been substituted in a multipage document.

Infrared radiation of documents consists of placing the material to be examined under infrared illumination and either photographing it using infrared film; or viewing it with an infrared sensitive video camera or a snooperscope to determine if different elements of a document: paper, or ink that appear the same under visible light, react differently under infrared illumination.

Ultraviolet illumination is a similar technique for examining documents. Typically a document is illuminated with different wavelengths of ultraviolet light, commonly referred to as long-wave or short-wave ultraviolet light. Under this illumination certain materials will fluoresce as visible light, which can be seen by the naked eye. As with the infrared, the purpose is to determine if one portion of the document reacts differently than the rest of the document, thereby indicating an addition or alteration.

The Video Spectral Comparator by Foster and Freeman is a video imaging system designed for examining suspect documents utilizing infrared absorption, infrared luminescence, and ultraviolet florescence. It consists of a video camera with a spectral range of 400 to 1,100 nanometers, an integral monitor zoom lens, a variety of light sources, and a wide range of interchangeable camera filters that enable document examiners to view questioned documents under various lighting conditions (including sidelighting) and to enlarge the image up to twenty-five times its size.

Some document examiners scan documents into their computer and study them on the computer screen. Using a graphics program, the document examiner can remove background noise or overwriting in order to see the handwriting more clearly. The examiner can enlarge the computer image and make exhibits for court or deposition.

WHAT SERVICES DOES A DOCUMENT EXAMINER PROVIDE?

Forensic document examiners study documents in order to draw conclusions about their authenticity including the complete document or any part of the document. Document examination covers alterations, substitutions, and counterfeiting of documents in addition to a comparison of handwriting.

Document examiners also conduct research in order to complete their assignments. Research can cover any phase of document examination including researching the background of an opposing examiner. Experts may have to find comparable documents to determine authenticity, research documentary stamps, paper, ink, writing instruments, penmanship systems, or any other material that affects a case.

Document examiners can conduct tests on materials to draw conclusions about documents in question. Most of these tests are nondestructive. Document examiners may also reproduce documents in question to determine how they were created, by working backward to arrive at the starting point or origin of the documents.

After examiners have completed their review, they give an oral opinion and, if requested by the client, write a letter of opinion or an affidavit. Document examiners prepare detailed reports on request and in federal court cases, prepare exhibits to graphically demonstrate their findings, and, when necessary, testify in deposition and in court concerning their opinions.

Document examiners also work as consultants. Besides educating attorneys about document examination, experts can assist an attorney in preparing a case involving questioned documents, prepare questions for deposition of opposing experts, review their depositions for inconsistencies and misinformation, and help prepare cross-examination questions and give the attorney enough information to properly litigate a case.

FEE STRUCTURE

A document examiner should be able to supply a fee agreement contract for her services that spells out the retainer fee, hourly rate, and charges for expenses. Some document examiners charge a flat fee for a case, but most have an hourly rate. Fees cover preliminary opinions, written opinions, consultation, case review, technical investigation, laboratory work, report and exhibit preparation, precourt conferences, travel time, and time spent in court and in deposition testifying as an expert witness. Out-of-the-area expenses include airfare, ground transportation, lodging, and sometimes meals. See Figure 1.1.

WHY DOCUMENT EXAMINERS DISAGREE

Document examiners come to the same conclusion in most of their cases, however, there are cases in which document examiners do not agree and oppose each other in court. Disagreement among document examiners over the authenticity or spuriousness of documents is the result of various factors relating to the material examined, the skill and health of the writer, and the skill and integrity of the document examiner.

The document examiner needs to consider all of the material used, in both the questioned documents and the known exemplars. This includes the type of paper and its properties, the writing instrument, the writing surface, and the environment in which the documents were signed. Other considerations may also include the type of lighting, the location, and the position of the writer at the time of the signing.

Document examiners are frequently presented with inferior documents and asked to render an opinion. Poor quality documents can hamper the examiner's ability to correctly interpret the evidence.

Some documents examiners rely on too little comparable material. They fail to get sufficient material to cover the range of the writer or they fail to get comparable material, that is, material that is similar in nature to the questioned documents or from the same time period. The amount of writing available may be too limited although the document examiner may feel that the available exemplars are sufficient.

Figure 1.1
Fee Agreement

Forensic Document Examiners

FEE AGREEMENT CONTRACT FOR DOCUMENT EXAMINATION SERVICES

Retainer Fee (payable in advance) Covers first 2 hours.	$400.00
Additional fee per hour	$200.00

Our professional staff is capable of handling large cases in a timely manner.
Fees cover preliminary opinion, written opinion, consultation, case review, technical investigation, laboratory work, report preparation, precourt conferences and travel time.

Additional Expenses

Deposition or court appearance per hour (minimum 2 hours)	$400.00
Out of Local Area (over 50 miles each way — minimum 4 hours)	$800.00
Out of State/Country — per day	$1,600.00
Day set aside for court appearance or deposition unless notified in advance	$400.00

Court Exhibits

Exhibit preparation per hour (Plus photographic and reproduction costs)	$100.00

Travel Expenses

Auto Expenses:	$.35 per mile.

Out-of-the-area expenses include: airfare, ground transportation, and lodging.
Client shall be responsible for the cost of any time spent in court as a result of this case.

Please remit upon receipt of invoice. Balances over 30 days are delinquent and subject to 1 1/2% interest per month. In the event it becomes necessary to refer any unpaid bills to an attorney for collection, the client agrees to be responsible for all costs to said reference including court costs, private process, and attorney's fees of 20%. Clients agree that cases will be filed in county in which Forensic Document Examiners maintains its office.

Please sign a copy of this fee agreement and return to me. No work will begin until the fee agreement has been signed and returned with the retainer fee.

____________________________ ________________

Client's Signature Date

Forensic document examiners may come to a difference of opinion if they compare different exemplars. Attorneys need to provide their experts with all relevant material so that examiners have everything they need to draw proper conclusions. Each document examiner should have access to the same material. Examiners should ask for a chance to review all the material that the opposing examiners used to come to their conclusions.

Material used to compare known documents with questioned documents should be representative of the writer. If the exemplars or the questioned material are disguised or forged, the document examiner may draw incorrect conclusions about the authenticity of the documents.

There are many factors that affect an individual's handwriting. These factors must be made known to the document examiner if they have an impact on the material being examined. Failure to account for mitigating factors leads to erroneous conclusions.

The well-being of the writer includes his physical and mental health at the time of the signing of the documents. It may also include his emotional state or any impairment that he may have suffered at that time.

The amount of experience that the examiner possesses can affect her opinions. The experience of examining thousands of handwriting samples enables a document examiner to weigh the value of individual handwriting characteristics more accurately than a less experienced examiner since she knows the frequency with which these characteristics show up in the general population.

Difficult cases may result in differences of opinion based on the document examiners' interpretation of the evidence.

Disagreements arise among document examiners because:

- They examine different material.
- They do not compare enough samples of handwriting.
- They fail to get suitable material for comparison.
- They fail to get material from the proper time period.
- They are given disguised exemplars.
- They are given forged documents for comparison, represented to them as genuine handwriting exemplars.
- They are trying to work with poor quality copies.
- They fail to find out about conditions that may have altered a writer's normal handwriting in the particular matter in question.
- They fail to consider disguise.
- They base their opinion on matching letter forms only.
- They interpret the same evidence differently.

QUESTIONS TO ASK WHEN RETAINING AN EXPERT

1. Are you a certified document examiner?
2. By whom are you certified?
3. Were you required to pass any tests in order to be certified?
4. What is your formal training in the field of document examination?

5. Did you serve an apprenticeship to an experienced document examiner?
6. Who was your mentor?
7. Are you a member of any document examiners' organizations? Which ones?
8. What seminars have you attended on document examination?
9. Have you presented papers at any seminars?
10. How long have you been a document examiner?
11. How many questioned document cases have you handled?
12. Do you participate in proficiency testing?
13. What is your percentage of accuracy?
14. How many times have you testified in court and in deposition?
15. Have you ever failed to qualify as an expert witness in court?
16. Do you maintain an office and a laboratory?
17. Can you give me the names of several attorneys who have used your services?

SUMMARY

Forensic document examiners draw conclusions about questioned documents. They may conduct experiments, engage in research, test materials, and provide written reports on request. They also testify as expert witnesses in court cases involving questioned documents.

Forensic document examiners obtain their training from various sources such as correspondence courses, apprenticeships, independent study, and research.

Any expert that is hired should be recognized through certification as an expert in his field. Determine if the expert is certified and the process used for certification.

Document examiners should maintain an office and a laboratory.

It is also important to verify the expert's credentials and check references.

The amount of experience a document examiner has had in the field of questioned documents reflects her ability to assess the uniqueness of individual characteristics.

2

Questioned Document Cases

WHAT IS A DOCUMENT?

A document is any material on which a permanent or semipermanent message has been imprinted. Forensic document examiners work with any substance that can impart a written message. While documents most frequently consist of paper written on with pen or pencil, document examiners have studied typewritten materials, carbon copies, graffiti on walls or locker doors, blackboards, mirrors marked with lipstick, cardboard boxes, and blotting paper. The types of documents examined include wills, checks, bank signature cards, contracts, credit cards, deeds, anonymous letters, and other business forms.

WHAT IS A QUESTIONED DOCUMENT?

A questioned document is a document whose origin or content is in dispute. The provenance or circumstances regarding its discovery may also be questioned. The document may contain substitutions or alterations such as additions and deletions; fraudulent information regarding handwriting and signatures, typewriting, printing, or rubber stamp impressions, or be a counterfeit document. A questioned document can also be called a suspect document.

WHAT IS AN EXEMPLAR?

An exemplar is a handwriting sample that is known to be genuine. Exemplars are compared with questioned material in order to determine the authenticity or spuriousness of what is questioned. The authenticity of the exemplar must be verifiable. Genuineness of the exemplars can be proven by the admission of the person who wrote it, by witnesses who saw the person writing or who heard the person acknowledge his handwriting, or by acceptance of the documents in the normal course of business. An exemplar is also called a standard.

There are two classes of exemplars; those executed in the normal course of business known as informal exemplars, and request writing samples called formal exemplars. Request writing is usually collected by a police officer, a private investigator, an attorney, or a document examiner.

Exemplars can also be typewritten samples from a specific typewriter or printed samples from a particular printer.

WHAT CAN A DOCUMENT TELL US?

- The writer or originator of the document.
- The origin of the document.
- The number of people who created the document.
- If the document has been altered.
- The age of the document.
- The type of writing instrument(s) used on the document.

Document examiners are also called on to determine:

- The sequence of writing on typewritten or handwritten documents.
- If material was added to the contract after it was signed. (This often involves interdelineation of lines of writing and typewriting.)
- Whether or not a page has been added or substituted in a multipage document.
- If medical records have been altered or fabricated.
- If anyone is embezzling money by manipulating company books.

Document examiners can also identify:

- The industrial spy leaking confidential information to competitors.
- The writer of anonymous letters.
- The writer who placed incorrect information on architectural drawings.
- The author of the hold-up note dropped at the scene of the crime.
- If the accused wrote the confession of murder or if someone is trying to frame him.
- Whether the corporate minutes were created after the fact or reflect ten years of work.
- What can be deciphered from charred documents or indented writing.
- If the bank signature cards that add another party to an existing account are genuine.
- Who scribbled obscenities on the locker doors.
- If the beneficiary's typewriter was used to type a will.
- If the amount of the check has been raised.

Embezzlement, industrial espionage, threats, extortion, and blackmail are among the types of cases that a document examiner may be called on for help.

- Who is the rightful heir in a contested will case?
- Who has sent threatening anonymous letters?
- What is the chronological order of the writing on the document?

Information about documents includes:

- When was each piece of paper first manufactured based on its watermark?
- What kind of typewriter or printer was used to create the document?
- What kind of ribbon did the typewriter use?
- What type of pen or pens were used?

WHAT TYPES OF PROBLEMS CAN BE SOLVED?

Forensic document examiners are called on to solve many different types of problems that arise involving documents. A document examiner may be asked to determine if the document has been altered in any way. Documents may be altered for many different reasons and in many different ways. The amount of a check may be raised or the name of the payee changed. Wills are altered to benefit a family member at the expense of the rest of the family. Contracts are modified after they have been signed. Pages are substituted in multipage contracts or other negotiable instruments.

ALTERATIONS

Document examiners are often asked to make determinations about alterations on a document.

- Has the document been altered in any way?
- Has information been erased from a document?
- Has important information been obliterated?
- What was written on documents under blackout or whiteout?
- Has additional information been added to a document after it was signed?
- In what sequence has information been written or printed on the document?
- When was the alteration completed?
- What is the age of a document and/or entries on the document?
- Has the document been damaged?
- Can the document be repaired?

SUBSTITUTIONS

- Have pages been substituted in a contract or will?
- Has a genuine signature been photocopied onto a suspect document?
- Has material been substituted or added to a page after it was signed?
- Have numbers been raised on negotiable instruments?

AGE OF DOCUMENTS

In order to determine the age of a document (or entries on a document) a handwriting expert may have to determine the age of the paper and/or the ink used on the paper.

- What was the source of a watermark?
- When was the watermark first manufactured?
- Has the paper been artificially aged by heat, chemicals, or staining and wrinkling?
- Can the age of the ink be discovered from chemical tags?
- What type of pen was used to create the document?
- Was the type of pen in existence when the document was purportedly executed?

TYPEWRITER IDENTIFICATION

Identifying the typewriter or printer used in a questioned document case may be vital to solving the age or the authorship of a document.

- What kind of typewriter was used?
- Was a particular typewriter used?
- Was the document created on a printer with the aid of a computer?
- What type of printer was used to create the document?

HOW MUCH INFORMATION CAN BE DISCOVERED ABOUT DOCUMENTS?

Some information about documents is easily obtained. For example, a watermark can identify the date the paper was first manufactured. This information can be procured from the dandyroll factory that manufactures the watermarks or *Lockwood-Post's Directory of the Pulp, Paper and Allied Trades* published by Miller Freeman Publications. A new edition of *Lockwood-Post's* is published each year.

An important part of a document examiner's work is knowing what can be determined and where to get the needed information. Document examiners may need to send documents to an ink chemist or an expert on paper for laboratory analysis; or they may need to research items used to create a document such as rubber stamp impressions and embossed seals. A document examiner should maintain a list of resources.

In some cases, the forensic document examiner may be able to assist in the restoration of damaged documents. The document examiner should be able to refer a client to a conservator who can restore damaged documents.

TYPES OF FRAUD

Embezzlement, medical malpractice cases involving altered or fabricated records, and industrial espionage are examples of other types of fraud that forensic document examiners encounter. In some of these cases, the document examiner will be looking for the originator of the questioned documents. In others, she is looking for alterations such as erasures and overwriting or material that has been added to a document at a different time. An expert may also identify sequential writing, that is, writing that has been done at one time instead of over a period of time.

EMBEZZLEMENT

Embezzlement is the fraudulent misappropriation of funds with which someone has been entrusted. Embezzlement usually involves a person who has been given a position of trust by his employer. In some cases document examiners work with accountants to decipher the system used to pilfer funds. The document examiner may be expected to match numbers to determine the identity of the embezzler or she may simply have to identify the writing on specific documents.

MEDICAL MALPRACTICE

Medical malpractice usually entails alterations or additions to medical records. Records can be doctored to reflect proper procedures on the part of medical personnel for the purpose of avoiding lawsuits or loss of their license. These alterations or additions are generally added after a lawsuit has been filed. The document examiner can determine if all the medical records were written at one time instead of on the dates indicated in the records. She can identify the insertion of material to make the record reflect proper procedures, and may be able to determine when the records were actually created.

INDUSTRIAL ESPIONAGE

Industrial espionage is the theft of valuable information from a company or place of business. It may involve disgruntled employees or undercover agents sent to steal formulas, specifications, blueprints, or other proprietary secrets.

INSURANCE FRAUD

Insurance fraud is the single largest area of white collar crime. Insurance fraud is a $100 billion a year industry with most of it directed to health care which involves forged signatures, fictitious patients, inflated fees, and falsified documents.

DOCUMENTS USED IN CRIMINAL ACTS

Murder confessions, hold-up notes, and death threats are also examined by document examiners. Kidnapping notes, extortion and blackmail, and prank mail, both viciously and sexually oriented, will be encountered. Graffiti and anonymous poison pen letters constitute some of the types of cases document examiners may be asked to solve.

MURDER CONFESSIONS, HOLD-UP NOTES, AND DEATH THREATS

Document examiners are asked to identify the author of hold-up notes or other handwritten threats, to uncover a bigamist, or to determine who put the wrong dimensions on an architectural drawing. Did the suspect write the murder confession or is he being framed? These are just a few of the scenarios that are encountered in the examination of documents.

GRAFFITI OR ANONYMOUS POISON PEN LETTERS

Graffiti and anonymous poison pen letters in a business environment cause a decline in morale in employees. Culprits are often surprised when they are terminated from the company for seemingly childish pranks. Occasionally a disgruntled employee will write a poison pen and/or threatening letter to a previous place of employment or a sexually explicit letter will be sent anonymously.

Graffiti often involves writing on media other than paper, such as walls, locker doors, or mirrors. It may be spray-painted, scratched with a sharp instrument, or written with lipstick or chalk. Whenever possible, the document examiner should arrange to study the original, although a good, clear photograph may suffice.

DISGUISE

Documents such as poison pen letters often contain disguised handwriting. Disguised writing is any conscious or deliberate attempt to alter the normal characteristics of one's handwriting habits to prevent recognition. Deciphering disguise and identifying the author of disguised writing falls under the purview of the document examiner. Disguise may also be found in falsified evidence, forged securities, embezzlement, and kidnaping notes or extortion. Some writers alter their signatures on documents in order to deny them at a future date.

COUNTERFEIT DOCUMENTS

Counterfeiting involves the fabrication of fraudulent documents in imitation of genuine documents. Counterfeiting involves making a copy of a legal or financial document without authority or a right to such a copy for the purpose of benefiting oneself at the expense of others. It generally involves money or securities but can include other items such as counterfeit credentials. Modern computers and color photocopiers make it possible to counterfeit many types of documents from gift certificates to counterfeit identification documents.

INTERDELINEATION OF LINES

Problems sometimes arise involving commingled writing. It may be necessary to determine which writing was placed on the document first. Lines that intersect can be studied to ascertain the sequence of writing. This includes written material and/or typed and computer-generated documents.

INDENTED WRITING

Occasionally document examiners are confronted with cases involving indented writing. Indented writing is created when sheets of paper sitting under the original page receive the impression from the pressure of the writing instrument. While ink adheres only to the first page, indentations may affect three or four subsequent pages of writing.

The impression of writing on a page may need to be deciphered. It may be possible to sidelight the document and photograph it, or place it on an Electrostatic Detection Apparatus (ESDA) to reveal the indentations.

INSERTIONS

Material is sometimes fraudulently added to a contract or other legal document after it has been signed. This material can drastically change the intent of the document. It is more difficult to detect additions that are skillfully added to a document than erasures. It becomes the task of the document examiner to determine if the addition or alteration was made after the document was executed.

CUT AND PASTE

Modern photocopiers enable one to cut and paste a document and copy it so that any insertions or substitutions cannot be detected from the altered document. Genuine signatures are glued to fraudulent documents and the photocopy is presented as authentic. Without an original document, it is difficult to determine if a fraudulent alteration or insertion has taken place.

ELECTRONIC ALTERATIONS

Original signatures can be scanned into computers and printed onto other documents, thereby making the printed signatures appear to be genuine original signatures to the naked eye. Documents of all kinds are scanned into computers, data is manipulated, and new documents are printed and presented as authentic. Document examiners can identify computer-generated documents.

IDENTITY THEFT

Identity theft is the fraudulent use of another person's good name and reputation. For example, the unscrupulous are stealing the reputation of victims by impersonating the victim when applying for credit. The thieves steal information about a person's family, credit history and financial status in order to use that person's identity to steal from banks, credit card companies, or merchants.

Some perpetrators are giving the victim's identification when arrested for criminal activity. When these criminals are sentenced, they often destroy the victim's reputation.

OTHER TYPES OF FRAUD

Any type of document can be forged. While forgers concentrate primarily on legal documents and financial obligations, they also falsify college diplomas, letters of recommendation, and identity papers. Legal documents include wills, deed, contracts, and agreements. Financial documents that impart an obligation involve checks, credit card transactions, letters of credit, securities, gift certificates, and refunds.

OPPORTUNITY

Opportunity is the catalyst that propels individuals into white collar crime. Many individuals take advantage of an opportunity to forge a will or raise the amount on a check. Many cases that fall under the document examiners purview involve opportunists.

SUMMARY

Forensic document examiners are called on to solve many different types of cases involving fraud. Document examiners determine the authenticity or spuriousness of questioned documents. They compare handwriting to determine authorship, decipher cross-outs and indented writing, determine line sequence, or pinpoint alterations on documents; identify writers of anonymous notes; and assist in determining the age of documents. Document examiners examine all or any part of a questioned document.

3

Working with a Document Examiner

WHAT DOES A DOCUMENT EXAMINER NEED TO KNOW ABOUT THE CASE?

Since the field of document examination is small, an examiner is sometimes contacted by both parties involved in litigation. To avoid a conflict of interest, a document examiner should be told the names of the litigants and their attorneys before any information about the case is discussed.

A document examiner needs a basic description of the problem involved with a suspect document to determine if she is qualified to handle it. An expert needs to know if the case involves equipment or services that she can provide. A description of the documents available should enable the document examiner to determine if they are sufficient for drawing conclusions. She needs to know what control documents and exemplars will be available for comparison purposes. Lack of proper documents can limit the opinions that can be drawn about a questioned document.

It is necessary for the document examiner to have sufficient information to make an intelligent decision concerning the authenticity of documents. Providing the document examiner with this information at the beginning of the case may reduce the time needed to complete the assignment.

In order to maintain objectivity, the document examiner should not be told what the attorney hopes the outcome of the examination will be. For example, instead of saying to the examiner, "My client says his signature has been forged," an attorney should say, "The signature of John Doe is in question. Can you determine if the signature is genuine or not?"

Inform the document examiner about any hearings, depositions, court appearances, or any other deadlines that are important to the case. The document examiner needs to make sure that she prepares exhibits in a timely manner and that she will be available for the proceedings of the case.

All relevant information must be supplied to the document examiner on the provenance of the document, that is, the purported history or whereabouts of the document and how it came into the presenter's possession. Sometimes the information given doesn't match the condition of the documents. For example, a document that has been stored for many years should not look like a newly-created document.

The following is a list of suggested questions that the document examiner may need answered concerning documents.

PROVENANCE OF THE QUESTIONED DOCUMENT

The document examiner should be given any relevant information about the provenance of the questioned document.

1. How was it created?
2. When and where was the document found?
3. Where was the document stored?
4. Who presented the document?
5. What is his interest in the document?
6. What does the document purport to do?
7. Are there any discrepancies in the history of the document?
8. Is the document in the same condition now as when it was first presented?

PHOTOCOPIES

If there is no original questioned document or the original is not produced, the document examiner will want to know the following:

1. Where is the original questioned document?
2. Why hasn't the original questioned document been produced?
3. Is the original questioned document available?
4. Can the original questioned document be sent to the document examiner's office?
5. If not, can the original document be made available to be examined and photographed by the document examiner?
6. If the original questioned document is not available, why not?
7. Have photographs been made of the questioned document? If so, where are they?
8. Has the photocopy of the questioned document been reduced or enlarged?
9. What generation photocopy do you have?

EXECUTOR OF THE QUESTIONED DOCUMENT

1. Who created the questioned document?
2. Was the questioned document the work of one or more persons?
3. How many people contributed to the creation of the questioned document?
4. Was the writer assisted, as in guided-hand writing, when signing the questioned document?

5. What do any creators of the questioned document have to say about their participation?

WITNESSES

1. Are there witnesses to the preparation, execution, or presentation of the questioned document?
2. Do the witnesses have a personal interest in the determination of authenticity of the questioned document?
3. What is the reputation of the witnesses?
4. Have the witnesses supplied complete details as to time, place, and circumstances of the execution of the questioned document? If not, why not?
5. Are the signatures of the witnesses in question?
6. Were all of the signatures notarized? By whom?
7. Is the notary signature in question?
8. Has the notary been contacted to verify the signature(s)?
9. Did the notary actually witness the signing of the questioned document?
10. Did the notary correctly identify the signers of the signatures?
11. Did the notary examine proper identification?
12. What identification did the notary examine?

PHYSICAL AND MENTAL CONDITION OF THE WRITER

What was the physical condition of the writer when executing the document in question?

1. Did the writer suffer from any handicaps or long-term illnesses?
2. Was he addicted to drugs or alcohol?
3. Was he intoxicated or suffering from the side effects of drugs or medication at the time the document was written or signed?
4. Was there a sudden deterioration in his health?
5. Had he been in an accident or had surgery?
6. Was the writer dyslexic?
7. What was his mental state at the time of the writing?
8. Was the writer angry?
9. Was he upset?
10. Was he depressed?
11. Did psychological factors affect his writing?
12. Were there any neurological disturbances?
13. Was mental illness a factor?

MECHANICAL FACTORS

What part did mechanical factors play in the formation of his writing?

1. What type of writing instrument was used?
2. What type of writing surface was involved?

3. Was the writer writing from an unnatural position?
4. What was the position of the person when writing?
   a. Was he standing or sitting when he signed the documents?
   b. Was he lying down or reclining?
5. Did poor lighting or bad eyesight affect the writing?
6. Was he using an unusual writing surface such as writing on a wall, the steering wheel of a car, or a body part such as his hand?
7. Was the signature a guided-hand signature?

EDUCATION AND SKILL OF THE WRITER

The amount of formal schooling and the system of penmanship learned can also provide important clues.

1. How much education did the writer have?
2. Was the writer semi-literate?
3. What penmanship system did the writer learn?
4. Did the influence of foreign handwriting systems affect the writing?
5. What level of education did the writer have?
   a. Did the writer drop out of high school?
   b. Does the writer have an advanced degree?

The skill level of the writer is another important consideration.

1. Was the writer a skilled penman?
2. Did the writer's work require that he write frequently?
3. Did the writer employ special characters in his work such as a draftsman?
4. Was the writer an unskilled laborer who seldom wrote except to sign his name?

DATING INFORMATION

It may be necessary to verify the date on the document or to determine its date of origin.

1. Is the date on the document correct?
   a. Is the document a printed form containing a date of origin?
   b. Does the paper contain a watermark?
2. Does the date coincide with other information about the document?
3. Is the date of the document consistent with the movements of the author of the document?
   a. With his physical and mental condition at the time?
   b. With the habits of its purported author at the time in question?
   c. Have you considered hospitalization, injuries, vacations, business trips?
4. Have other documents issued at the time of the document in question been presented to the document examiner to verify their agreement with the said document?
5. Was the document presented in a timely manner based on its date?
6. If not, where has the document been and why?

7. Is the number on the document, such as a check or invoice number, in proper sequence by comparison with companion documents of the same vintage, or has it clearly been predated or postdated?

EXEMPLARS

To help the document examiner support her opinion to the satisfaction of the court, collect as many valid exemplars as possible at the beginning of a case.

1. Are the exemplars genuine? (While many legal and business papers are accepted in court, they may also be fraudulent.)
2. How can you be sure the standards are valid?
3. What proof do you have? (Documents have been incorrectly validated based on fraudulent exemplars.)
4. Have you provided the document examiner with technically adequate, provable, and legally admissible exemplars?
5. On what merits has the writing been assumed to be authentic?
6. Can the writing be verified as genuine in court?
7. Are the exemplars suitable for comparison?
8. Do they reflect the condition of the writer at the time of the questioned writing?
9. Have you collected exemplars dated around the time of the questioned document?
10. Do you have some exemplars dated prior to the incident involving the questioned documents?
11. Have you collected exemplars that are similar to the questioned material?
12. Do the exemplars contain suitable material for comparison such as similar letter combinations and spacing?
13. Are the standards genuine, internally consistent with themselves, and properly dated?
14. Have you collected all available documents? (See Table 4.1).
15. Are the exemplars originals? If not, why not?
16. Where are the original documents?
17. Can original exemplars be made available to the examiner?

REQUEST WRITING

1. Do request writing standards show any signs of attempted disguise?
2. Do they contain suitable material for comparison such as similar letter combinations and spacing?
3. Have they been properly taken and properly witnessed?
4. Have the exemplars been created for the purpose of litigation?

Unless precautions are taken, request writing samples can be worthless as a forger will disguise his requested handwriting to avoid detection or exemplars will be obtained that are not suitable for comparison purposes.

OTHER DOCUMENT REPORTS

Once your document examiner has given her opinion, any reports generated by an opposing expert need to be shared with your examiner.

1. Has any other document examiner looked at the documents in this case?
2. Have any reports been generated by any other document examiners in this case?
3. Have all of the exemplars used by other document examiners been presented for comparison? If not, why not?
4. Did the other examiner conduct any tests? If so, what tests and what are the results?
5. Did the opposing examiner look at original documents?
6. Did he prepare any exhibits?
7. What is the opposing document examiner's background?

Any exemplars utilized by an opposing expert need to be given to your expert so that she has the same documents to compare and surprises in court can be prevented.

Any testimony by any witnesses that has an impact on the handwriting should be given to your expert.

All parties involved will want to know:

1. The length of time the opposing expert has worked as a document examiner.
2. The number of cases in which he has been involved.
3. The proportion of cases for plaintiff versus defendant.
4. The background of the examiner, especially education and training.
5. The titles and locations of any articles or books published by the examiner.

TYPES OF DOCUMENTS THE EXAMINER NEEDS

Document examiners prefer to work with original documents whenever possible so they can observe any alteration of the original. Modern office equipment is sophisticated enough so that documents can be modified without leaving evidence of the modification. Photocopies can be cut and pasted to create composite documents without leaving any evidence of the process used to create the alterations. Scanning enables the fraudulent duplication of original documents that pass for genuine documents. Scanned documents can also be manipulated to create new documents that defy detection. Because of the ease of altering photocopies, document examiners prefer to work from the original documents.

Most document examiners have portable laboratories that can be taken to the courthouse or an attorney's office in order to study original documents when the documents cannot be taken to the examiner's laboratory.

Do not wait until the court date before showing the document examiner the original documents. There is always the possibility that the original documents could contain evidence that changes the examiner's opinion on the case.

ORIGINAL DOCUMENTS

Original documents are the actual documents that have been created, whether printed, typed or handwritten, and signed. Original documents reveal the most information about their nature. They provide the best detail regarding line quality and pressure patterns, and they pick up tapered initial and terminal strokes. While some indication of these qualities are present on photocopies, originals provide the most valuable information.

Some examinations can only be conducted on original documents. Originals are needed to identify alterations and insertions into the material on the document as well as to determine line sequence. Originals may contain indented writing that will be of assistance by revealing important information. The paper and the ink may need to be tested. Document examiners keep original documents in mint condition by careful handling and storage.

PHOTOGRAPHS

The questioned document should be photographed and photocopied. When original documents cannot be sent to a document examiner's laboratory, photographs of the documents can be used for examination purposes. Photographs provide an accurate record of the original condition of the evidence.

Photographs can be in black and white or in color. The photographs should be at least a one-to-one ratio since a reduced photograph may not contain enough detail. Photographs can be enlarged to show fine detail more easily than photocopies. A good quality photographic enlargement often reveals information that is difficult to detect without magnification. The photographer should add a measuring device to the document when photographing it to show the original size of the questioned material. See Figure 3.1.

Document photography frequently involves microphotography and macrophotography. Microphotography involves photographing documents through a microscope. Macrophotography is close-up photography in which photographs are enlarged so that minute details are exposed. These specialties require the services of a forensic document photographer. Many document examiners have been trained in document photography and there are some specialists who only handle this specialized field.

PHOTOCOPIES

Photocopies are frequently sent to document examiners because they are easily obtained and transported. A document examiner can work with a photocopy as long as it is an accurate reproduction of the original document. In cases where there is no original document, and the court accepts a copy as best evidence, a document examiner will give a conditional opinion subject to examination of the original document.

Figure 3.1
Type of Measuring Device Used in Photography

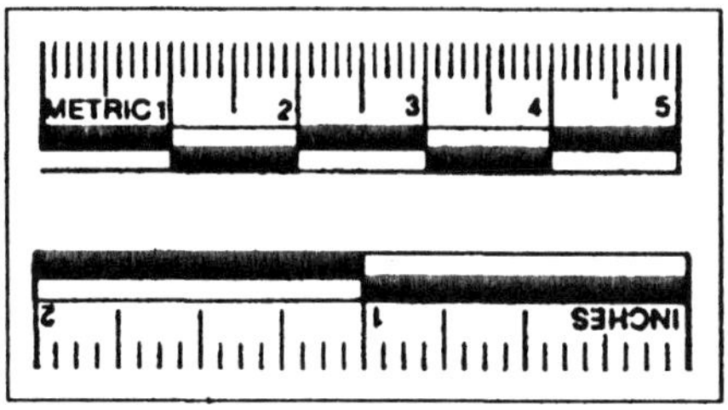

Document examiners who participated in proficiency testing performed extremely well when presented with photocopies instead of originals, therefore, photocopied documents can accurately be analyzed. Opinions on photocopied documents will be valid as long as the photocopy is a true representation of the original. However, most photocopies are multigenerational documents that have lost considerable line quality and therefore have limited use in the comparison of documents. Also, photocopies can be altered in such a way that the alteration cannot be detected.

Photocopies of the questioned document should be made to show the whole document in its normal size. Details can be enlarged on the photocopier to assist the examiner in her examination.

A photocopy made from an original is called a first generation photocopy. A photocopy made from that first generation copy is a second generation photocopy. Each time a copy is made from an earlier generation, the quality of the photocopy deteriorates, line value is reduced, and details are lost.

It is important to work with the earliest generation available. Document examiners are often presented with multiple generated documents that have lost so much detail that they are unable to draw conclusions from the poor copies. If there is no original document, the document examiner should be provided with the earliest generation photocopy available.

Colored photocopies are easily obtained and may prove useful in some document cases. When documents from a case have different color backgrounds and/or ink, colored copies help identify the source documents.

FAX DOCUMENTS

With the proliferation of modern facsimile machines, document examiners are being asked to examine faxed documents. Can anything be determined from a faxed copy?

The earliest facsimile machines produced crude copies with large jagged lines. See Figures 3.2 and 3.3. Modern facsimile machines can transmit a much finer line that can hardly be distinguished from a photocopy. As technology continues to improve fax transmissions, working with faxes will not be any different from working with photocopies.

A photocopy gives us a clearer picture than a faxed copy as seen in Figure 3.4. A faxed copy that is repeatedly photocopied will lose some of the jagged lines seen on the original fax.

A document examiner should ask for a better copy than a fax when rendering opinions. Only a conditional opinion should be given on a faxed copy, subject to examination of the original document. A document examiner should request a better document before a final opinion is given. A photocopy is considerably better evidence than a faxed copy and should be easily obtainable.

What can and cannot be determined from facsimiles? Line quality and pressure patterns cannot be determined from faxed documents. Most other handwriting characteristics can be ascertained from good quality faxed documents. Proportions can be measured and compared; utilization of space between letters, words, and lines of text can be determined; as well as, page layout, margins, and baselines can be studied. Writers tend to use consistent letter forms that can be compared. Initial and terminal strokes, hooks and ticks, and any other peculiarities of a writer can be recognized from faxed documents.

Significant differences in letter forms are also evident in faxed copies. The method of construction of letter forms can sometimes be discerned from faxed copies, and since the method of construction is a crucial element in making determinations of genuineness versus spuriousness, some conclusions can be drawn from faxed copies.

Figure 3.2
Typewritten Letters That Have Been Faxed

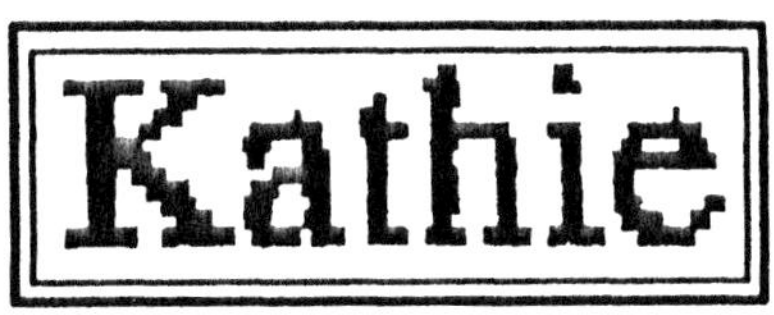

Figure 3.3
Sample of Handwriting That Has Been Faxed

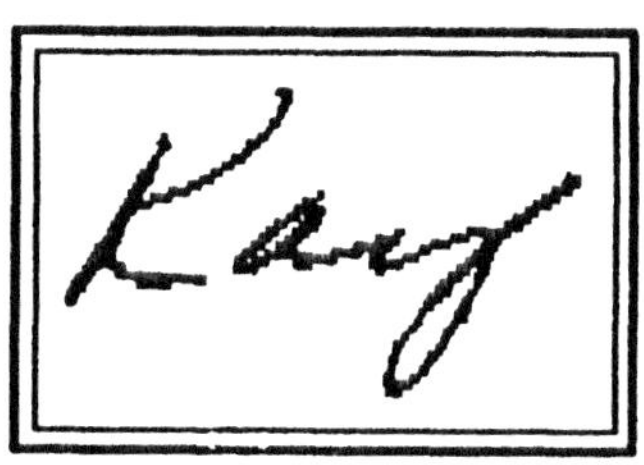

Figure 3.4
Comparison of a Photocopy with a Faxed Document

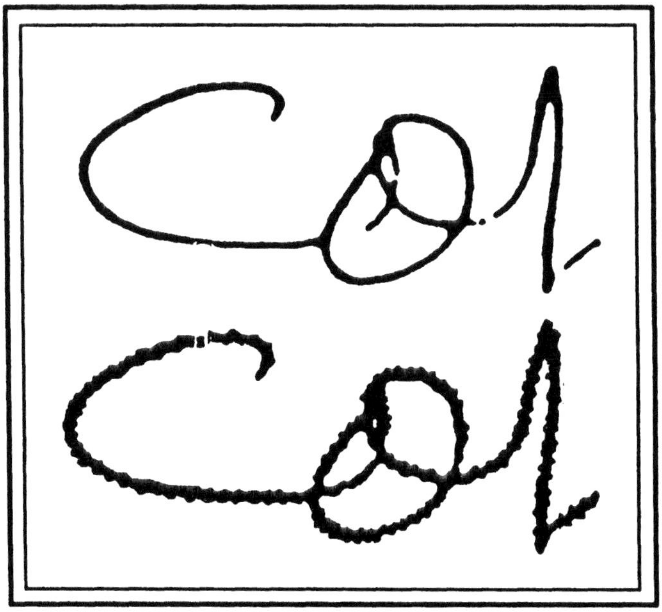

Enlarging faxed documents increases the jagged lines. The larger the enlargement, the more jagged the lines. Therefore, enlarging a faxed document distorts, not clarifies it.

MICROFICHE

Many modern documents are put on microfiche after which the originals are destroyed. Document examiners prefer to examine the original microfiche whenever possible. More information is available from a microfiche than from a photocopy of the microfiche.

SUMMARY

Document examiners need to know the names of the litigants in order to avoid a conflict of interest. They needs specific information about a document and its signers. Document examiners need to examine all of the documents in a case, both questioned and known. They should be supplied with original documents whenever possible. If no original documents exist, document examiners should be supplied with the earliest generation photocopies.

Document examiners must be informed of any unusual circumstances or problems that could affect the outcome of the case. This includes the physical and mental condition of the writer at the time the document was signed.

If other examiners have reviewed the documents, your examiners needs access to any reports presented as well as the documents examined. Inform your experts of any deadlines and court appearances. Examiners must be fully appraised of the circumstances surrounding the signing of the questioned documents in order to make an intelligent and accurate assessment of the case.

Document examiners prefer to work with original documents. If original documents are not available, a detailed photograph can be substituted. If photographs are not available, a photocopy that is an accurate reproduction of the original is the next best evidence. A faxed document can reveal some information but it is not as useful as other methods of reproduction.

4

Collecting and Preserving Documents

EXEMPLARS

To help the document examiner support her opinion satisfactorily to the court, provide her with as many valid exemplars as possible at the beginning of the case. Exemplars, also called standards, are legally admissible authentic samples of handwriting used for comparison with questioned writing. They are used by the document examiner to enable her to form an opinion concerning the authenticity of handwriting in dispute. There are two kinds of exemplars (informal which are documents previously executed and known to be genuine) and formal (which are request writing samples). Exemplars are also called known handwriting samples.

Handwriting identification depends on the quality of the known writing. One of the most important steps in the investigation of suspected or disputed writing is the procurement of sufficient genuine writing samples. Legal advisers and investigating officers must be able to anticipate the document examiner's needs in the way of comparative material. Sufficient suitable material facilitates the work of the expert in establishing the master pattern or habits of the writer in order to avoid errors and inconclusions. A document examiner who must work with insufficient writing has a more difficult task and may not be able to draw adequate conclusions from the limited material.

Informal handwriting exemplars are more reliable for comparison purposes than request writing. Since informal writing was written in the normal course of business, it more accurately reflects the subconscious habits of the writer. Self-consciousness or conscious-awareness enters into the request writing process. Even when there is no attempt to disguise request writing, it may not represent the normal subconscious habits of the writer.

If informal exemplars are not sufficient or suitable for comparison purposes, request writing should be taken from the victim as well as any suspects. Often the only way to obtain comparable handwriting samples is through request writing. There are some disadvantages to request writing that must be taken into consideration.

DISADVANTAGES OF REQUEST WRITING SAMPLES

Request writing taken after the incident may not be as close to the date of the questioned writing as informal documents executed in the normal course of business. Courts consider request writing taken after the fact as self-serving and may not allow it.

Some writers will deliberately disguise their request handwriting. The person taking the request writing needs to take this into consideration. Suggestions for taking request writing are covered later in this chapter.

It may be difficult or impossible to duplicate the writing environment of the suspect document in order to obtain comparable documents. The writer may not be available for request writing or circumstances may have caused changes that make it impossible to obtain similar request writing samples.

POST LITEM MOTAM SIGNATURES

Post litem motam signatures written by the client to prove his innocence may be disallowed by the court. According to J. Newton Baker in the *Law of Disputed and Forged Documents*, "Writing made after the controversy arose or made for the occasion may not be used by the party who wrote them to corroborate his testimony. All such writings offered in evidence are subject to the discretion of the trial judge for admittance as standards of comparison" (p. 85). These handwriting samples are written after the fact and may be considered self-serving. Court citations to eliminate post litem motam signatures as evidence are covered in Chapter 18.

COLLECTING INFORMAL EXEMPLARS

Exemplars must be suitable for comparison with the questioned writing. Since handwriting can be found on many different types of surfaces, comparison materials should, when possible, duplicate the conditions under which the questioned document was executed. While this is usually done with request writing, it may be harder to locate informal writing samples that meet this criteria. Locating material to be used as evidence may require considerable effort on the part of the investigator.

Comparison materials should, when possible, be written under the same conditions under which the questioned documents were executed. While this is the standard method of taking request writing, it is impossible to control the writing environment of informal writing samples.

Try to obtain signatures that are similar to the questioned signature. If the questioned signature is in ink, get signatures in ink, if it is in pencil, get documents written in pencil for comparison. If the questioned document is on lined paper, find documents written on lined paper. If the questioned document contains handprinting, collect documents that are handprinted.

Where no similar documents are available, try to locate documents whose authenticity can be verified such as canceled checks that have been accepted by a bank. Other documents executed in the regular course of business are also suitable. A list of possible places to locate signatures for comparison can be found in Table 4.1.

The date of the questioned writing must be taken into consideration when looking for suitable comparable documents. While an adult's handwriting may remain constant for many years, writing habits normally change over time so that an outdated standard may be unsatisfactory for comparison purposes. All writing samples are not of equal value and some may be of no value at all.

When gathering handwriting for comparison purposes, it is necessary to keep in mind that various factors cause changes in handwriting. Age and illness may lead to the deterioration of writing skills, which can be an important consideration in a disputed will case. A teenager's handwriting may change drastically in as short a time frame as a year. A drug addict may undergo a radical change in handwriting as his addiction takes over. Handwriting samples taken prior to the addiction are not going to accurately reflect later writing.

Handwriting changes gradually over a person's lifetime but some factors can cause drastic changes in handwriting in a short period of time, therefore it is essential to compare handwriting from a similar time frame and under similar conditions. Trauma such as stroke, illness, or loss of a spouse; or medication, or substance abuse can affect handwriting. If a person's writing has changed drastically around the time the questioned document was executed, there may not be comparable material available.

Ideally, writing executed around the date of the questioned material should be used for comparison purposes, some dated shortly before and after the date of the questioned material. What time frame is considered suitable? Documents executed within two to three years are most suitable. If these are not available, documents dating further from the questioned material may be used. Do not rely on present-day writing exclusively, if possible.

Make sure the handwriting exemplars are not in dispute and that they can be authenticated. Any uncontradicted testimony of competent eye witnesses who saw the execution of the writing can be used to verify its authenticity. Courts accept the testimony of the author admitting genuineness or someone to whom the author has admitted genuineness. The testimony of a person who received writing from the author and acted on it is also valid, though not necessarily accurate. Documents executed in the normal course of business are frequently used for comparison purposes which includes negotiable instruments such as checks, contracts, and other business documents.

Table 4.1
101 Places to Search for Documents

1. Account Books
2. Affidavits
3. Assignments
4. Autographs
5. Auto Insurance Papers
6. Auto License (MVA)
7. Auto Title Papers
8. Bank Deposit Slips
9. Bank Safe Deposit Entry Slips
10. Bank Savings Withdrawal Slips
11. Bank Signature Cards
12. Bank Statements & Receipts
13. Bible Entries
14. Bills of Sale
15. Bonds
16. Books, Signatures of Owners
17. Building After Hours Registers
18. Business License Applications
19. Charity Pledges
20. Check Book Stubs
21. Checks including Endorsements
22. Church Pledges
23. Convention Registrations
24. Contracts
25. Cooking Recipes
26. Corporation Papers
27. Criminal Records
28. Credit Applications
29. Credit Cards & Charge Slips
30. Deeds
31. Deeds of Trust
32. Depositions
33. Diaries
34. Divorce Papers
35. Dog License Applications
36. Drafts
37. Drive-it-yourself Applications
38. Driver's Licenses & Applications
39. Druggists' Poison Registers
40. Employment Application
41. Envelopes, addresses
42. Fishing Licenses
43. Funeral Attendance Registers
44. Gas Service Applications
45. Gate Records at Defense Plants
46. Greeting Cards
47. Hospital Papers
48. Hotel & Motel Guest Registers
49. Hunting Licenses
50. Identification Papers
51. Inventories
52. Leases, Real Property
53. Letters, Personal & Business
54. Library Card Applications
55. Light Company Applications
56. Life Insurance Papers
57. Loan Papers
58. Mail Orders
59. Manuscripts
60. Marriage License Papers
61. Medicare Cards & Papers
62. Membership Cards: Social, Occupation
63. Memoranda of all kinds
64. Military Papers
65. Mortgage Papers
66. Newspaper & Magazine Subscriptions
67. Occupational Writing
68. Package Receipts
69. Parent's Signatures on Report Cards
70. Partnership Papers
71. Passports
72. Pawn Tickets
73. Payroll Receipts
74. Pension Applications
75. Permit Applications
76. Petitions, Referenda, etc.
77. Photograph Albums
78. Pleadings, Civil and Criminal
79. Postal Cards
80. Probate Court Papers
81. Promissory Notes
82. Property Damage Reports
83. Receipts for Rent
84. Registered Mail Return Receipts
85. Releases
86. Rental Contracts for Equipment
87. Reports
88. Sales Slips
89. School & College Papers
90. Social Security Cards & Papers
91. Sport & Game Score Cards
92. Stock Certificates, Endorsements
93. Surety Bonds Applications
94. Tax Returns and Estimates
95. Telephone Service Applications
96. Time Sheets
97. Traffic Tickets
98. Voting Registration Records
99. Water Company Service Applications
100. Wills
101. Workman's Compensation Papers

Document examiners have given erroneous conclusions based on forged exemplars. When the exemplars have been fabricated by the same writer as the forged material, an opinion of authenticity based on false information will occur. Document examiners mistakenly identified Adolph Hitler as the author of the Hitler Diaries because they used forged exemplars of Hitler for comparison.

HOW MANY SAMPLES OF HANDWRITING ARE NEEDED?

The type of case determines the number of exemplars that the document examiner needs for comparison with the questioned documents. Always try to collect as many samples as possible because it is more important to have suitable undisputed samples than a large quantity of little comparable value. Cases have been won in court using a single known signature to support the authenticity of a questioned document. One signature is sufficient when all the characteristics of handwriting match. When proving that an individual did not write a questioned document, it is necessary to obtain a larger range of writing and one hundred signatures may not be enough. An average would be twenty to twenty-five signatures and four to five pages of normal handwriting and/or handprinting preferably written at different times.

More known documents are needed if the writer has a wide range of variation or an oversimplified signature, while only a few signatures would suffice if the writer is consistent. An oversimplified signature is one that contains few changes of direction and is usually an illegible scrawl. Oversimplified signatures are easier to imitate than more complex signatures that contain more changes of direction and more stylized letter forms.

When a questioned signature shows obvious signs of forgery not present in the known signature, one known signature should be enough to prove non-genuineness. Forged writing often contains tremor or has a drawn look.

A single signature would be sufficient to determine the facts when the questioned signatures are written with a higher skill level than the suspected writer could execute. However, it is better to have more exemplars whenever possible. The document examiner must evaluate the exemplars to determine if she has sufficient suitable material to render an accurate opinion.

SUITABLE EXEMPLARS

Canceled checks, contracts, applications, and business letters make suitable exemplars or standards. The writing can be properly identified, the date can be verified, and the habits of the writer can be studied. Additional standards may be needed if the words on the disputed writing do not match the exemplars.

Ideally, original writing should be available for the scrutiny of the document examiner. Original writing is always better than a photocopy or a facsimile. If it is impossible to obtain original documents, a first generation photocopy should be supplied. The original documents should be requested whenever a photocopy is supplied by the adverse party. Intermediate tones are almost always lost in a photocopy because it aims to secure the greatest possible contrast. Subsequent generations of photocopies may drop sufficient detail, rendering them worthless to a competent document examiner.

According to the FBI Law Enforcement Bulletin published in September, 1970, handwriting identification depends on the quality of the known writing. "A's cannot be compared with G's — 'John Jones' cannot be compared with 'Samuel Hansen' — The J's must be compared with J's and the 'ohn's' with 'ohn's.' Handwriting cannot be compared with handprinting."

Documents similar in nature will make the best exemplars. Contracts should be compared with contracts, and canceled checks with canceled checks. Try to procure like signatures. An "A" should be compared with "A," an "Al" with "Al," and handprinting with handprinting. Documents written with ink should be compared with other documents written in ink. Try to find writing on similar documents. People often have more than one style signature depending on the document being executed. Checks may be executed in a more careless manner than wills and contracts. Do not use signatures written while the writer was intoxicated unless the questioned documents were written under similar circumstances.

Some handprinting can be compared with handwriting and vice versa. Some writers use handprinted letters and handwritten ones interchangeably. Most common is the use of handprinted capital letters in place of cursive. Other writers use the same letter form for both handprinted and cursive writing.

There are many characteristics of handwriting that can be compared besides letter forms and connecting strokes. Document examiners compare line quality, pressure patterns, size and proportions, spacing, slant, baseline, and utilization of space. Document examiners can compare similar letters such as "N" and "M," and "P" and "R"; circle letters and loops can be compared. Therefore, all available handwriting samples should be given to a document examiner.

While it may be possible to make a match with only a few exemplars, the more exemplars available the better. Collect as many samples of handwriting, including signatures, as possible. It is necessary to collect enough handwriting samples to enable the expert to render a professional opinion. How much is enough? Enough would be sufficient exemplars to eliminate any other writer as the author of a document.

QUESTIONS ABOUT EXEMPLARS

- Are all the exemplars genuine?
- Can they all be properly identified?
- Are there sufficient standards for the purposes of making comparisons?
- Are the exemplars consistent, that is, are they written by the same writer?
- Are the dates of all of the exemplars similar to the questioned signatures?
- Are similarities due to class characteristics or individual characteristics?

CASES IN WHICH NO EXEMPLARS ARE NEEDED

There are some cases in which no exemplars are needed to prove spuriousness. Since no one can write his signature exactly the same way twice, identical signatures are generally evidence of nongenuineness. This would include traced forgeries, scanned signatures, or even freehand simulations, as well as cut and paste signatures.

Some writers use signature stamps and autopens as legitimate signatures making it is necessary to determine the nature of the signatures before an opinion of nongenuineness is given.

Signs of forgery are indicative of nongenuineness. Documents that contain indications of tracing can be identified without known signatures. Evidence of tracing the signature would be a groove or guide line along the signature line or residue of pencil or carbon. See Figure 4.1 for evidence of a traced signature.

An example of writing that contains obvious tremor due to being slowly drawn instead of written can be found on Figure 4.2.

When a questioned signature matches the handwriting of another writer, an identification can be made that the writing was penned by that individual. In this case, no known signatures of the victim are needed for comparison.

Figure 4.1
Example of Tracing by Indentations Along the Signature Line

Figure 4.2
Type of Tremor Characteristic of Forgery

Writing of the impaired or illiterate can be identified as spurious if the questioned writing exceeds the ability of the known writer. A high skill level signature of an impaired individual can be rejected without comparison documents.

REQUEST WRITING

Request writing exemplars are handwriting samples made at the request and under the supervision of the police, document examiners, or attorneys for comparison with questioned writing. The writer is asked to complete forms containing all the uppercase and lowercase letters plus numbers and punctuation marks. See Figure 4.3. Dictated material is also used. Dictation should include the material in question as well as additional writing.

Care must be taken to insure that request writing is suitable for comparison purposes since the writer may attempt to disguise his writing. Normal writing is a result of subconscious habit. The quality of writing is recognized by repeated significant characteristics executed with ordinary attention to the writing act. Certain precautions can insure that the exemplars are suitable.

The document examiner should take the request writing exemplars whenever possible. The examiner is then in a position to determine if the writing is normal writing or if the writer is trying to disguise his handwriting. Lawyers frequently have their clients write their name ten times on a sheet of paper. This is not an appropriate handwriting sample. When taking the request writing samples, follow established procedures.

Figure 4.3
Handwriting Specimen

Copy the following:

Arthur Bob Charles	Don Edwards Frank
George Henry Imig	John Kenneth Lamb
Mary Nan Olson	Paul Quentin Robert
Samuel Tom Umphrey	Vernon Will Xavier
Yolanda Ziffman	Abel Baker Charlie
Daniel Eugene Fell	Geronimo Harry Ingalls
James Katherine Luther	Michael Norman Othello
Pat Q. Romeo	Stanley Tomas Uranus
Victor Wally	X. Y. Zambene
1234 N. East Ave. S. W.	5678 S. West Blvd. N. W.
9012 E. North Pl., S. E.	3456 W. South St. N.E.
Signature	Witness
Address	Date

PROCEDURE FOR TAKING REQUEST WRITING

1. Use a questionnaire to validate any circumstances that could affect the writing (See Figure 4.4). Illness, injury, or drug abuse may alter the writer's handwriting.
2. The writing conditions of the questioned document should be duplicated. If a suspect writing is handwritten, get handwriting for proper comparison. If a suspect document is printed in uppercase printing, the request writing should be uppercase printing as well.
3. Compare ballpoint pen with ballpoint, pencil with pencil, and so on. Duplicate the writing instrument.
4. Duplicate the writing environment. Photocopy the document, whiteout the suspect writing and duplicate the form several times. Have the suspect sign the samples one at a time, removing each sample as it is completed so that he cannot copy from his earlier work. If the questioned document is not available, use similar size paper to make up exemplars.
5. If the questioned document is written under unusual circumstances, these circumstances should be duplicated. If the writer was standing while signing a questioned document, the writer should be asked to write in a standing position.
6. Give specific instructions and make a note of the instructions given. For example, the writer was asked to print using all uppercase letters.
7. To prevent the writer from disguising his exemplars, increase the speed of dictation to rush the writer. Distract him between handwriting samples. The writer will not be able to maintain his disguise if he is distracted.
8. Have the suspect write with both hands. Indicate which hand is being used on each form that is signed.
9. Date and sign all request writing with your initials; number the documents in the order in which they were executed; and include any special instructions that you gave the writer such as, "Use all uppercase."
10. Additional request writing can be worded to include words, expressions, letters, names, and combinations found in the questioned writing. When a case involves numbers, have the suspect write his numbers from one to one hundred. Organize a diversity of alphanumeric characters into a paragraph such as the ones that follow.

Questions About Writing Standards

- Do request writing standards show any signs of attempted disguise?
- Have they been properly taken and properly witnessed?
- Do they contain suitable material for comparison such as similar letter combinations and spacing?

Figure 4.4
Request Writing Worksheet

Document Examiner:______________________________ Case No.______________

Attorney:____ Date:________________

Writer:____ Age:_________________

Male: ________ Female: ________ Right Handed: ______ Left Handed: ______

Level of Education: ____________________ Country Educated in: ___________

Physical Handicaps: ____

Illness or Chronic Conditions: _____________________________________

Medications Used: ____

Alcohol Consumption: None: ____ Light: ____ Moderate: ____ Heavy: _________

Present Physical Condition: ____

Other Pertinent Information: ____

Type of Exemplars: ____
(Such as Forms, Simulated Documents, Signatures, etc.)

Material Was: Copied: _____ Dictated: _______ Spontaneous: ______

Number of Exemplars: _____________

Starting Time:___________ Time Finished: _________ Total Time: ___________

Witness: ____

LETTERS FOR DICTATION

The London Letter:

> Our London business is good, but Vienna and Berlin are quiet. Mr. D. Lloyd has gone to Switzerland and I hope for good news. He will be there for a week at 1496 Zermott St. and then goes to Turin and Rome and will join Col. Parry and arrive at Athens, Greece, Nov. 27th or Dec. 2nd. Letters there should be addressed: King James Blvd. 3580. We expect Chas. E. Fuller Tuesday. Dr. L McQuaid and Robt. Unger, Esq. left on the 'XY' Express tonight.
>
> Sincerely,

A more modern dictation follows:

My Dear Zeb:

Very soon now tax returns must be made to the United States Department of Internal Revenue by the American citizen, whether he lives in New York City or Zenia, Ohio. Here are some key pointers:

1. Forms are provided.
2. List all dependents.
3. Blind people get extra credit.
4. Employees must list all wages.
5. Get the forms from your company.
6. Jot down expenses.
7. Keep a record of donations.
8. Personal deductions over $1,000 must itemize. (The law allows you 10%).
9. Husband and wife can file jointly.
10. Quarterly payments must be made by self-employed.

The zero hour is coming! What other questions can I answer for you?

TYPEWRITING STANDARDS

Questions arise about typewritten documents that require standards for comparison purposes. Standards are taken from typewriters in a similar manner to gathering handwriting samples. Both informal and formal samples can be acquired. Informal samples consist of material typed on a specific machine during the normal course of business. Formal samples are material specially typed on the machine. All the keys on the typewriter need to be copied. See Figure 4.5.

Figure 4.5
Typewriter Exemplar

'1234567890-=	~!@#$%^&*()_+
qwertyuiop[]\	QWERTYUIOP{}¦
asdfghjkl;'	ASDFGHJKL:"
zxcvbnm,./	ZXCVBNM<>?

Or:

The quick brown fox jumps over the lazy dog.
The quick brown fox jumps over the lazy dog.

Several pages of type should be taken. If there is a questioned text, the material from the text should be typed. Follow the guidelines for taking handwriting exemplars.

ADDITIONAL STANDARDS

Other types of printed material for comparison purposes may need to be collected. Faxes, photocopies, and computer-generated documents may need to be studied. They can be collected in a similar manner to collecting typed documents.

In one case a document examiner needed to determine if documents had been faxed from one fax machine to another. An enlarged photocopied document did not exhibit jagged edges usually representative of faxed material. The fax machines were delivered to the document examiner's laboratory. Similar documents were generated from the sending fax machine to the receiving fax machine. The documents were enlarged on a photocopier, duplicating the document in question. The reproduced document showed the same characteristics as the questioned document. The duplication process had eliminated the rough edges.

Once the standards are collected they can be enlarged by photograph, photocopy, or scanner. Earliest generation photocopies are the best. As photocopies are copied and recopied, their value diminishes as subtle details are lost with each subsequent copy. Enlargements of multigenerated photocopies have lost so much needed detail that they deteriorate; gaps appear where none exist on the originals, and details are distorted.

DOs AND DON'Ts FOR COLLECTING EXEMPLARS AND STANDARDS

- **DON'T** rely on too little writing. How much is enough? Enough to show the range of handwriting characteristics of the writer.
- **DO** obtain sufficient handwriting exemplars, at least twenty to twenty-five signatures or four to five pages of handwriting or handprinting.

- **DON'T** rely exclusively on writing that differs significantly from the questioned.
- **DO** collect similar samples: handprinting with handprinting, ink signatures with ink signatures, lined paper with lined paper, same size with same size.
- **DON'T** rely on documents recently written if the comparison documents were written many years ago.
- **DO** collect standards dated at approximately the same time as the questioned.
- **DON'T** compare writing written under abnormal conditions (for example, when the writer was intoxicate) with normal writing.
- **DO** collect documents that duplicate the writing environment: checks with checks, contracts with contracts.
- **DO** instruct the writer in order to obtain similar exemplars. For example, print with all uppercase letters.

THE CARE AND HANDLING OF DOCUMENTS

Ideally, evidence is collected, safeguarded, and preserved throughout the litigation process. It is necessary to safeguard documents while they are in your possession and to present them to the document examiner intact.

Documents are easily damaged and must be carefully preserved because improper or careless handling can inflict severe damage. Papers can be damaged by folding, tearing, or crumbling as well as staining from rust, food, soil, and grease. Unnecessary handling also harms documents so they should be handled as little as possible. If the documents are going to be tested for fingerprints, wear cotton gloves when handling them. Hold original documents by the edges since body oils can soil documents.

Pins, staples, glue, and other fastening devices also injure paper. Do not staple original documents or mark them in any way. Do not circle or highlight material to be examined. In short, do not fold, spindle, or mutilate documents in your care.

Do not write on top of documents. Sometimes indented writing appears on evidence because careless writers made notes while the original documents were underneath. Mark envelopes for documents before inserting the documents.

Erasing information from documents whether by abrasion or chemical eradication damages paper fibers and the finishes on paper. Contact with rough surfaces can also injure the finish on paper.

Original documents should be placed in mylar folders to protect them while being handled to reduce the chance of unintentional damage. Some documents can be secured by stapling the jacket around the document. Photocopies of small standards can be stapled to a larger sheet to prevent loss.

Documents that are being transported should have cardboard sheets placed around them. These sheets should be taped, not stapled.

Paper and ink are sensitive to the elements, especially light, heat, and water. Sunlight fades paper and ink; heat makes paper brittle; water dissolves some types of ink causing the ink to spread across the paper making the paper swell. When the paper dries, it does not return to its original size.

Documents should be stored in a suitable environment away from sunlight and excessive heat or moisture. Original documents should be kept in a fireproof safe or a fireproof file cabinet when they are not being examined.

It is best to examine documents before they are tested for fingerprints as the chemicals used to bring up prints may obscure evidence. Ninhydrin sprayed over pencil writing makes it illegible.

Only nondestructive tests may be performed on any piece of evidence unless you acquire written permission from the court for destructive testing. Any alteration to the original document is destructive testing even if only a small sample is used.

Documents should be photographed and photocopied and these materials used for examination as much as possible. A good close-up photograph may reveal more information than the original document viewed without magnification.

It is the responsibility of document examiners to preserve the documents while in their care and to return them intact.

CHAIN OF CUSTODY

Evidence must be protected whenever it is transferred to another party. If the evidence must be sent by mail, use registered mail, restricted delivery. Certified mail is not sufficiently protective when dealing with original documents. Many people use Federal Express to send documents because they provide fast efficient service and track the location of packages, which maintains the chain of evidence. Make sure the carrier is instructed to hand deliver the evidence to the proper person. Courier services hand deliver documents, providing a safe method of transferring documents.

A paper trail tracking original documents needs to be maintained. The document examiner must be able to verify control of the documents at all times. A chain of custody form signed by each person who handles the documents should be maintained by the document examiner. A copy should also be kept with the documents. See Figure 4.6.

Never relinquish possession of any original documents to anyone without first establishing that the person or agency is authorized to receive the document. Make sure to get a valid detailed receipt and place it in your files.

If these procedures are followed whenever possible, the integrity of the documents will be preserved and the chain of custody maintained.

RESTORATION OF DOCUMENTS

The paper industry continually makes improvements to the quality of its paper so that modern paper is more durable. Various finishes are put on paper to protect and preserve it so that it is impervious to agents such as insects, mold, and mildew.

Figure 4.6
Chain of Custody Form

CHAIN OF CUSTODY					
DATE	TIME	RECEIVED FROM	SIGNATURE	RECEIVED BY	SIGNATURE

However, as paper goes through its normal aging process, it becomes brittle and discolored. Some treatments to paper actually destroy it. Lamination, adhesives affixed to paper, and some ink formulas are destructive to paper.

Soiled documents can be cleaned, including documents damaged by soot and smoke, or dirt and soil. Paper can be washed to flush out impurities deposited into the fibers. Washing not only removes the dirt from the paper but puts moisture back into the fibers.

Water-soaked papers can be dried and separated. Some papers need to be freeze-dried in order to separate the pages; others can be hung to dry or blow-dried. Once the papers have dried sufficiently, the pages can be individually separated and laid on a flat surface to finish drying.

Fire-damaged and charred documents may be salvageable. Charred paper is brittle and needs to be handled carefully because if it is mishandled it will disintegrate. Spraying the paper with an acetate will strengthen it so that it can be moved and handled. Charred paper should be placed on cotton batting or firm paper for transport. It may be necessary to spray it with a fine mist of water to put moisture back into the pages. It is a good idea to photograph it at its original site.

Documents that are brittle from age or heat should also be handled very carefully. Many old papers are held together with cellophane tape that has yellowed and attempts to remove the tape may destroy the paper.

Pages that are stuck together with glue may be separated by carefully steaming the documents to soften the glue. These restorations should not be attempted by an amateur.

Slightly damaged documents can be restored. No method should be used by anyone who is not properly trained as more harm could result from improper attempts at restoration. Damaged documents are restored by conservators. There are several centers in the United States that offer restoration services on documents. Conservators also provide information on proper preservation to prevent deterioration of fragile documents.

SUMMARY

Exemplars are known handwriting samples used for comparison with questioned documents. There are two types of exemplars, formal and informal. Formal exemplars are request writing samples. Informal exemplars consist of documents executed in the normal course of business. Proper procedures should be followed when taking request writing.

Attorneys must take steps to protect documents entrusted to their care. Documents are fragile and require special handling. Not only must documents be kept in their original condition, but a chain of custody must be maintained to ensure the integrity of the documents. If everyone who handles document evidence takes the necessary precautions to ensure the integrity of the documents, evidence will be properly preserved for court proceedings.

Part II

Handwriting Identification

5

The Evolution of the Written Word

THE HISTORY OF WRITING

Writing consists of messages that convey ideas to others in a permanent or semipermanent form. This definition includes pictures and drawings as well as penmanship systems. Writing evolved because mankind had a desire to communicate thoughts to others in different locations. Writing developed independently in all major cultures. All primitive people had an oral language and an early stage of writing, or something resembling writing. Mankind devised a means of communicating through visible signs that could be understood by others. Records have been chiseled into stone, notched into sticks, carved into wood, knotted on ropes, pressed into clay tablets, and marked on animal skins.

Writing grew out of pictures; cave drawings were the first written record of mankind. Gradually pictures came to represent words. Word pictures known as ideographs were used by the Sumerians, Chinese, Aztecs, Mayas, and Egyptians. Most notable were the Egyptian word-pictures, called hieroglyphics.

Pictures were then modified into symbols and symbols represented syllables. A symbol representing a sound or a syllable is known as a phonograph. This developed into simplified phonetic symbols called the phonetic alphabet. The Sumerians, who assigned a symbol to each sound, are generally credited with the development of the first alphabet. The Phoenicians spread this alphabet throughout the known world.

THE FIRST ALPHABET

The Phoenician alphabet consisted of twenty-two letters. They separated their words with periods and their sentences with slash marks. Their writing went from right to left. Figure 5.1 gives you an example of the Phoenician method of writing.

Figure 5.1
Phoenician-Styled Writing

/metsys.gnitirw.naicineohP.fo.elpmaxE

The word alphabet comes from the Greek words for the first two letters, "A" and "B," which were alpha and beta. The Greeks changed the writing direction making it left to right and added vowels to the alphabet. Their alphabet consisted of twenty-four letters.

The Romans borrowed the alphabet from the Greeks and gave our letters their abecedarium names of "A", "B", "C." For several centuries Roman writing consisted of disconnected capital letters. Roman scribes invented the lowercase letters patterned from the capital letters. These letters simplified the forms and made it easier to copy manuscripts. Ascenders and descenders to the letter forms developed from the copying process.

Gradually connecting strokes, also known as ligatures, were added to connect the letters within words. Many styles were used over the centuries but the most prevalent is the garland connecting stroke that resembles the letter "u".

Today the influence of the early alphabets is seen throughout Europe and America. The European explorers brought the alphabet to the new world. North and South American systems are based on the Germanic system and Romance languages, which are derived from the Romans. Most of the countries in Central and South America use Spanish, except for Brazil which uses the Portuguese language and alphabet. The United States and Canada share the same language and penmanship systems.

The Greek alphabet is still used in Greece, Cyprus, and Crete. The Cyrillic alphabet, derived from the Greek, is used in Russia and Eastern European countries. This alphabet was introduced by Saints Cyril and Methodis who proselytized the Slavic tribes of East Europe in the ninth century. The Cyrillic alphabet is an adaptation of the Greek alphabet.

The Armenian alphabet and Hebrew text are found in the middle eastern countries. Arabic is used in this part of the world, as well as in northern Africa, although our American alphabets are taught in many of the African countries. There are many different languages in Africa. Africa is home to Arabic and the modern Roman alphabet, along with many dialects such as Ethiopian.

India, Mongolia, Tibet, and Asia have their own writing systems. India has two main alphabets, Hindu and Urdu, with many dialects. The Burmese alphabet is a combination of Indian Sanskrit and Pali Script of the Buddhist scriptures.

The major far east alphabets are Korean, Chinese, and Japanese. The Korean alphabet was designed rather than evolving like our other alphabet systems and is considered the only perfect alphabet. Japanese writing was adapted and simplified from the Chinese. Japanese is normally written in kanamajiri. Chinese writing is the most complex. See Table 5.1.

Table 5.1
Alphabet Systems

Germanic Alphabet
English Alphabet
- United States
- Canada
- The British Isles
- Australia
- New Zealand
- South Africa

German Alphabet
- Liechtenstein
- Switzerland (part of)
- Austria
- Belgium (part of)
- German

Dutch Alphabet — The Netherlands
- Belgium (Part of)

Danish Alphabet — Denmark
Norwegian Alphabet — Norway
Swedish Alphabet — Sweden
Finnish Alphabet — Finland
Icelandic Alphabet — Iceland
Afrikaans — South Africa
Celtic Alphabet — Ireland

Romance Languages
French Alphabet
- France
- Monaco
- Switzerland (part of)

Italian Alphabet
- Italy
- Switzerland (part of)

Portuguese Alphabet
- Portugal
- Brazil

Romanian Alphabet — Romania
Spanish Alphabet — Spain
- South American Countries
- Argentina • Bolivia
- Chile • Colombia
- Ecuador • Paraguay
- Peru • Uruguay
- Venezuela
- Central American Countries
- Mexico • Costa Rica
- El Salvador • Honduras
- Nicaragua • Panama
- Parts of the Caribbean

Based on Greek Alphabet

Cyrillic Alphabet
- Bulgaria
- Russia
- Ukraine
- Mongolia
- Lithuania

Greek Alphabet
- Greece
- Cyprus
- Turkey
- Crete

Slavic Alphabet
- Poland
- Czechoslovakia
- Hungary
- Yugoslavia
- Latvia

Other Alphabets
- Cherokee • Hawaiian

Some nationalities have independent alphabets, such as the Celtic alphabet of Ireland. In 1823, Sequoyah invented an alphabet of eighty-six characters for the Cherokee Indian nation. The Hawaiian alphabet has only twelve letters: "a", "e", "h", "i", "k", "l", "m", "n", "o", "p", "u", and "w".

Knowledge of the systems of writing assists the document examiner in distinguishing characteristics shared by a large number of people from the individual characteristics of a particular writer.

PENMANSHIP SYSTEMS

The principal influence on our twentieth century scripts were the Spencerian system of penmanship and the system of Payson, Dunton, and Scribner. Modern commercial hands were developed from these systems near the turn of the century by several penman, the most well-known being the Palmer method and the Zaner-Bloser system. Since the early 1900s, over sixty-two different systems have been created. The D'Nealian, created in 1962, is popular with modern school systems because students can make an easy transition from printscript to cursive.

The advent of the typewriter in 1873 reduced the need for exquisite handwriting. Penmanship schools became extinct early in the twentieth century as the typewriter replaced the penman in modern business offices.

HANDPRINTING

Handprinting comes under a variety of names. It has been called hand lettering, lettering, pen and pencil printing, print script, print writing, printing script, and script writing, and the school system refers to it as manuscript writing. Lettering is generally recognized as handprinting, that is, a precise style of printing used by architects, draftsman, engineers, and commercial artists.

Children are introduced to handprinting when they enter the first grade. Cursive writing is usually introduced in the second or third grade. After they are taught to write, printing is discarded. Some adults prefer handprinting and incorporate printed letter forms within their writing, or use handprinting instead of cursive.

Printed styles can be more diversified than handwriting. People who print do not stay with the letter forms they were taught as children. Most writers mix uppercase and lowercase letters; some combine printed letters with cursive. As a result, a document examiner can compare and identify printscript, as printing contains as many individualized characteristics as cursive, if not more.

SIGNATURES

A signature is a person's name as written by that person. Barron's Law Dictionary describes it as "a writing or other mark that is placed upon an instrument for the purpose of authenticating it or giving it legal effect" (p. 453). A signature is the only universal sign of identity.

A signature may be handwritten, printed, stamped, typed, or engraved. It is used in legal and financial transactions to attest to the validity of the document being signed, and on identification documents. Most signatures consist of a person's first and last name and may include a middle initial or name, as well as a title. A signature may also include Senior or Junior after a name.

Signatures have been used from early civilization to transfer property. When most people were illiterate, marks or seals were used to sign a document. Scribes would write the signer's name and the signer would add his mark, which usually consisted of a cross and was called the signum.

Modern writers pen their signatures more than any other combination of letters. Most people have stylized their signatures into a form that is comfortable for them and easily executed.

NUMBERS

As writing evolved, symbols were developed to represent numbers. Our numbers were derived from the Arabic. Most penmanship systems taught proper forms for numbers. These numbers are similar in their construction among penmanship systems with slight variations in embellishments.

Since number styles are limited, most people do not realize that their number forms are distinctive and can be compared and identified. While there is less variation in numbers than in written or printed letters, identifying characteristics will be present in most cases.

Many document cases involve numbers. These include alterations of numbers on checks and other negotiable instruments, changes in dates, embezzlement of funds, and addresses on anonymous letters.

GRAMMAR

In addition to studying numbers, document examiners will review punctuation for individual habits. Quotation marks, question marks, exclamation points, periods, commas, colons, and semicolons may contain distinctive patterns. The amount of indentation of a paragraph can assist a document examiner in making an identification.

The misuse of punctuation can also assist in identification. Writers have been identified because they make mistakes in punctuation such as ignoring proper punctuation for commas and periods or placing commas and periods in the wrong places. An excessive use of punctuation (or lack of punctuation) also leads to identity.

The method of writing a date or dollars and cents can assist in identifying the writer. The Bradford check classification system for identification relies on the habits that a writer develops when completing a check because these habits are consistent. These habits consist of placement, motor memory, and the style chosen to complete the check.

While a document examiner cannot rely exclusively on misspelled words, spelling idiosyncracies can contribute to the identification of an individual.

It is the document examiner's responsibility to review all the data on a document when rendering an opinion about the authenticity or spuriousness of a questioned document.

SUMMARY

Document examiners should be familiar with the penmanship systems in use during the twentieth and twenty-first centuries as well as systems from other countries that may influence handwriting. Familiarity with class characteristics from the major penmanship systems enables a document examiner to distinguish individual characteristics from class characteristics.

6

Handwriting Characteristics

CLASS CHARACTERISTICS

When document examiners study handwriting for identification, they compare the characteristics of writing for similarities and differences. There are two types of handwriting characteristics; class characteristics and individual characteristics.

Class characteristics are the most common traits used by most people. In handwriting identification, class characteristics refer to the standard rules of penmanship that the writer attempts to follow when he is learning to write. Some deviations from penmanship standards are so common that they fall into the category of class characteristics even though they are not part of any penmanship system. An example would be printed capital letters in place of cursive. The Greek "E" is another characteristic that is utilized by many writers.

Individual characteristics are those deviations from the norm that writers make when they change the writing from the form they were taught. Writers do not adhere closely to the rules of penmanship. Individual peculiarities creep into everyone's handwriting as they modify and stylize their writing. These modifications provide the strongest identification. No writer duplicates exactly all the peculiarities that show up in any other writer's handwriting.

What are the characteristics that make up writing? The individual features of handwriting are categorized for identification purposes. When a writer puts pen to paper he utilizes movement, spatial relationships, and form.

THE WRITING MOVEMENT

The writing movement includes direction, slant, rhythm, speed, and line quality. The direction of writing is dictated by the rules of penmanship. It is necessary for document examiners to know the normal development of writing in order to determine deviations from that norm. Slant is part of the direction of writing but is measured independently; rhythm and speed are affected by the direction of writing; and pressure is also related to the writing movement.

DIRECTION

Rules of penmanship dictate that writing progress from left to right on a horizontal plane. Each line is placed below the preceding one from the top to the bottom of the page. Letters return to an imaginary baseline in a rhythmic motion. Most penmanship systems begin their letter formations at the baseline and move upward and left or right, depending on the form of the letter.

Writing requires a movement through space. The writer starts at or above the imaginary baseline and moves up or down to form letters; and horizontally and diagonally forming loops and circles as well as straight lines.

The writer will try to adhere to the rules that govern the location of each letter, either above or below the line of writing. He is taught to divide writing into three zones: upper zone, middle zone, and lower zone. He is taught the proper proportions between the zones of writing. The writer knows the rules for size, slant, and spacing between letters and written words.

SLANT

Slant, also called slope, refers to the direction in which the letters lean. All letters lean forward or backward, or they may be vertical. Slant may also be variable. When a writer tries to disguise his handwriting, he will usually change the slant since that will change the pictorial effect of the writing. Note the difference in slant by two different writers in Figure 6.1.

RHYTHM

Rhythm refers to the even return to the baseline by the writer. Skilled writers possess more rhythm than unskilled writers. Rhythm can be even or erratic; it usually falls somewhere in between. Rhythm is usually disrupted when a writer attempts to copy another writer's handwriting. Rhythm is a significant characteristic in the identification of a forgery.

SPEED

The amount of time it takes a writer to execute a handwriting sample varies. Some writers think fast and try to write as fast as they think. Slow writers may be deliberate and meticulous or less familiar with the writing process. An individual can vary his speed of writing any time he chooses. Writers trade speed for legibility. The faster the writing, the more difficult it is to read.

CHARACTERISTICS OF FAST WRITING

There are numerous indicators of speed in writing of which line quality is the principle one. Fast writers simplify their letter forms and slur the endings on words. I-dots are jabbed and carelessly placed. T-bars are sweeping or tapered and may be joined to the following word. Word endings become blurred and decrease in size. Endings are abbreviated and impossible to read. Fast writing generally slants forward with firm steady strokes.

Rhythm is smooth and natural with good line quality, that is, the line is smooth and even. Pressure patterns are usually evident with strong downstrokes and lighter upstrokes.

CHARACTERISTICS OF SLOW WRITING

Generally, slow writing is stiff and labored. Slow writers make carefully executed letter forms that are generally consistent and exact. Many strokes of writing are retraced and cramped. T-bars are carefully placed and balanced, often with blunt endings. I-dots are more rounded and close to the stem. Beginning strokes and word endings are generally blunt to the point that bulbs may be observed without the aid of magnification. These bulbs are found at the beginning of letters and occasionally at the end of the writing as well. They are caused by the pen sitting still for a few seconds, leaving a thicker inkspot on the ink line.

Slow writers generally have a more vertical slant. Pressure is often monotonous without the differences in pressure seen in fast writing. Poor line quality may result if the writer is not proficient. Slow writing is easier to imitate since forgers generally write slowly when copying someone else's handwriting.

Figure 6.1
Comparison of Slant on Handwriting Samples

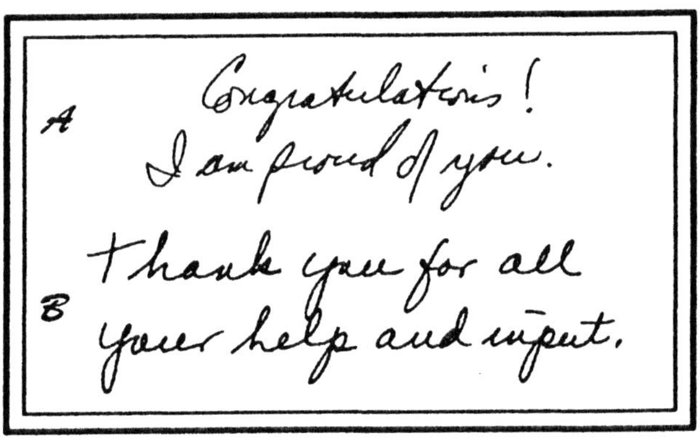

LINE QUALITY

The speed of the writing affects the line quality or line value. Line quality represents the smoothness of the line. Writing is normally rapidly executed. Good line quality is smooth and even, without tremor or corrugation. Line quality can be the most important criteria of identification.

Poor line quality is the result of slow writing, which may indicate forgery. When creating a forgery, the forger draws the signature instead of writing it. The art of drawing is slow and laborious resulting in tremulous strokes of writing. Some writers naturally write more slowly than others, however, there is a difference between slow writing and slowly-drawn writing.

PRESSURE PATTERNS

There are two types of pressure in handwriting. One is grip pressure and refers to the grasp of the writing instrument; the other is the amount of pressure used to push the writing instrument across the paper resulting in indentations in the writing line.

Most writers use lighter pressure on upstrokes when they are pushing the pen away and heavier pressure on the downstrokes when they pull the pen toward themselves. These pressure patterns are individualized and subconscious and, therefore, they are strong identifying factors in handwriting.

SPATIAL RELATIONSHIPS

Spatial relationships refer to the writer's use of space. This affects the size of the writing as well as the alignment. Spatial relationships can be significant identifying characteristics since writers frequently disregard the rules of penmanship when spacing their writing. Idiosyncrasies in vertical alignment or horizontal expansion help identify a writer. Unless spatial relationships are highly individualized, forgers overlook this aspect of writing.

SIZE

The normal size of writing is dictated by penmanship systems. Young children are taught to write using larger strokes and by the time they have mastered the basic letter forms, they are expected to reduce the writing size in half. The size of writing varies according to personal preference and available space.

PROPORTIONS

Proportions usually are consistent in writing regardless of the size of the writing. When a writer changes the size of his writing, his letters remain proportional. Document examiners compare the letters in each zone of writing. They compare the looped letters with middle zone letters. Capital letters are also compared to upper looped and lower looped letters and middle zone letters. Proportions include the horizontal expansion of the writing in relationship to the vertical strokes of the letters.

SPACING

Spacing refers to the amount of space between letters, words, and lines of writing. Writers are taught to space their letters evenly on a horizontal plane. The rules of writing dictate one to two letter spaces between each word. Sufficient space must be left between lines to prevent intermingling of upper and lower loops. Deviations in spacing can occur between letters, groups of letters, words, and lines of writing.

UTILIZATION OF SPACE

When a writer is given unlimited space, he will proceed to write in a size that is comfortable. Writing can be small, large, or variable.

A writer's utilization of space is affected by the parameters of the writing environment. He must adjust the size of his writing to fit into a specific area. Some writers plan ahead and space their work evenly in the space available while others miscalculate and must compress some of their writing to fit it into a tight space. How the writer adjusts size to accommodate the available space is an identifying factor.

ARRANGEMENT

Writers are taught to arrange their writing on a page by leaving margins all around the writing area. Depending on the type of paper, writers are trained to leave a one inch margin at the top and bottom of their paper and a smaller margin along the sides. Deviations from these norms help to reveal a writer through his personal pattern of arranging margins. Deviations include wide margins, no margins, irregular margins, or decreasing and increasing margins.

The amount of indentation at the beginning of a paragraph is another identifying characteristic. Some writers do not indent; some indent more than others. Some writers will not bother to separate their work into paragraphs; others will form paragraphs at inappropriate places.

ALIGNMENT

The baseline is the imaginary line on which writing sits, or actual lines on a document such as ruled paper or signature lines. Writing goes above and below the baseline but always returns to this baseline. The return to the baseline is a significant feature as few writers bring all of their letters exactly to the baseline. Some writers stay above the line, some sit on the line, and others drop the bottom of their letters below the line. Some writers form an arch along the baseline and others drift upward at the end of the line. Writers usually are consistent in their baselines. People copying another's writing rarely give consideration to the way the writer arranges his letters on the baseline.

FORM

Most people recognize form as the shape or design of the letter. Penmanship classes introduce the basic strokes of writing that make up the design of all of the letters. Penmanship instruction included the connectors between letters and the lead-in and terminal stroke formations of each letter. Legibility is also a consideration when assessing form.

LETTER DESIGNS

The writing strokes consist of lines and curves in various directions forming individual letter shapes. Lines can be vertical, horizontal, or diagonal. Curves are loops, circles, or parts of circles. Each letter has a distinguishing element that makes it unique. For example, the "t" has a cross bar, the "i" has a dot and the "f" is the only lowercase cursive letter that spans all three zones of writing.

Everyone has a mental image of what a letter should look like. Many of these designs deviate from standard penmanship forms. A person may adopt someone else's letter design that he admires. A writer may experiment with variations of letter designs until he finds one that he likes or he may simply make a design that he feels represents the letter form he is creating. Most people do not recognize the uniqueness of their individualized forms.

Many writers use more than one design for an individual letter. It is not unusual to see two or three different letter designs in one handwriting. It is important when collecting handwriting samples to obtain enough writing to cover the variations that a person has in individual letter forms.

Letter designs are the most easily identifiable feature of handwriting. Many document examiners rely on similarities and differences in letter designs to determine the authenticity or spuriousness of handwriting. Since forgery usually involves imitating letter forms, it is necessary to include other characteristics of handwriting in examining and comparing handwriting in order to draw proper conclusions.

METHOD OF CONSTRUCTION

Forgers concentrate on imitating the letter forms of their victim's handwriting, however, when copying each letter, they generally fail to follow the same method of construction that the victim uses. Writers develop consistent habits regarding the construction of letter forms. They start their letters in approximately the same place whether on the baseline or above it. They move the writing instrument in the same direction and join strokes at the same location each time. They terminate their letters in a similar manner. The more habits the forger fails to imitate, the easier it is to identify fraudulent writing.

INITIAL STROKES

Important parts of letter forms are the lead-in and terminal strokes that people use to begin and end their letters. Many of these are highly personalized strokes that assist in identifying a writer.

Lead-in strokes are found at the beginning of letters and words. They may be straight, curved, or hooked; long or short. The initial placement of the pen to begin each letter form is a highly individualized characteristic. Forgers rarely copy the beginning point of a letter and writers rarely deviate from these habits.

TERMINAL STROKES

Terminal strokes are ending strokes on letters and words. They also may be straight, curved, or hooked; long or short, and are consistent with writers. These are also frequently overlooked by forgers unless the terminal stroke is very distinctive.

MEDIAL STROKES

Medial strokes are those strokes found within words. These letters may be different than the initial or terminal letters. Some writers use different forms of a letter depending on its location in a word. The letter immediately before or after a medial letter may affect the design of a letter. The type of connecting stroke may also influence the form of a medial letter. Stand alone letters may be made differently than connected letters.

LIGATURES

Ligatures, also called connectors, are the strokes that join letters together. There are four types of ligatures: garlands, angles, arcade, and thready writing. Garlands are rounded strokes that go down to the baseline and up to the beginning of the next letter in a wide u-shape. They are the most common type of joining strokes. Angles consist of abrupt changes of direction. Arcade strokes are arched connecting strokes and thready connectors consist of ill-formed connections that resemble a line with a slight wiggle to it. Writers may use one or more of these connectors to link their letters together.

Letters in a word may be connected or disconnected. Some writers join (or do not join) some or all of their letters; some writers consistently join (or do not join) specific letter combinations. The document examiner studies the various methods of connecting letters as part of his analysis.

EMBELLISHMENTS

Embellishments were once considered an important part of letter forms but modern penmanship systems do not use embellishments. Calligraphers will embellish their letters with flourishes but the average writer does not, therefore any hooks, ticks, or flourishes that appear in handwriting assist in the identification process. Flourishes are extra strokes added to letters to improve their appearance. These flourishes are curved and wavy lines added to the beginning or ending of letters. Some writers have modified flourishes into underscores found below their signatures.

Hooks are small semicircular strokes executed subconsciously by a writer. Hooks may be found at the beginning or ending of words although some will appear in the middle. Ticks are abrupt changes in direction that form an angle to the writing line. This angle is usually less than 90 degrees. Writers subconsciously incorporate hooks or ticks in their writing. The hook or tick is not part of the letter design since they are strokes that go in the opposite direction of the lines that make up each letter.

LEGIBILITY

When handwriting deviates sufficiently from the traditional forms of writing, the reader must guess at the content of the material that has been written. Letter forms blur and merge with other forms to create new forms. An "o" may resemble an "a" and an "i" cannot be distinguished from an "e." In many cases the letters are completely illegible or improperly designed.

The degree of legibility of the writing is a factor that assists in the identification of a writer. A writer can vary the legibility of his writing by increasing or decreasing his speed. Increasing speed tends to decrease legibility. A writer must balance legibility by regulating speed and the precision needed to form clearly defined letter forms.

BODY MOVEMENT

In addition to writing movement, document examiners evaluate body movement. Writing is executed with finger movement, hand movement, forearm movement, whole arm movement, or a combination of any or all of these types of movement.

Finger movement occurs when the writer only moves his fingers to progress through a line of writing. This type of writing is seen primarily in people who have not developed a lot of skill in writing. When the writer uses only his fingers to manipulate the writing instrument, he must continually adjust the writing instrument while moving his hand across the paper to complete a line of writing. Finger writing is frequently employed when copying another's handwriting or signature.

In hand movement, the writer swings his hand around in a small arc as he forms the letters using his wrist as a center of action. He makes adjustments less frequently than the finger mover and may employ some finger movement in combination with the hand movement.

Forearm movement occurs when the writer uses his elbow as the center of action with most of the movement coming from the arm. It is the most difficult type of writing to imitate.

Whole arm writing uses the entire arm to complete the writing act. Whole arm writing is used to write in large strokes on large boards such as blackboards.

Body movement relates to penscope, that is, the distance the pen covers before the writer has to pause and adjust his hand to continue writing.

Pen position is also included with body movement. Pen position refers to the angle at which the writing instrument is held in relation to the surface of the paper. Modern writing instruments do not produce shaded writing that was prevalent during the nib pen or fountain pen era. Therefore, pen position is not frequently addressed by modern document examiners.

EVALUATION OF SKILL LEVEL

A person develops his handwriting to a skill level that suits his needs and ability. A wrier cannot exceed his skill level. The line quality, the rhythm of the writing, intricacies of letter forms, and body movements reveal skill level.

The smoothness of the line of writing represents the line quality, speed being the important determinate when measuring line quality. Slow writing is tremulous, lacks uniformity, and is the result of either a lack of skill or of copying another's style. It can be an important consideration in the identification of a writer.

Rhythm is another indicator of skill level as the writer who has a well-developed rhythm is a more highly-skilled writer than one whose rhythm is poor. The intricacies of the letter form as well as embellishments are also part of line quality.

It is easier to imitate a poor quality, lower skill level writer than one who has developed his writing to a high skill level. It is easier to copy oversimplified signatures that consist of a line and a squiggle than a complex signature that contains many intricate designs and changes of direction in the writing line.

GRAMMAR

Spelling and punctuation assist in handwriting identification. Spelling and punctuation cannot be used exclusively to identify handwriting but they can aid in identification. Adherence or lack of adherence to the rules of grammar helps identify a writer as well.

RANGE OF WRITING

All of the characteristics that make up an individual's handwriting represent the range of the writer. This includes class characteristics as well as individual characteristics; all of the deviations from the method taught, and all the idiosyncrasies of the writer. Most cases can be solved without having the full range of the writer's habits as there are usually sufficient identifiers in four or five pages of a person's handwriting to make an identification or elimination.

ELIMINATION

Any significant fundamental characteristic that is not part of the writer's range of writing indicates a different writer. If an apparent difference can be explained, then it is not a significant difference. Explanations for differences include accidentals or deliberate disguise; and outside factors such as health problems and aging. Deviation from the method of construction of letters, words, and signatures indicate a different writer.

Writing is a habit that requires almost no conscious awareness of the writing act, and is frequently beyond the control of the mind or the hand. This is evident when someone tries unsuccessfully to disguise his handwriting. The habits are so ingrained that the writer cannot eliminate all the characteristics that encompass his writing style.

INDIVIDUAL CHARACTERISTICS

Individual characteristics are strong identifying characteristics when comparing handwriting samples. Their value is weighed by the number of people who make a particular individual characteristic. Some individual characteristics are copied by many people, others are rarely seen in handwriting. The more handwriting samples a document examiner studies, the more accurate her assessment of the value of an individual characteristic since she knows how frequently that characteristic is likely to show up in other handwriting samples.

Individual characteristics can be categorized as consciously acquired habits and as subconscious acquisitions. Consciously acquired habits are those the writer deliberately cultivated in his writing. The subconscious habits crept into his handwriting without his awareness. Since the writer is not aware of these subconscious characteristics, he cannot change or delete them from his handwriting.

Consciously developed habits are easier to modify although a writer may forget them when attempting to disguise his handwriting. The most obvious methods of disguise are a change in slant, use of unusual letter designs, regulating the speed of writing, and altering the skill level.

A writer practices penmanship until he is satisfied with his development. Each writer possesses the ability to develop skills to his own comfort level.

Writers often make adjustments in some characteristics of writing without giving them much thought, such as in the utilization of space. A writer must adjust his writing to fit into an available space. The writer may not think about this while doing it even though he is aware of adjusting the size of the writing.

Subconscious developments are more subtle. Most writers are not aware that these elements exist in their writing. Hooks and ticks may creep into their letter forms. Pressure patterns develop without conscious awareness. Deviations in other handwriting characteristics may go unnoticed. The more subconscious the habit, the stronger the identifying factor because of the difficulty in changing these subconscious characteristics.

SIGNATURES

Just as a writer develops his handwriting, he also fashions a signature as a means of identification. Most people devise a signature that differs slightly from their handwriting. Some writers use one style of signature for signing checks or routine documents executed in the normal course of business and another for more formal documents such as contracts or deeds. Other writers use a specific form such as their first and last name with a middle initial for all of the documents that they sign. Because the signature is the most frequently written combination of letters that a writer makes, it is more habitual and more fluidly written.

INITIALS

Initials consist of the first letter of a person's first, middle, and last name. They are used to mark changes in contracts or to identify each page of a will. Since initials consist of two or three capital letters, it is more difficult to make a determination of authenticity or spuriousness when dealing only with initials.

SUMMARY

Handwriting characteristics can be categorized under movement, spacial relationships, and form. Movement includes direction, slant, rhythm, speed, and pressure patterns. Spacial relationships include size, proportions, the utilization of space, baseline alignment and page and paragraph arrangement,and spacing between letters, words, and lines. Form covers letter designs, the method of construction of letters, and the strokes that join the letters together. Initial and terminal strokes are part of letter design.

The identification of handwriting includes many factors other than the actual formation of the letters. These handwriting characteristics are important aids in determining the author of a writing sample. See Table 6.1.

Table 6.1
Characteristics of Writing

MOVEMENT
Fluency
- Rhythm
- Writing speed
- Line quality
- Level of skill of the writer

Slant
- Forward, backhand, or vertical
- Variable

Pressure
- Depth of pressure
- Pressure patterns
- Horizontal pressure such as T-bars

Penstroke movement
- Finger movement
- Hand and wrist movement
- Arm movement
- Combination

SPATIAL RELATIONSHIPS
Size and Proportion
1. Overall size of the letters
   - Capital letters
   - Middle zone
   - Height of upper/lower zones
   - Width of letters
2. Zonal Proportions
3. Relationships
   - Baseline with capitals
   - Length of words
   - Relationship of T-bars & I-dots

Alignment
1. Margins
   - Left/right/top/bottom margin
   - Even margins
   - Increasing or decreasing margins
   - Irregular margins
2. Utilization of Space
   - Space between letters, words, lines
   - Size of letters in relationship to space available
3. Baseline
   - Writing sits on baseline
   - Writing sits above/below baseline
   - Regular return to the baseline
   - Peculiarities in relation to the baseline

LETTER FORMATIONS
1. Structure of the letter formations
   - Lead-in strokes
   - Terminal strokes or finals
2. Method of Construction
   - Initial stroke of the letter
   - Direction of the line
   - Intersections or junction of lines
   - Ending point
3. Individual characteristics & peculiarities
   - Stylized letter formations
   - Flourishes and embellishments
   - Idiosyncrasies
4. Letter forms
   - Copybook style
   - Stylized
   - Flourishes and embellishments
   - Simplified
   - Deteriorated
   - Ill-formed
   - Handprinted forms
5. Legibility
   - Legible
   - Illegible
6. Connecting strokes
   - Garlands
   - Arcades
   - Angles
   - Thready
   - No connectors
7. Position of letter in word
   - Initial stroke
   - Medial stroke
   - Terminal stroke

Skill of the Writer
- Highly skilled writer
- Average writer
- Low skill level
- Illiterate

RANGE OF WRITING
- Establishment of the master pattern
- Unexplainable differences

Grammar
- Grammatical errors
- Spelling
- Punctuation

7

Factors That Influence Handwriting

BASIC PRINCIPLES

The principles of handwriting identification are built on two basic principles. The first and foremost of these principles is that *no two people write exactly alike.* The use of our signature in legal and financial transactions is based on the unique features that occur in each person's handwriting distinguishing it from every other person's handwriting. This principle enables document examiners to differentiate genuine and nongenuine writing and to identify the author of a handwriting specimen.

The second principle states that every writer has natural variation in his handwriting so that no two signatures by the same author will be exactly the same. It is the job of a document examiner to distinguish between this natural variation and a different writer.

Writing is a skill which results from a variety of factors that combine to create an unique style for each individual writer. The process begins in young children through the visual observation of one's surroundings. Children see many forms of writing that they will eventually identify and duplicate. They develop a concept of what writing looks like. Gradually they learn to recognize the letters of the alphabet and numbers.

Writing is influenced by what we see and what we remember. We are surrounded by stimuli that influences our understanding of letters and words. Billboards, posters, magazines, and television all contribute to our learning the identity of letter forms.

At the same time children are learning to recognize letters, they begin to develop hand-eye coordination. By imitating their elders, children's play is preparation for adult activities. For example, children pretend to write by scribbling on any available surface from paper to walls. Young children actually begin learning to write when they start scribbling with a pencil or a crayon. Coloring is a precursor to writing and helps children develop coordination.

Writing begins formally when children are given paper and pencil and taught to create basic letter forms following a model. They trace the letter design with their pencil several times and then attempt to duplicate that letter form. They struggle to control their movements until they can easily copy each letter. Many physical factors play a part in the development of each writer. The size of the hand, flexibility of the wrist, and grip pressure on the pencil all contribute to the individuality of writing.

Children are taught handprinting in the primary grades. Cursive writing is introduced by the end of the second grade or the beginning of the third grade.

Students deviate from the standard penmanship forms from the time they begin to write. In fact, copybook style writing is so rare that anyone who writes perfect Palmer could easily be identified.

Each writer reaches his own skill level in handwriting based on his visual impressionability, capacity for graphic expression, and his ability to overcome mechanical and physical impediments. Writing is a complex act that takes years to master. Habitual writing is reached when the motor skills of the writer are fully developed and the writer no longer has to focus attention on the act of writing. At this point, the writer concentrates on content and lets his subconscious handle the execution of the writing act. The writing has become a habit.

Graphic maturity is reached when all writing movement is made from the habituated neuromuscular patterns. According to Robert Saudek, graphic maturity occurs at about fourteen years of age. In many people it occurs when they reach adulthood (eighteen to twenty-one years of age). Some people never reach graphic maturity; their writing remains at a low form level. The writer may not have mastered writing for many reasons such as lack of formal schooling or lack of a need to write.

INFLUENCES

An individual's handwriting changes somewhat during his lifetime. The most obvious change takes place from childhood through adolescence. Although graphic maturity is generally reached at the end of adolescence, changes will continue to occur gradually over time. Many factors will affect the act of writing although few factors will alter the handwriting so that it cannot be identified.

The penmanship system we are taught in our introduction to learning to write influences our handwriting. The primary systems being taught in our school systems are the Palmer, Zaner-Bloser, and D'Nealian. While these systems are similar, there are some differences in letter forms and methods of construction. The characteristics learned from a penmanship system are class characteristics because they are common to a large number of people.

Even though students learn the same system of writing, each develops unique characteristics that distinguish his writing from all other writers. These are individual characteristics of writing that are either consciously created or subconsciously executed. A writer will copy a style or letter form that he admires. A writer will experiment with different letter designs to add unique and individual letter forms to his writing; the more mature the writer, the more individual the letter forms.

Some writing habits are so subtle that the writer is not aware of them. Like breathing, they occur without conscious effort. Hooks and ticks are examples of writing habits that fit into this category. The writer is unaware of the flick of the wrist that creates these hooks and ticks on various letters which may be found in any letter form, usually at the beginning and ending of words.

Family members often share handwriting characteristics identified as familial characteristics. Children observe and copy their parents' handwriting. Siblings imitate each other's writing. Some children practice their parents' handwriting until they become fairly proficient at imitating it.

Groups of people who share a common bond develop handwriting characteristics that are unique to that group. Accountants, engineers, and draftsman fall into this category. People from foreign countries also share some common characteristics due to the system of writing they were taught. Unless the document examiner is aware of these influences, she could mistake national or group characteristics for individual characteristics of writing.

PRINCIPLES THAT ASSIST IN THE IDENTIFICATION OF HANDWRITING

- No two people write exactly alike.
- Individual characteristics that are unique to a particular writer exist in every person's handwriting distinguishing it from every other handwriting.
- The act of writing is a skill learned through repetition until it becomes a habit.
- A person's normal form of writing is based on mental images of learned letter designs.
- People stylize their writing starting with the penmanship system they were taught.
- People adopt writing styles by copying those they like.
- Many writing habits are subconscious and cannot be changed by the writer.
- A person's handwriting changes over the course of his lifetime.

FACTORS THAT CAUSE CHANGES IN HANDWRITING

Once a writer has reached the permanent condition of automatic writing, he has reached graphic maturity, which continues until some physical or mental disturbance interferes with his ability to write.

Robert Saudek in *Experiments with Handwriting* (p. 40) tells us that we are capable of writing fluently, easily and automatically only when we have obtained the following conditions.

1. We are familiar with the letters so that the mention of a letter conjures a graphic image of that letter in our minds.

2. We have control of the writing instrument and the mechanical factors (paper, pen, and writing surface) do not impede.
3. We are free of any physical impediment that would hinder writing.
4. We know how to spell the words so that we do not have to concentrate on spelling.
5. We are writing in our native language.

Obviously there are other factors that can affect our writing such as mental illness, emotional stress, even the mood we are in when we are writing. The type of document being written may cause us to write more or less formally and neatly. Many factors combine to affect handwriting.

What are the basic factors that influence our writing? The level of education attained affects the development of writing. An illiterate writer makes clumsy, halting strokes. As writing skill increases, the writing becomes smooth flowing and well executed. If a child continues in school until he reaches graphic maturity, his writing will be more highly developed than a student who drops out of school before he has mastered this skill. Some children take more pride in writing well and work to develop a high skill level.

Mechanical factors affecting our handwriting include the writing instrument, paper and writing surface, as well as the position of the writer when writing. Poor lighting conditions may adversely affect legibility.

Our physical well-being causes changes in our writing ability. Illness and injuries can alter a person's handwriting temporarily or permanently. Medication and substance abuse can also modify our handwriting.

The emotional state of the writer influences the appearance of our writing. When we are excited or angry our writing is more expansive and hurried. Our writing becomes compact when we are pensive and introspective. When we are tired our writing line and our word endings tend to droop.

The psychological factor, that is the writer's physical makeup and personality, influences the writing act, according to J. F. McCarthy in "Some Aspects of Normal Behavior: Their Use in Understanding Problems Encountered by Document Examiners" published by the *Journal of Forensic Science* in January, 1976:

> Handwriting most certainly reflects some aspect of the writer's personality. . . . Handwriting is in essence nothing more than a form of visual behavior, graphically recorded and relatively permanent. It is the result of the writer's physiological, psychological and environmental life. (p. 201)

Lack of familiarity with the material has an impact on handwriting. Difficult words, foreign words, and complex concepts may interfere with the smooth flow of normal script.

The major factors contributing to handwriting will now be considered in more detail.

TIME SPAN

Handwriting changes over time. It changes most strikingly from childhood to adolescence until we reach adulthood. Handwriting continues to develop until the writer reaches graphic maturity when it stabilizes. Subtle changes may continue to take place over time, more for some than others. Handwriting will deteriorate as the aging process robs us of our physical skills.

Penmanship was once a major subject in classrooms around the country but modern schools do not devote much time to teaching proper penmanship. With less emphasis on conforming to traditional writing systems, children are developing their own individual style of writing at an earlier age.

The Palmer method of penmanship and the Zaner-Bloser system are still the most popular penmanship systems taught to students. The D'Nealian system is gaining acceptance as it is easy to adapt the printed forms to the written script. Other penmanship systems similar to the Palmer and Zaner-Bloser are being taught throughout the United States.

As children grow into adolescence, their handwriting often shows drastic changes in many handwriting characteristics. Teenagers will experiment with different styles of writing, changing letter forms until they find a style they like. By the end of the teen years, a young adult's writing has stabilized into an adult style that changes gradually over the years.

Once graphic maturity is reached and writing movement is made from the habituated neuromuscular patterns, a basic style has been adopted that generally continues throughout a person's life although various factors continue to alter and modify the writing.

Changes in mature handwriting occur gradually, however, a dramatic event can cause sudden changes. President Nixon's writing changed drastically following Watergate. The writing of a man whose wife died of cancer changed so dramatically over the course of her illness that he had to sign new bank cards in order to cash a check.

Changes take place in our handwriting as we grow older. Handwriting skill usually declines in elderly writers. Legibility is reduced, writing lacks uniformity, and coordination is impaired. Elderly writing develops tremor due to loss of muscular control. The quality of the writing suffers and letter forms deteriorate. Ordway Hilton describes the deterioration of handwriting of the elderly and infirm in his book, *Scientific Examination of Questioned Documents*, "Writing of this nature is characterized by lack of fluency in execution and inaccuracy and inconsistency in details of form" (p. 324).

Since a signature is a stronger habit than other aspects of our handwriting, signatures normally do not deteriorate as rapidly as other writing. Many people maintain the ability to sign their name after they lose the ability to write anything else.

HEALTH

According to Patricia Wellingham-Jones, "Speech, gestures, handwriting, and other expressive behaviors are overt manifestations of neurological and mental functioning" (*Drugs and Handwriting,* p. 3). A person's mental and physical condition affects his ability to write, therefore, the document examiner must take the mental and physical condition of the writer into consideration when comparing handwriting so that writing for comparison purposes is taken from a similar set of circumstances.

Sudden traumatic changes in a person's life can alter handwriting. Any illness, either chronic or transitory, can cause changes in handwriting, either temporarily or permanently. It is important to compare handwriting from a similar point in time and under similar circumstances.

A writer who is under severe stress from an injury or is in excruciating pain will not write in his normal manner. In fact, writing will deviate sometimes to the point of not being identifiable.

A long-term debilitating illness such as cancer or Parkinson's Disease will cause handwriting to slowly deteriorate. The deterioration is not necessarily a steady decline. There may be some temporary improvement in writing although the writer never regains his optimum skill level.

Writers who lose the ability to write with their dominant hand, learn to write with other parts of their body such as the opposite hand, foot, or in the case of quadriplegics, with the pen held between the teeth. When a person becomes fluid in writing using an alternate method such as other-hand writing or footwriting, they will have retained many similar characteristics to their previous writing. Even mouthwriting, while more awkward than handwriting, shows remarkable similarities to previous handwriting samples.

Once a handicapped writer has mastered writing with an alternate body part, the examiner may not be able to distinguish from previous dominant handwriting. The mouthwriting of quadriplegic Joni Eareckson Toda is similar in many ways to her writing before her accident though there is some loss of fluidity. See Figure 7.1.

BLINDNESS

A sighted writer who becomes blind must rely on his previous knowledge of graphic movement to continue writing without the ability to visually check his progress. There is a tendency for the blind writer to write passages continuously so that he doesn't lose his place. A writer's script tends to rise in the middle of the page and then to drop as the writing hand is extended across the page forming an arch.

A person born blind has a more difficult time learning to write. He uses a special guide to gauge his spacing. Each letter is placed inside of a box using the sides of the box to control the size and form of the letters, which gives the writing a stilted appearance.

Figure 7.1
Mouthwriting

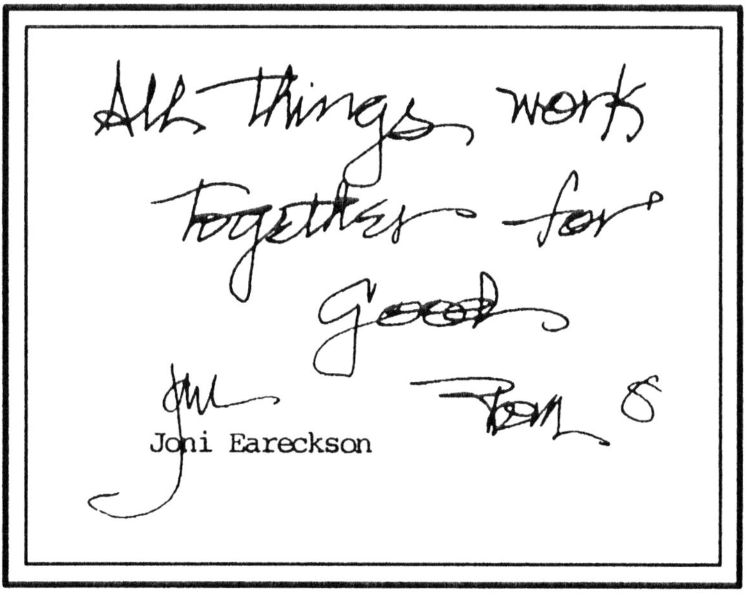

MENTAL ILLNESS

A person's mental state can affect the appearance of his writing. Mentally ill people often have difficulty expressing themselves in writing. Depending on the severity of the illness, the writing may deteriorate into illegibility. Severe disturbances can cause writing to become a series of lines, in some cases short vertical strokes while in others horizontal wavy lines. None of these can be deciphered. In most cases, mental illness does not diminish or destroy the habitual writing habits although it may cause them to be altered.

Suicide notes and letters usually show some deterioration of the quality of the writing, although the normal writing habits of the person are present. Mental depression affects the writing but does not destroy the habitual characteristics. The mood of the writer can modify the appearance of the writing. Is the writer happy, angry, excited, or depressed?

DRUGS AND MEDICATION

Every drug has an effect on the person taking it. Many of these effects are undesirable side effects that cause changes in a person's writing style or even his ability to write.

Patricia Wellingham-Jones tells us in her book, *Drugs and Handwriting*, that almost every drug has many effects but we cannot state that a particular drug causes a particular result. Side effects can also distort handwriting. What are some of the other adverse reactions?

1. Tiredness	5. Confusion	9. Tingling
2. Dizziness	6. Tremor	10. Pain
3. Nervousness	7. Restlessness	11. Paralysis
4. Spasm	8. Parkinsonism	12. Muscle Relaxation

Confusion and dizziness may disturb the overall writing of an individual causing the overlapping of lines and a disturbed baseline.

Euphoria causes increases in the size of the writing. The writing may also drift uphill. Nervousness and restlessness result in erratic pressure, tremor, or other irregularities in the writing. Spasms are sudden involuntary muscle contractions that create jerks and glitches in handwriting. Tremor is an involuntary inconsistent oscillation altering the direction of the writing temporarily and repeatedly. Tremor caused by caffeine is vibratory and transitory.

Psychic and psychotic changes will be variable, with disturbed rhythm being the most obvious. Depression usually causes writing to droop and drift downward.

Some drugs will cause Parkinsonian symptoms resulting in micrographia (small writing) that trails off. Muscle relaxants can cause writing to trail off as well. Light, erratic, or fading pressure can also be the result of muscle relaxants.

ALCOHOL AND DRUG ABUSE

In addition to the side effects of medication, drug abuse (including alcoholism) causes other adverse effects on handwriting. Alcohol reduces inhibitions causing larger, more rapid handwriting. As the level of intoxication increases, writing becomes more slurred, while extremes of size and spacing occur.

Alcoholics have general deterioration in their handwriting. However, as the disease worsens, the handwriting may actually improve when the alcoholic is intoxicated and deteriorate when he is sober.

Alcoholism causes uncontrolled muscular movement, jerking, and tremor. Breaks in pen lines, irregular strokes, and overwritten parts produce an erratic action without semblance of order.

Drug abuse also alters handwriting. Different types of drugs produce different side effects. A question of authenticity of the signature of a drug addict requires comparison of signatures from the same time period, and as many signatures as possible, under similar circumstances. Drug abuse over a period of time causes continual deterioration of the handwriting as well.

TREMOR IN HANDWRITING

Tremor is indicated by an involuntary recurrent erratic movement of the pen. These tremulous strokes are instant changes from the desired direction of the pen and are attributed to nervous impulses affecting the muscles indicating a loss of control of the pen.

There are many different causes of tremor in handwriting, for example, aging, illness, and drug abuse. Other causes are writer's cramps and pathological or neurotic disorders. Pathological tremors resulting in a convulsive manner of writing are independent of the will and therefore beyond the control of the writer. These tremors are often rhythmic to and fro movements that are practically impossible to imitate with the same writing speed and pen pressure. While wavering and broken strokes form the letters of a signature, they generally retain sufficient individual characteristics to be recognizable for identification of the writer.

The tremor of illiterate and uneducated individuals is more varied because of the unfamiliarity of the writing process. There is a lack of control but the writing line is firm. The strong lines of the illiterate writer can be distinguished from the tremulous lines of the more experienced writer, whose tremor is usually lighter, weaker and finer.

The tremor of fraud or criminal tremor results when one is attempting to copy another's writing. The act of creating slowly drawn writing lines causes corrugation. The corrugation is very fine and uniform and can be seen most clearly under a microscope.

Tremor is difficult to imitate. An error can easily be made by overlooking the line quality. A forger trying to imitate tremor usually fails to corrugate the line in the right places. He has a tendency to make smooth curves that the genuine writer is incapable of executing.

MECHANICAL FACTORS

Mechanical factors may temporarily alter handwriting. A change of body position may have an effect on the appearance of the handwriting since the writing deteriorates when a writer attempts to write from an awkward position. If the writer is lying down, his orientation will be affected and the ink in the pen may not flow properly. Without adequate support, the writing loses uniformity and pressure patterns are affected. Leaning across a bed also distorts the appearance of the writing.

What is the writer's normal writing position? What was his position when executing the document in question? Was the writer seated at a desk? Standing? Was the paper on a flat surface, a ledge, the steering wheel of a car, the writer's lap? Try to determine this information in order to duplicate the writing condition when taking request writing samples.

Inadequate lighting may affect the handwriting. Dim light may make it difficult for the writer to see what he is writing. Bright light may temporarily blind the writer so that the writing is distorted. Writers depend on feedback from viewing the line of writing in order to make adjustments to their writing.

The type of writing instrument can affect the appearance of the handwriting. A broad pen point creates a different effect than a fine point. Ballpoint pens produce a different appearance than fiber tip pens. Pencil writing causes other changes in the appearance of handwriting. Problems with the writing instrument such as ink flow or a damaged or leaky pen may impede writing.

The type of paper and the flow of the writing instrument affect handwriting. Poor quality paper can make writing difficult. Ink may not flow evenly, particularly with ballpoint pens that goop on curves. Some papers are more absorbent so that the ink spreads into the paper. Poor quality paper can snag a pen causing glitches in the writing. If the writer is having difficulty with pen or paper, he may have to change the pressure and speed of writing. A microscopic examination may reveal coarse paper or a poor ink flow.

The writing surface affects the indentations in the paper. A rough writing surface can also create grooves and patterns on the paper. If writing is done on a soft surface, the pressure appears to be heavier as the indentations into the paper are deeper. A hard writing surface under the paper reduces the depth of the indentations into the paper.

People attempt to create conditions conducive to comfortable writing. Occasionally this is not possible, so the writer must adapt his writing to the conditions present. Writing may be done on various surfaces such as a rough wooden table or desk, a glass or metal surface, even on a body part such as a lap or a hand.

Environmental factors can influence writing pressure. Extreme temperatures or the amount of humidity in the air may affect writing. Writing while riding in an automobile can alter handwriting.

There are also nontraditional writing instruments that have been used and must be examined by document examiners. For example, spray paint on walls and furniture, lipstick on mirrors, writing scratched into metal with a stylus, and chalk on a chalkboard. These nontraditional instruments affect writing, but many of the characteristics will still be identifiable.

SUMMARY

The document examiner needs to be informed of any factors that could influence the handwriting being examined. The principle factors considered include age, health, substance abuse, and mechanical factors. Health factors include physical and mental health and any medication that may affect handwriting. Mechanical features cover the writing surface, writing instrument, and lighting. The writing position may also affect the writing act.

8

Principles of Handwriting and Handwriting Identification

The courts require that an expert adhere to the standard principles of his discipline. What are these principles? The works of the recognized experts in the field have been culled and the following accepted principles pertaining to handwriting and handwriting identification have been identified.

PRINCIPLES OF HANDWRITING

1. **The act of writing is a skill learned through repetition until it becomes a habit.** Any series of repeated movements tend to become easier to execute as a person practices these movements. We call the result a habit. To develop a habit, one must repeatedly focus attention on the action to be acquired. The action must be consciously repeated until the senses recognize their respective tasks and the muscles respond accordingly. As the habit develops, the effort involved diminishes and decreasing attention is needed to focus on the act to be accomplished. The desired achievement requires less and less conscious awareness until the writer can repeat the action automatically.
2. **Handwriting requires the concerted effort of the brain, muscles, and nerves.** Writing is a complex act, resulting from a combination of coordinated actions between the eye, brain, and muscles of the arm, hand, and fingers. It is the result of skill developed by long continued, painstaking effort. While conscious awareness isn't necessary, the writer must have his faculties intact in order to write. No one can write when he is unconscious.
3. **No two people write exactly alike.** Each writer is unique. A writer brings different experiences to the act of writing. A writer's concept of letter designs deviates from other writers, effort and self-discipline vary, and coordination develops at different rates and to different skill levels.
4. **Individual characteristics that are unique to a particular writing exist in every person's handwriting distinguishing it from every other handwriting.** As handwriting skill develops, the writer experiments with different letter designs and methods of creating these designs. He develops individual characteristics that

distinguish his writing from all others. Even handwriting that is copybook style is unique as no one adheres exactly to copybook writing.

5. **There is natural variation in everyone's handwriting.** Normal variation in natural writing is the variance in the strokes, forms, and features of the writing that occurs from the inherent inability of the human hand to write with mechanical precision (Robinson p. 142). The variability in writing is different for each person. Most writers have more than one style of writing and more than one mental pattern for each letter form. Letter forms can also vary based on their position in a word.
6. **No one can duplicate exactly anything he has written.** Handwriting cannot be accurately reproduced in all its intricate features. Therefore, any duplicate signature is suspect as it has to be a copy of the original signature or a mechanically produced one.
7. **There is less range of variation in writing executed at the same time and under the same circumstances.** Writing executed at the same time is more consistent than writing over a period of time under different circumstances using different writing materials.
8. **No one can write better than his skill level.** Skill is the level of ability in writing that a writer has achieved through repeated practice. A person can write on a lower skill level than his own but not on a higher skill level.
9. **People adopt writing styles.** Writers imitate styles they like. They will also experiment and make up letter forms.
10. **People stylize their writing, deviating from the method they were taught.** Most writers deviate from the penmanship system they were taught. They will individualize letter forms and ignore some of the rules of penmanship; change slant, size, proportions, and spacing; simplify their writing or add embellishments; introduce printscript into their cursive writing; copy styles they like; and experiment with variations in their signatures.
11. **Many writing habits are subconscious and therefore cannot be changed by the writer.** Writing becomes automatic to the point that the operation not only requires almost no deliberate attention, but is frequently beyond control of the mind or the muscular system.
12. **A writer can be identified by his subconscious habits.** The habits are so ingrained that the writer cannot eliminate all the characteristics that encompass his writing style even when he tries to alter or disguise his writing.
13. **A person's normal form of writing is based on mental images of learned letter designs.** Normal subconscious writing occurs when the graphic image is firmly fixed in the mind of the writer and the writer no longer pays attention to the details of writing. The writer concentrates on the message being written and not on the method of writing.
14. **A person's handwriting changes gradually over the course of his lifetime.** There are many causes for the changes that take place, both natural and traumatic. A person generally reaches graphic maturity as he approaches adulthood. Writing generally changes gradually and may deteriorate in one's declining years.
15. **Substance abuse affects handwriting.** Substance abuse generally causes writing to expand. The form level deteriorates depending on the degree of impairment. Habitual drug abuse leads to the deterioration of handwriting.
16. **Some illnesses, trauma, and emotions may affect changes in handwriting.** Many of the changes caused by illness and emotional upheaval are temporary. Long-term

illness can cause deterioration and severe trauma can cause sudden abrupt changes in the handwriting that are permanent.

17. **It is not possible to determine what caused a change in the handwriting from studying the handwriting characteristics.** Since many different factors affect handwriting, a document examiner cannot look at the writing and identify the cause of the change.
18. **If the writer places the pen on the paper before starting to write, the lines will have blunt initial strokes.** Some writers habitually place the pen on the paper before starting to write, resting the pen on the paper long enough to leave a small blob of ink at the beginning of the writing line.
19. **If the writer stops his pen before lifting it from the paper, he will leave a blunt ending on his terminal strokes.** These writing habits are usually consistent for a writer.
20. **If the writer has the pen in motion when he begins and ends writing, initial and terminal strokes will be tapered or faded.**
21. **When a writer changes the size of writing, proportions between uppercase and lowercase letters generally remain the same.** Writers adjust the size of their writing to accommodate the space available without altering the size relationships.
22. **The amount of pressure that a writer uses to push and pull the pen through the strokes of writing will be seen in the variations of the pressure patterns.** Pressure is affected by the grip on the pen as well as the downward pressure against the paper.
23. **Most people create heavier strokes when the pen is descending toward the writer with lighter strokes when the pen is being pushed away from the writer.**
24. **The writing surface affects the depth of pressure.** A softer surface such as a pad of paper results in deeper impressions in the paper while a hard surface limits the depth of the indentations.

PRINCIPLES OF HANDWRITING IDENTIFICATION

1. A writer can be identified by his subconscious habits.
2. Identification requires determining if differences in handwriting are due to natural variation of a writer or a different writer.
3. Writing can be identified as belonging to an individual when there are sufficient individual characteristics of writing and no basic structural differences when compared with known writing.
4. Any fundamental unexplainable difference in writing is sufficient to prove that the writing being compared does not belong to the same writer. It must be a significant fundamental structural difference.
5. Determination of lack of genuineness depends on multiple factors, that is, more than a single indicator unless that indicator is a significant fundamental difference.
6. One distinctive characteristic is generally not sufficient to identify a writer.
7. Handprinting and numerals can be compared and identified.
8. Imitated writing intentionally bears resemblance to the writing from which it is being copied.
9. Imitated writing is usually drawn, not written.
10. Drawn writing generally lacks variations in pressure.

11. Imitation tends to conform closely to a fixed form and does not display the unconscious abandon that in genuine writing produces natural variation.
12. Forgers do not recognize the natural variation of handwriting and therefore they make their words and letters alike.
13. Identical original signatures can only be obtained by tracing the original signature, using a signature stamp, creating a robot signature with a writing machine, or scanning the signature into the computer and printing it.
14. A tracing doesn't have to be an exact copy of the original from which it is traced.
15. A tracing may have less detail than the original from which it is traced.
16. A tracing may deviate from the original due to slippage of the tracing paper or the deliberate moving of the paper to distort the copy.
17. No one can duplicate all of the intricate subconscious writing habits of another, however, some forgers are highly skilled in imitating others' handwriting on a limited sample of writing.
18. Freehand simulations by a skilled writer can be difficult to detect as obvious signs of forgery are not always evident.
19. Obvious signs of forgery include patched writing, hesitation as revealed by ink blobs and breaks in the line of writing, pauses in the writing, tremor causing poor line quality, and erasures.
20. Presence of any of the signs of forgery does not suffice to indicate that the document in question is not genuine as any of the signs could be part of the writer's normal habits.
21. Lack of any sign of forgery does not indicate genuineness.
22. Blunt initial and/or terminal strokes can indicate forgery but the presence of blunt strokes is not proof of forgery.
23. Individual characteristics in writing are deviations from class characteristics and are valuable in determining the identity of the writer.
24. The more diverse and unusual the accumulation of mutual characteristics and individual handwriting habits, the more positive the identification of the writer.
25. Forgers make mistakes.
26. Forgers tend to copy the pictorial effect of the writing but they overlook the idiosyncracies and subtle habits of the writer.
27. It is impossible to maintain a successful simulation of a lengthy document. The longer the text, the more the writing reverts to the natural characteristics of the writer as his concentration wanes.
28. In a comparison of handwriting it is necessary to compare line quality, pressure patterns, rhythm, letter forms, the method of construction, initial and terminal strokes, connecting strokes, diacritics, t-bars, punctuation, spacing, size and proportions, idiosyncracies, slant, alignment, and any hooks or ticks on letter forms.
29. Some characteristics that are not taught in any penmanship system have become class characteristics because they are shared by many writers. An example would be a Greek "E" or a t-bar connected to the next letter.
30. Family members frequently share handwriting characteristics, called familial characteristics.
31. There can be striking resemblances between two individual handwritings.
32. A writer can intentionally alter or distort the appearance of his normal writing.
33. It is not possible to identify a writer if there is a lack of sufficient material for comparison.

34. Some characteristics of the writer will be evident even when a writer alters or distorts his handwriting.
35. The average writer cannot sustain the intense concentration needed to maintain a disguise through extended writing samples. The more he writes, the more the writing reverts back to his natural characteristics.
36. Numerals and punctuation are rarely disguised.
37. Disguise is rarely consistent.

SUMMARY

Document examiners should understand the principles of handwriting and the rules that govern handwriting identification.

Handwriting identification is based on the fact that no two people write exactly alike. Equally important is the fact that no one can exactly duplicate anything that he has previously written. It is the function of the document examiner to determine the difference between natural variation and a nongenuine writing.

Part III

Documents

9

Materials from which Documents Are Made

WRITING MATERIALS

Writing materials usually consist of paper, a writing instrument such as a pen or pencil, and ink. Paper includes every type of paper from bond paper to carbon and carbonless paper. Writing instruments cover all types of pens and pencils as well as crayon, chalk, and other instruments used for writing.

Documents can also be imprinted with seals and stamped with rubber stamps. They can be held together by fasteners and binders. Material can be affixed to paper with tape, glue, paper clips, staples, or nonsticky note paper. Documents can be altered with erasers and correction fluids, or be damaged by fire or water.

Modern writing instruments also include typewriters, computers, photocopiers, scanners, and printers. Modern writing instruments will be covered in Chapter 10.

PAPER

Throughout history many substances have been used as writing surfaces including rocks, clay, and similar materials found in nature. The Egyptians made paper from a reed known as papyrus. The Chinese made paper from the inner bark of bamboo and hemp. Europeans began manufacturing paper, using cotton and linen around the twelfth century. Today most paper is made from wood pulp and may contain some cotton; higher quality paper uses cotton rag.

Papermaking has become a scientific process that employs highly sophisticated equipment in the manufacture of thousands of varieties of paper for a variety of uses. Paper is treated to obtain characteristics to meet various needs. Paper comes in a variety of styles, colors, weights, and finishes. It is identified by many of its qualities.

Properties of Paper

The first property of paper is its color. Paper comes in many different colors and finishes; even white paper has different shades. Color can be measured by spectral reflectance with a visible wavelength spectrometer. Paper is coated with finishes that are dull or shiny, smooth or rough.

Paper is sold by its weight. Lightweight paper takes longer to manufacture and is therefore more expensive.

Paper is also categorized by its strength. Strength is measured as tensile strength and as tear strength. Tensile strength is the amount of force parallel to the plane of the specimen required to produce failure. It is used to determine the durability of paper. Tear strength refers to the internal tearing resistance. Bursting tests are used to measure paper's ability to resist breaking when pressure is applied to one side of the paper. Puncture tests are also used.

Durability is used to ascertain the wearability of books, book covers, and edges. Modern paper can also be acid-free which adds to the life of the paper.

The thickness of paper varies considerably and is a notable characteristic of paper. Document examiners measure the thickness of paper with a micrometer to determine if a substitution has been made in a set of papers.

Paper is considered for its brightness and opacity. Paper receives its brightness from additives such as calcium carbonate and titanium dioxide. Finishes are applied to help whiten paper. There are chemical tests that can be used to determine the composition of the paper. The simplest test consists of illuminating the paper with ultraviolet light and studying the intensity of the florescence. Opacity refers to the amount of light that can pass through the paper. Opacity is determined by using transmitted light or an opacimeter.

Water absorbability, water resistance, and water repellency are significant features of paper that can be measured. Ink absorption is an important consideration as various papers have different absorption rates which can affect the appearance of the writing line. Paper is also tested for its wet strength. Paper can be identified by its properties.

Document examiners may want to know:

- Is paper stiff or limp?
- Is it porous or impermeable?
- Is it soil resistant?
- What additives have been added in the manufacturing process?
- What brighteners?
- How flammable is it?

All these properties of paper are taken into consideration when manufacturing paper to fill various needs. These same properties aid in the identification process when a question is raised about the paper in a document case.

PAPER TESTING

Paper can be tested for any of its properties. There are several laboratories that routinely test paper for brightness, creasing quality, tear resistance, gas permeability, density, curling tendencies, folding endurance, moisture content, porosity, ink permeability, sizing, softness, spot stain, static properties, and water vapor permeability.

Paper content can be identified including the amount of groundwood and additives. Fiber analysis is available. Heat testing is used to determine the relative stability of paper. The grain or machine direction can be identified.

Document examiners utilize nondestructive testing to identify paper by its qualities. Their examinations consist of studying the paper under various types of lighting including ultraviolet and infrared as well as conventional lighting, both direct and transmitted. They also examine paper under the microscope for identifying features.

Paper can be measured for size and thickness. Has the paper been cut from a larger piece? Has the paper been torn from a notebook? Paper torn from a notebook can be matched to the pad from which it came if the pad is also available for comparison.

Marks on papers can be examined and identified: paper clips leave impressions on paper; staple holes can be located; and indented writing may be found. Paper may have been laminated or treated with chemicals or glues.

WATERMARKS

A watermark is a trademark of a paper manufacturer. The watermark consists of a design that is pressed into the paper during the manufacturing process. The paper passes over a dandyroll that imprints the watermark onto the paper. The watermark consists of a thinner area on the paper.

The dandyroll contains the design of the watermark in a metal form that pushes the paper fibers aside leaving an imprint in the paper. Most sheets of paper contain a single watermark but some paper such as safety paper may contain multiple repeated designs. The dandyroll may also make the imprint for the woven or laid papers. See Figure 9.1.

Paper manufacturers use distinctive designs as their watermarks. Watermarks identify the paper manufacturer. Not only do they identify the manufacturer, but the dandyroll manufacturer keeps a record of when a particular watermark was first used. This information can be used to prove that a document dated prior to the manufacture of the paper it is written on is obviously misdated.

CARBON AND CARBONLESS PAPER

A mixture of beeswax, lampblack, and grease were combined and coated on paper to create carbon copies. In the early 1900s carnauba wax was used to make carbon paper. Modern carbon paper is coated with a mixture of pigments and waxy oily substances.

Typewriter carbons are generally black. A carbon paper intended for use with a pen is usually blue. The advent of the photocopier has eliminated the need for most carbon copies in the office environment.

NCR (No Carbon Required) paper is carbonless paper introduced by the National Cash Register Company in 1954 and has become a staple on business forms. Carbonless paper is used in multipage documents.

When two pieces of the specially treated paper come in contact and are written on, they transfer the writing from a top sheet to the sheets below. Document examiners can draw some conclusions from the examination of documents consisting of carbonless paper.

ENVELOPES

Envelopes can reveal information of value to a document examiner. It may be necessary to compare envelopes to determine if they come from the same source. Envelopes can be distinguished by their shapes and colors, the method of folding the envelope, and the type of glue on the flap. It may be important to know if the envelope was opened and resealed. The usual method of opening an envelope surreptitiously is by steaming it to soften the glue. That person may then use additional glue to reseal the envelope. The flap of the envelope will be wrinkled if it had been steamed open and may contain extra glue. The envelope should also be checked to see if it was accidentally torn when it was opened.

Figure 9.1
Watermark Found on Quality Paper

The method of completing the address on the envelope may help the examiner make an identification. Some writers place each line directly under the other lines while others indent each line. In some anonymous note cases, the handwriting on the envelope is the only writing available. The postmark and the stamp on the envelope may provide clues that assist the examiner.

SAFETY PAPER

Safety paper is specialized paper designed to reveal any attempts at altering the material on the surface of the paper. Safety paper is manufactured for use with negotiable instruments and identification documents such as stocks and bonds, and passports and drivers licenses. It is designed to reveal any alterations such as raising the amount of a check or changing the payee. Safety paper contains backgrounds that change color when chemical ink eradicators are applied. Safety paper frequently contains fugitive inks. Fugitive inks cannot be seen until a duplicate is made on a photocopier or a scanner or the paper is treated with an ink eradicator. These inks will print the word, copy, on the photocopy. They will reveal the word, void, on the safety paper.

While safety paper prevents alterations such as raising the amount of the check, it is readily available so counterfeiters are making bogus documents using the same technology used for creating legitimate documents. Safety paper does not stop the flow of counterfeit checks on fictitious accounts or forged endorsements on stolen checks. A clever forger can soak a genuine check in a chemical solution and remove all of the ink and reuse the check. Fugitive inks do not react to these chemical solutions.

Any negotiable instrument is susceptible to counterfeiting. Checks, bonds, stock certificates, gift certificates, and winning lottery tickets are some of the items being counterfeited.

Identification papers include birth certificates, licenses such as marriage licenses and drivers licenses, photo identification documents from colleges and workplaces, immigration documents such as passports and visas, and badges authorizing entry into secure places.

These documents incorporate other security features to make them more difficult to counterfeit. However, with the proliferation of modern day computer equipment, quality printing with the same security features is now readily available. Modern-day forgers have the means to create excellent fraudulent documents that defy easy detection.

OTHER SECURITY FEATURES

In addition to safety paper, documents contain other security features to prevent alteration or imitation. These include special inks that fluoresce under ultraviolet light, fugitive inks that develop when documents are chemically altered or copied, special seals and embossing, plastic threads imbedded in the paper, and lamination, to name a few. Copyproof papers are being developed that cannot be photocopied or scanned into a computer for duplication. Companies are ordering special paper with limited access that is not available to anyone not authorized to use it.

EMBOSSING DEVICES

Notaries emboss documents with their notary seals. Government agencies emboss documents when they certify the copies of records in their control. Stock certificates and other negotiable instruments frequently contain embossed seals. Some organizations use embossed seals for their certificates. Stationery embossers are available to enhance stationery with monograms or other designs.

Document examiners conduct a microscopic examination of embossings to determine if they are authentic. They can also determine if commingled writing was done before or after the embossing.

RUBBER STAMPS

Documents may be stamped with many different kinds of rubber stamps. Some executives use signature stamps on company checks. Letters are postmarked with canceling stamps. Certified checks are authenticated with special stamps. Official documents are stamped with their agency information. These stamps may present clues to the identity of the creator of a counterfeit or forged document.

FASTENING DEVICES

Papers are held together by many different types of fastening devices such as paper clips, staples, clamps, and paper fasteners. Fastening devices such as paper clips and staples may assist a document examiner in determining if pages have been substituted in a multipage document. Paper clips leave indentations on pages when they have been left on a document for any significant period of time. They may even leave rust marks on paper.

Staples leave staple holes on documents. A document examiner will check a multiple page document to verify that the holes and indentations align. The number of staple holes can be compared to see if each page has the same number of staple holes in the same locations. It is also possible to determine if the staples have been removed and reinserted into the same holes.

BINDERS

There are many types of presentation binders used to keep multiple pages of documents together as a unit. These include spine binders that slip over the left edge of a small number of pages as well as binders using metal prongs that are pulled through holes in the document, usually on the top or side of the document.

Three ring binders come in various sizes for organizing documents. Pages can easily be inserted and removed from these binders without leaving any evidence.

TAPE AND GLUE

Many different types of tape and glue can be found on documents. Documents are patched with transparent adhesive tape, usually a permanent tape. Removable tape is used to hold items on a page temporarily. Gummed tape is used for labels. Documents may have additional material attached to them with tape or glue. Anything that is placed on a document may provide information about the origin of the document. Labels and seals attached to documents can be studied microscopically. The type of tape or glue used may give clues about the originator of a particular document.

OTHER DEVICES

Documents may be bound with rubber bands. They may be stuck with pins or hammered with nails. Mounting tape and mounting adhesives are also applied to paper. Laminating machines are used to apply a plastic coating on paper to protect documents such as drivers licenses from being altered. Paper can be sprayed with solutions to strengthen it or protect it from damage.

CORRECTION FLUIDS

Various types of correction fluids have been on the market since the 1950s beginning with Liquid Paper, which is a liquid tempera paint. Powdered correction paper is also available. The powder was affixed to a tape that was spooled and inserted onto a typewriter. This made it easier to make the correction as the typist did not have to manually hold the correction paper. It was struck in the same manner as the ribbon was struck.

Most document examiners know how to read writing under whiteout. Documents can be photocopied using special techniques that reveal the writing under the sections covered with whiteout. This process does not alter the document and the photocopies can be used in court as evidence.

DAMAGED DOCUMENTS

Intentional damage may be done to paper to make it appear older than it really is. Counterfeiters artificially age paper with chemicals and other stains. Tea or coffee grounds are sometimes applied to paper to age it. Paper may be soiled with dirt to alter its appearance. Paper can be ironed with a hot iron or baked in the oven to make it more brittle. It may be folded and torn or mutilated in other ways as well.

PAPER PROBLEMS

What types of questions are document examiners asked to determine about paper? The date may be at issue. Is the date correct? Identifying the age of the paper may be important. The paper manufacturer and the dandyroll factory maintain records on the date of origin of their watermarks. Sometimes the composition of the paper tells its age. Additives found on the paper may not have existed on the date written on the paper. The Hitler Diaries contained whiteners and plastic filaments in the labels that were not in existence during Hitler's lifetime.

The document examiner may be asked to compare two sheets of paper to see if they are similar. Has a substitution of a page been made in a set of papers such as a will or a contract? Properties of paper can be compared to identify differences between several pages of a document. This generally requires various types of lighting and magnification and may require chemical testing.

Indented writing may be found on a page that could assist an examiner in deciphering a questioned document. Indented writing can be read using sidelighting. It is often easier to read a document that has been photographed using sidelighting. The sidelighting casts a shadow over the indentations so that the writing becomes visible.

It may be necessary to match edges of pages torn from a pad of paper. If the paper tears erratically, it can be matched. Some documents have arrived in the document examiner's laboratory in pieces and they must be put together like a jigsaw puzzle. A semisticky paper can be used to hold the documents in place until the entire page has been reassembled.

Documents soiled by fire or water may need to be professionally cleaned or dried. Document examiners may need to use special techniques to restore damaged documents.

QUESTIONS TO ASK ABOUT PAPER

- What kind of paper was used?
- Was more than one kind of paper used on a multipage document?
- Are the watermarks consistent on all of the pages?
- Do the watermarks all face in the same direction?
- Is the paper the same size, thickness, and color?
- Are there any marks on the paper?
- Was the paper torn or damaged?
- Did the paper come from a pad? Can the tears be matched?
- Does the paper contain lines?
- Is the paper soiled, crumbled, or faded?
- Has the paper been cut by hand? Is it smaller than standard paper?
- Are there any discolorations or stains on the paper? What caused them?
- Did ink from another page bleed through?
- Are there any indications of indented writing on the paper?
- Are there any signs of erasure through abrasion or the application of chemicals?

- Are the margins on the paper all the same?
- Was the document held together with staples or paper clips?
- Are there any holes where the paper may have been stapled?
- Are the holes consistent on each page of a multipage document?
- Has the page been altered in any way?
- Has the document been taken apart and restapled?
- Is it likely that the document contains fingerprints that could be helpful in this case?

OTHER WRITING SURFACES

Document examiners are sometimes asked to examine other writing surfaces. Anything that can hold a permanent or semipermanent message may contain information for examination. This includes (but is not limited to) mirrors, windows, walls, locker doors, and cardboard boxes, in fact, any flat surface. Messages have been scratched with sharp objects onto cars, doors, rocks, trees, and other rough surfaces. Traditional writing surfaces such as blackboards and whiteboards may contain questioned writing.

WRITING INSTRUMENTS

Writing is applied to a surface by adhesion or absorption. An example of adhesion is the result of a pencil being pushed against the writing surface so that pieces of graphite cling to the paper following the path of the writing instrument. It is a dry method that places marks on the surface of the paper. Other adhesive media include charcoal, chalk, and crayons.

Absorption causes a liquid (ink) to penetrate the paper. The ink flows from a pen onto paper and must dry quickly to prevent smearing. Paper is treated so that the ink is absorbed without feathering or running on the paper.

Pencils

Pencils are pushed against the paper and leave particles of graphite on the writing surface. These marks can be removed by brushing off the particles with a rubber eraser.

Pencils are disposable or mechanical. A standard pencil is a wooden cylinder with graphite in the center. The graphite is a composition of graphite mixed with clay. The mechanical pencil is filled with a stick of graphite which can be replaced. The term lead or lead pencil is incorrect as the instruments contain no lead.

Colored pencils also contain clay and wax but the graphite is replaced by pigments and dyes.

Pencils containing graphite are used because pencil writing is easy to remove and replace, leaving little evidence of the alterations.

Pens

While many types of pens have been used over the years, most of the documents that forensic document examiners study are contemporary documents that have been penned with a modern writing implement. Improvements in pens continue to develop and these new innovations are appearing in the marketplace at an unprecedented rate.

Lewis E. Waterman invented the fountain pen in 1884. Fountain pens were widely used until the invention of the ballpoint pen in 1945. While fountain pens are still popular, the ballpoint pen has continued to gain in popularity so that it is the pen most frequently used and most frequently encountered by a document examiner.

Today the writer can choose between fiber-tip pens, felt-tipped pens, and rollerball pens in addition to fountain pens and ballpoint pens.

A fountain pen consists of a bifurcated metal nib, a reservoir to hold ink, and a feed channel to move the ink from the reservoir to the tip of the penpoint. All but the nib are enclosed in a barrel or housing unit.

A ballpoint pen is a precision instrument consisting of four major parts: the ink, the tube, a small ball that rotates, and the ballholder. The ink must flow without clogging and yet dry quickly on the paper to prevent smearing. The rotating ball draws ink from the tube and rolls it onto the paper as it is being pushed across the page.

In 1979 the Paper Mate Company began marketing the Eraser Mate, an erasable ink pen. The ink in these pens is thicker than normal ballpoint ink. The ink can be erased until it "sets" or dries. The tightness of the paper fibers determines the amount of time it takes the ink to set but it dries in only a day or two in any case.

Fiber-tip pens, also known as porous tip or felt tip pens, contain similar components as the fountain pen with the nib being made of a porous material instead of metal. Modern felt tips come in a variety of pen tip widths and colors.

The rollerball pen is similar in design to the ballpoint but the water-based ink it uses is much thinner and flows more easily onto the paper. Waterproof rollerball pens came on the market in 1988.

The Micro Permaroller by Pentel was the first rollerball pen that contained permanent waterproof and fadeproof ink.

Gel pens are the latest innovation offered to the public by the pen manufacturers. These ballpoint pens give writers a wide variety of colors. These are waterbased inks with fadeproof pigments instead of dye. See Table 9.1.

Identification of Pens

Document examiners distinguish the type of pen used to create a handwriting sample by considering the characteristics of the pen and the ink used to create the sample. The fountain pen leaves parallel grooves that penetrate the paper, leaving a slightly heavier line of ink along these grooves. The ink is waterbased and is easily absorbed by the paper. Flowback of the ink at the end of the groves is also characteristic of fountain pens.

The ball from a ballpoint pen leaves a groove in the paper in the center of the line of ink which can be seen under a stereoscopic microscope. The heavy ink of the ballpoint pen sits on the paper. Ballpoint pens are susceptible to gooping. The ink collects on the rim of the ball housing on curves and deposits a blob of ink onto the paper when the pen position changes.

Fiber tipped pens use a fluid ink. The porous pen point leaves flat even inking sometimes accompanied by hairline dragging of ink along the edge of the line. The rollerball has a similar water-soluble ink but the ball leaves a slight indentation in the paper similar to the ballpoint.

Table 9.1
Dates Pens Were First Manufactured

1884	Lewis E. Waterman introduced the fountain pen
1945	Ballpoint pens first marketed in NYC
1951	Felt tip markers were introduced
1964	Fiber tip pens entered the market
1979	The Eraser Mate Pen marketed by Paper Mate
1988	Waterproof rollerball pens came on the market
1991	Gel pens appeared on the market

Other Writing Instruments

Stick charcoal is popular among artists. It is easy to apply and can produce fine delicate lines as well as broad heavy strokes. Charcoal is made from carbonized wood that can easily be pulverized into powder. Charcoal does not penetrate paper. In fact, the major disadvantage of charcoal is its tendency to smear and smudge the paper.

Chalk is composed of a mixture of dry pigments and binders. There are many combinations used in the manufacture of chalk today.

Crayons are composed of waxes and pigments. These waxes adhere to the surface of paper and are difficult or impossible to remove.

COMPOSITION OF INKS

Ink is a liquid solution containing dyes and/or pigments used to make visible marks on a writing surface. Ink is manufactured for pens, rubber stamps, and stamp pads. Ink is also manufactured for typewriter or printer ribbons and for commercial printers. Each use requires a different type of ink with different properties.

Ink consists of a coloring agent (dyes or pigments), a solvent to make it fluid, and a fixing agent to maintain its consistency.

There are presently four types of ink on the market. The first kind of ink is water-based and dissolves in water. This ink is mixed with dyes and used in rollerball pens and fountain pens. Water-based inks are absorbed into the paper fibers when applied to the surface of paper. The second kind of ink is alcohol-based and is used primarily in commercial printer's ink. The third type of ink is glycol-based ink used in ballpoint pens. This ink needs to be thicker in viscosity than other inks. Ballpoint pen ink can be identified by its glossy appearance and its burr striations. See Figure 9.2. Burr striations are bands of ink that form a pattern on the paper as the result of uneven depositing of ink on the paper. Ballpoint ink is not absorbed into the paper. Glycol-based ink is used in number machines and check protectors and for rubber stamp pads. Finally, the fourth type of ink is solvent-based ink used in broad-tip markers including those used to write on glass.

Drawing inks contain dye, water, shellac, and solvents in a homogeneous fluid. Inks may be opaque or semi-opaque. Sometimes pigments are substituted for dyes. Pigments will not fade and are therefore considered permanent.

SPECIAL PURPOSE INKS

There are also some inks that are invisible to the naked eye but will fluoresce under ultraviolet light. These are used for security purposes.

Another type of invisible ink is fugitive ink (also called void ink) that develops a strong color when treated with ink eradicator. These are frequently found on checks to prevent alterations and are so named because the word, void, appears when the ink is developed.

Fugitive inks have been developed that appear when a document is copied or scanned into the computer. These fugitive inks prevent the duplication of negotiable instruments on a photocopier or scanner. These usually read as void or copy.

UNUSUAL WRITING FLUIDS

Document examiners may have to analyze documents that have been marked with unusual writing instruments. Lipstick on a mirror is one example. A stylus or other sharp instrument may be used to scratch a message onto a metal surface. Whiteout, nail polish, and other chemicals are sometimes used as writing fluids. Vegetable juices and body fluids have been used for writing in invisible ink. These types of ink are revealed when the document is heated.

Spray paint is popular with graffiti artists. Since writing is a well-developed habit, handwriting characteristics can be revealed in spray-painted graffiti. Letter shapes will be similar to written letter forms. The arrangement of the writing tends to remain the same and in many cases, identification of the graffiti artist is made.

CHARACTERISTICS OF INK

Ink has characteristics that can be compared and tested. Some basic properties of ink can be determined by observing the ink under magnification. Ink can be porous or viscous, (viscous ink is thick and nonporous). Ink can be shiny or dull depending on its chemical composition.

Figure 9.2
Burr Striations from a Ballpoint Pen

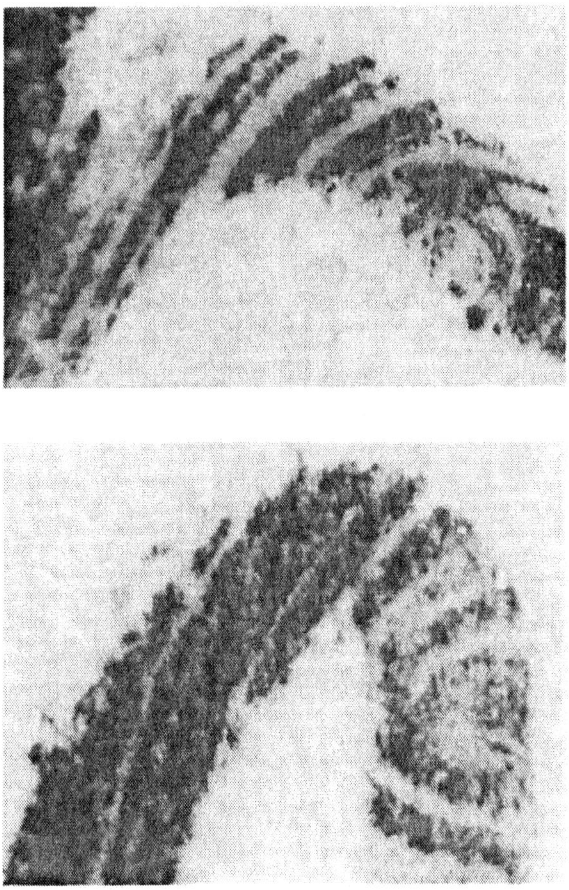

Document examiners can determine what type of ink has been used on a document. They can distinguish between water-based ink and glycol-based ink. They can detect different inks even though they appear to be the same color and they can identify the same ink on different documents. They can determine which line is on top of intersecting lines.

Ballpoint ink is shiny and forms burr striations that can be seen microscopically. It is viscous and therefore sits on top of the paper with very little absorption. Fluid ink found in fountain pens, fiber-tip pens, and rollerball pens has a dull appearance and is absorbed into the paper.

In 1975 ink manufacturers began adding chemical tags to their inks and changing these on an annual basis. Small amounts of rare elements were added to batches of ink. By determining the composition of ink, a forensic ink chemist can determine the year that the ink was first manufactured. Ink manufacturers discontinued this practice in 1994.

INK TESTING

Most testing conducted by forensic document examiners is nondestructive testing. Document examiners use strong lighting and magnification to make determinations about ink. The color of ink can be examined under various wavelengths of light ranging from ultraviolet to infrared. Ink may appear to come from a single source under natural light. Exciting the ink with infrared or ultraviolet illumination may show differences in ink, revealing that a document has been altered. The ink can be photographed microscopically using colored filters and special lighting conditions so that a permanent record can be made of the differences. Colors can be compared to determine whether the same or different ink is found on a questioned document.

A document examiner may have to decipher writing under blackout or crossed-out lines. Infrared and ultraviolet illumination may enable the material under the cross-out to be read. A thin plastic tape applied to the paper will outline the writing underneath. The tape used should be removable.

LINE DIRECTION

The line direction of ink can be determined in certain cases. Fluid inks show direction at line interceptions, revealing the ink that is on top. The ink on top has a continuous edge showing. The ink that intercepts another segment of line, sometimes dissolves some of the ink that was already on the paper and the dissolved ink will run.

Writers generally release their grip on a pen when pushing the pen away from themselves. The upstrokes are lighter when the grip on the pen is loosened. The downstrokes are heavier as writers pulls the pen toward themselves. Therefore, an examination of a fluid ink line should show lighter upstrokes and heavier downstrokes thus enabling the examiner to follow the direction the writer took.

Two characteristics of ballpoint pen ink show line direction. The first indication is the position of ink blobs on the writing line. As a writer changes direction with the pen, some of the ball that collects the ink does not touch the surface of the paper. The ink collects on the ball, which is scraped onto the housing of the ball and is deposited onto the line of writing when the writer again changes the position of the pen after the curve. Therefore, line direction is determined by the location of blobs of ink on the ink line immediately after the line has changed direction via a curve.

The second attribute of ballpoint ink is burr striations. Striations occur when some of the holes of the ball become clogged with ink and leave blank sections in the line of writing. Striations in a curve in the line move from inside to outside in the direction the writing instrument is moving.

Damaged ballpoint pens may leave markings on an ink line that are unique to a particular pen. These markings can be compared to demonstrate that a particular pen made repeated entries over a period of time.

DESTRUCTIVE TESTING

Destructive testing usually involves chemical testing. The most widely used chemical test on ink is thin layer chromatography. Small plugs of ink are removed from the questioned document with a hypodermic needle. The plugs are placed in a solvent and the ink separates into its organic components. The dye components separate and climb up chromogram sheets of silica gel using capillary action. The results are compared to other sheets in a standard ink library to match the separate dye components and identify the ink. This test can be used to differentiate inks on documents.

Court approval is needed to conduct any type of destructive testing. Any document subjected to destruction, even partial destruction, should be photographed before the destruction takes place.

PEN AND INK PROBLEMS

Document examiners are called on to determine if a document has been altered in any way. The amount on a check may be raised, names may be changed, terms on a contract may be modified, or medical records amended to reflect proper procedures.

Fraudulent documents are fabricated to hide criminal activity. Different pens may be used to make it appear that documents were created over a period of years when they were created at one time. In most cases, document examiners can recognize documents that have been fabricated by someone who simply alternated pens. A microscopic study of the burr striations of the ink line may reveal the true nature of the document.

CASE STUDY

A bookkeeper embezzled several hundred thousand dollars from her employer. She produced a set of books that she claimed to have written over a five-year period. The employer suspected that the books had been created after the embezzlement was discovered. The document examiner who inspected the books visually compared the ink line on all of the pages. The pens used to create these lines showed unusual burr striations which could be matched to entries covering the five-year span. It is highly unlikely that the same malfunctioning pens could be used repeatedly over the five-year span. The court agreed.

QUESTIONS ABOUT PENS AND INK

- What kind of writing instrument was used on the document?
- Was more than one type of writing instrument used?
- What kind of ink was used?
- Does the ink contain identifying marks?

QUESTIONS ABOUT CORRECTIONS

- What type of correction material was used on the document?
- What was written under the whiteout?
- What was obliterated with a black marking pen?

DOCUMENT PROBLEMS

There are many document problems related directly to the materials making up documents.

The sequence of writing may be questioned. Was the writing or typing done at the time indicated or was evidence manufactured after the fact to support a theory or claim? Document examiners can normally determine line sequence without destructive testing. The questioned material can be photographed through a microscope to record fine details.

Does the document contain alterations? A microscopic examination may be needed to determine if material has been altered or deleted from a document. It may be necessary to use side lighting to reveal what was written and erased from a document.

Does the document contain any attachments that reveal the nature of the document? Labels may be glued to the document in question. The document may be sealed or stamped with an embosser.

Questioned documents are frequently tested for fingerprints using ninhydrin. Ninhydrin turns the paper pink. Ninhydrin destroys indentations on a document and destroys the fine details that are important in document examiners' investigations. Document examiners should study and photograph documents before they are tested for fingerprints. Document examiners are trained to avoid handling the documents in a manner that will obliterate the fingerprints.

Documents may need to be tested with DNA to identify or eliminate a particular subject. An example would be an envelope sealed with saliva.

A question can arise about the sequence of writing in relationship to a fold in the paper. A fold damages the paper. It stretches the fibers in one direction and if the crease is sharp, it may break some of the fibers in the finish on the paper. A line written after a paper is folded will have different characteristics than writing done before the fold. The writing done prior to the fold will have a smooth break at the fold line. Writing completed after the fold will show skips where the pen came in contact with the fold and any ink that lands on the broken fold will spread into the paper.

DATING DOCUMENTS

The date that materials comprising a document first came on the market can assist a document examiner in cases when documents have been backdated. If the paper, the pen, or the ink was not manufactured at the time the document was dated, then the document has been backdated.

Watermarks are coded to identify the date they were first manufactured. The code may be a dash under or over a letter, or a slight change in design. The special symbol is changed frequently, sometimes yearly. Many fraudulent documents have been revealed when their watermark demonstrated that they were manufactured after the date on the document.

Paper that isn't watermarked can be dated according to the date that additives were first used in or on the paper. The Hitler diaries were proven to be fraudulent because the labels on the covers of the diaries contained additives that were not available when Hitler was alive.

Pens also have a first date of manufacture. The type of track the pen leaves on the paper indicates the type of pen used.

The ink plays an important roll in the identification of pens because of changes in ink formulas. The first date of production can be established by analyzing the composition of the ink and comparing its formula with other ink samples whose date of origin is known. Ink can be dated according to ink tags.

Some documents contain material on them that reveals the date they were first manufactured. Greeting cards contain numbers that can be matched by the manufacturer to the date the card was first offered to the public. The price on the card may help pinpoint the date of origin of that particular card. Preprinted forms often contain the date they were introduced or revised.

INK DATING

In addition to the first manufacturing date of ink, forensic chemists have devised a method of testing ballpoint ink samples to give a relative date of the writing. Ink dating can only determine the approximate date a message was penned on paper. According to Erich Speckin, an ink chemist with Speckin

Laboratories in a lecture to the National Association of Document Examiners, "In the field of forensic chemistry advances in technology have made it possible to date ink within six months or less."

Ink chemists determine the age of ink by the rate of extraction from the paper and the percent of extraction. They measure how fast the ink can be chemically removed from the paper and how easily it is removed. Ink dries chemically in approximately three and one-half years according to Erich Speckin. By using the rate of extraction, ink chemists can determine the age of the application of the ink to within six months. After the ink has completely dried, the chemist can only state that the ink is over three and one-half years old.

When no known ink samples are available in the ink library, ink chemists are using accelerated aging to determine the dryness of ballpoint ink. Two samples of ink are placed in separate containers and one is heated to artificially age the ink. A comparison is made between the two samples of ink using thin layer chromatography to determine how much the original sample of ink has dried in relation to the artificially aged ink.

Ink dating using any other method than date of origin of a particular ink is controversial. Aging conditions can affect the rate of drying. Ink on documents that are stored in a cool, humid environment will dry at a different rate than documents stored in a sunny, dry environment. Knowledge of aging conditions is extremely important when attempting to date ink.

It may be necessary to compare ink samples from a document to see if additions were penned onto the document at different times. When two writings on the same paper are compared with each other, a determination can be made about the relative age of the ink samples. Since the ink samples were maintained in the same environment by the fact that they were on the same document, a comparison can be made between the inks as to their relative age based on the extractability of the ink.

An exact date that ink was penned onto a document cannot be determined by any method. Relative ink dating can only offer a range during which ballpoint ink could have been placed on the document. The only definitive date that can be verified is the date of origin of a particular ink based on its composition.

QUESTIONS TO ASK ABOUT INK

- What type of ink was used on the document?
- Was more than one ink used to complete the document?
- When was the ink first manufactured?
- Could the ink be duplicated by anyone else?
- Does the ink contain chemical tags?
- What type of testing will be done on the ink?
- Has the ink been contaminated in any way?
- What controlled research studies do you have to support your method of testing ink?
- Can the tests be replicated by other qualified forensic scientists?

SUMMARY

Paper can be identified according to its properties. Document examiners conduct nondestructive testing on paper to determine if different pages of a document contain the same properties.

Many types of writing instruments are used on documents. The type of pen used to complete a document can be identified by its track on a document and the type of ink it deposits on the writing line.

Materials such as paper clips, staples, tape, and glue used to hold papers together can also be useful in the examination of questioned documents.

Documents can be dated based on their date of origin. The watermarks on paper are used to determine the date the paper was first manufactured.

Ink dating is also being done using the rate of extraction or accelerated aging techniques.

10

Office Equipment

Document examiners are called on to make determinations concerning documents produced on modern office equipment. There are many types of problems that can be solved concerning documents that have been typed or printed.

TYPEWRITERS

The manual typewriter contains typebars which throw the letters against the ribbon onto the paper. Because of their mechanical nature, manual typewriters develop defects that make each one unique and therefore identifiable.

Document examiners identify typewriters by the type that they produce. Different typefaces were used by typewriter manufacturers which helps in the identification of the particular model of typewriter.

The first typewriters used pica or elite spacing. Pica places ten characters to the inch on a line and elite places twelve to the inch. The lines of typing are arranged to be .165 inches apart or six lines per inch. See Figure 10.1.

The electric typewriter was introduced in the 1930s. These typewriters required only a light touch on the keys to activate them. This made it difficult to identify an individual typist by the force with which certain keys were pressed.

In 1961 IBM introduced the Selectric typewriter which used a typeball to place letters onto a document. The typeball, or element as it is sometimes called, fits into the typewriter and can easily be interchanged even with other model typewriters. This style became so popular that it was used by other typewriter manufacturers and replaced the typebars.

Another development in the typewriter was the daisywheel printer which uses a plastic or metal element that is shaped like a wheel with each spoke containing a different letter of the alphabet. The wheel spins to the correct character to be typed and that spoke hits the ribbon against the paper. Some modern printers use daisywheels as well.

TYPEWRITER IDENTIFICATION

Identifying typewriting is similar to identifying handwriting. There are two basic considerations needed to establish identity. First the typeface must be the same, that is, the size and the design of the letters and numbers. Second, the defects must match.

Most typewriter identification is made from an examination of the work produced by the typewriter. The type on the typebars tends to wear unevenly as it is used; some of the letters go askew, serifs break, and circles are filled with ink. The letters may twist or misalign. A visual examination of all the characteristics is usually conducted by the document examiner.

Mechanical defects produce individual imperfections that help to identify a typewriter. The rubber platen gets old and hard. Continuous striking of the keys can cause unevenness to develop on the platen which will affect the print alignment. The ribbon may be defective and cause only a portion of the letter to be typed. Insufficient carriage movement will cause incorrect spacing between letters.

The mechanical defects caused by the defective parts can be reduced to a combination of five kinds of problems. These are: (1) faulty horizontal alignment, (2) vertical misalignment, (3) slant or slope, (4) tilt, "off its feet," or footing, and (5) damaged type.

Alignment problems can occur with typeballs but they are usually very slight and they generally affect all the letters in the row or column. Most common is a rotating misalignment causing a horizontal alignment defect.

The typebar machine alignment affects only the single letter, both uppercase and lowercase while the typeball alignment affects all the letters in a row or a column.

Daisywheels are flexible so consistent misalignment is not likely. The spokes of the daisywheels break more easily than the typeball or the typebar.

Figure 10.1
Examples of Elite and Pica Styles

An example of PICA type on typewriters.
An example of ELITE type on typewriters.

INSERTIONS

Document examiners are asked to determine if typewritten documents contain insertions or deletions and alterations. Insertions on typed documents can be identified through misalignment of the text. Misalignments are caused by reinserting a paper into a typewriter to add material. It is almost impossible to realign material correctly. Vertical realignment is easier because typewriters contain paper guides and the edge of the paper sits against the guide. The horizontal alignment is much more difficult.

Slight differences in spacing between lines can be determined by measuring. Document examiners use typewriter grids to check for misalignment.

If the same typewriter is used to add to a page of text, it can be identified. Insertions of pages of typewritten text will be more obvious if a different typewriter is used.

Deletions and alterations are readily apparent on typewritten documents. When the key strikes the ribbon to the paper, it indents the paper. When the typist erases the letter or covers it with whiteout, the indentation remains. Even when correctable tape is used to lift the ink from the paper, the indentation remains and is visible under magnification.

QUESTIONS ABOUT TYPEWRITERS

- What kind of typewriter was used? Manual, electric, or electronic memory typewriter?
- What make and model was the typewriter?
- What type element? Typebar, typeball, or daisywheel?
- What is the spacing? Pica, elite, proportional, or other?
- Was each page typed continuously without the paper being removed and reinserted into the typewriter?
- If removed and reinserted how many times and what was written each time?
- Is the date of the document consistent with the age of the typewriter?
- Is the spacing uniform?
- Is there a carbon copy and is it identical?

WORD PROCESSORS

The most recent typewriter design is the electronic memory typewriter or word processor. Electronic memory machines store the key strokes either on a magnetic tape or disk or solid state chip. The material to be typed is keyed in and stored, retrieved as desired, and printed after it is edited.

Few mechanical defects develop in these machines, so that it may not be possible to identify a specific machine. These systems use either a daisywheel or a typeball. Typeballs and daisywheels are interchangeable and can be quickly replaced. Various font styles are available for each typeball or daisywheel.

RIBBONS

Typewriter ribbons assist in the identification of documents. The type of ribbon used gives additional information about the document.

Ribbons for typewriters and printers are sometimes interchangeable. The two main families of ribbons are fabric ribbons and film ribbons. The ink is transferred to the document by the impact of the typewriter key. Single-strike ribbons transfer all the ink onto the paper at one time, while multi-strike ribbons can be used over again. Some fabric ribbons can be re-inked. Some ribbons are half red and half black and some are half ink and half correction tape.

Single strike impact film ribbons consist of a polymer film coated with pigments, dyes, waxes, and oils. The ink is absorbed into the paper and can be covered with correction tape or fluid. Some of these ribbons print in double or triple rows of slightly staggered characters. Since the ribbon is only used once, the discarded ribbon can be deciphered by reading diagonally from top to bottom.

On the correctable film ribbon, the ink contains resins but lacks the dyes found in permanent ink. The ink sits on the paper instead of penetrating and can be lifted with a sticky tape before it sets. It is easily removed immediately after placement but becomes increasingly difficult to remove after it sets. It takes about twenty-four hours to set completely.

Correcting tapes impress a white coating over the letter to be covered. The typist strikes the incorrect letter and the white coating adheres to the letter. It is possible to identify the misplaced letter by looking at the letter under magnification, as the double impact leaves an indentation in the paper that is observable when properly enlarged.

QUESTIONS ABOUT RIBBONS

- What kind of ribbon was used? Film or fabric?
- Was the same ribbon used throughout the document?
- Has the ribbon been retrieved?
- Is the data on the ribbon readable?
- Is the date of the document consistent with the date the ribbon was made?
- Are there corrections and how were they made? Whiteout, correction ribbon, or lift-off tape?

COMPUTERS AND PRINTERS

Computers have replaced typewriters in modern offices. Today's documents are typed on a keyboard connected to a computer, mistakes are corrected, and the documents are printed on one of several printers connected to the computer system. With the decline in the use of typewriters and the increase in personal computers, typewriter companies switched to the manufacture of printers.

The dot matrix, ink jet, and laser printers have now taken over the market from earlier impact printers. The dot matrix has a series of small pins that press against the ribbon and stamp the paper. The design of the letter indicates which pins to press against the ribbon. The original nine-pin has been replaced by the twenty-four-pin that can input 360 dots per inch, producing letters that are high quality images.

Ink jet printers spray the ink onto the paper configuring the letter designs similar to the dot-matrix designs. The sprayed ink may run slightly, blurring the rough edges of the dots. Ink jet printers leave small spatters of ink next to the printed characters. These splatters can be seen under a microscope.

The laser printer is the fastest and sharpest technology in the printing field. A light source such as a laser exposes a photosensitive drum in a pattern of tiny dots to form an image. Negatively charged toner clings to the positively charged, sensitized areas of the drum. The toner is transferred to the paper, which has been given a positive charge. The toner is fused to the paper by heat and pressure. The quality of the laser printer is superior to other printing methods and is constantly being improved. Laser copy can be identified by the crisp straight edges of the copy.

COLOR PRINTERS

Color ink jet printers have practically replaced the black-only ink jet printers. Color-technology is an improvement over the black-only printers in that three additional colors: cyan, magenta, and yellow are added to make thousands of colors that can produce near photographic quality images. These printers are still relatively slow, taking several minutes to print a single 8" x 10" full-color page. Color laser printers are being introduced to the business world. Like the ink jets, they also use three colors to create an image while still possessing the crisp features and speed of a laser printer. Initial cost is high but it is offset by greater speed and lower cost per page when compared to color ink jets. This rapid advance in printing technology has presented opportunities for the unscrupulous to create authentic looking fraudulent documents from diplomas to stock certificates that are difficult to detect. Printed colored signatures are sometimes misrepresented to be original hand-signed signatures.

FONTS

Since the advent of nontypeface printers, a variety of fonts are available as residential and optional software programs for computers. Similar choices of fonts are found on multiple computer systems and individual computers can produce varied fonts. Most fonts are scalable so that sizes vary. The computer operator can change font size, word, letter and line spacing and other alignment features as desired.

DIFFERENTIATING SOURCES OF PRINT

Typewritten documents can be identified by their lack of technical sophistication when compared with computer generated documents. Observable features on typewritten documents include ragged right margins; uniform spacing between letters and words; six lines of type to the inch; and indentations from the typeface striking the paper. Close examination should also reveal any corrections that have been made on the typewritten document. The indentation from the corrected letter will be evident on the paper even though it has been covered with whiteout or lifted off with a sticky tape.

The type of printer can be recognized from the printed page but it is not possible to identify a specific printer as the source of a document. Pages printed from a computer system usually have flush right margins; spacing differences between letters and words; and material is easily centered and enhanced with italics, different fonts, and changes in the size of the letters. Distance between lines vary depending on the size of the print or the whim of the computer operator.

THE FACSIMILE MACHINE

The facsimile (or fax) machine consists of three basic elements: the scanner, the modem, and the printer. The scanner translates the material on the original document into electronic data. The modem modulates the electronic data so that it can be transmitted over the telephone lines. The receiving modem translates the electronic data and demodulates it so that the printer can make a facsimile of the original document.

The data is transmitted as small squares called pixels that are either black or white. Early facsimile machines transmitted vertical and horizontal lines without much problem but they left a staggered appearance on diagonal lines. This caused distortion of the original material when the document was reassembled into a printed page. The data tended to be transmitted unevenly as can be seen on the faxed and enlarged typewritten letters in Figure 3.2. Each letter should appear exactly the same each time it appears on the faxed copy but it doesn't. Handwriting is generally more distorted than typewritten letters since there are more lines in handwriting that are curved. In addition, other interference may occur in facsimiles such as blank spaces where there should be data and black vertical lines where they don't belong.

Modern fax machines have finer adjustments and smaller pixels so that the staggered diagonal lines are not as obvious. As technology advances, the quality of the data that is transmitted continues to improve.

The early fax machine used coated thermal paper similar to the early photocopier paper. This paper is sensitive to light and heat and the copy on these papers will fade and disappear over time. It is difficult to retrieve messages from faded faxes. Modern fax machines use plain paper.

The data on a fax transmission is reduced slightly in size during the transfer process. Reduction is about 1 percent. This is due to the transmitting terminal identifier (TTI) line that identifies the original facsimile machine and that appears on the top of the faxed document. The TTI line usually contains the name of the sender, the date and time the document is sent, plus the page number and the number of pages being transmitted. Since owners of fax machines set the data on the TTI line, it is possible to misidentify the name of the sender or to eliminate it altogether.

Businesses have turned to fax machines as a method of transmitting data quickly and inexpensively. As technology advances, fax machines have become standard office equipment in the past twenty years.

Fraudulent facsimiles can be identified by close examination under magnification. Faxed documents can sometimes be traced to their origin through the TTI line or the activity report (transaction report) from the receiving fax machine. Each manufacturer of fax machines uses a distinctive font that can assist in identifying a particular machine.

FADED FAXED DOCUMENTS

The print on a thermal fax copy may fade to illegibility. Document examiners have been successful in some cases in deciphering the data that was originally on the faxed copy. Several methods are used by document examiners such as scanning the document into the computer and adjusting the contrast and using infrared illumination.

CASE STUDY

A prominent business man testified in court that he had sent a fax from his office in one city to an office in another city. A document examiner contradicted the business man's testimony because his examination of an enlarged multigenerational copy of the material that was faxed didn't show the staggered lines evident in faxed transmissions. The business man hired a document examiner to demonstrate how the material had been faxed as indicated. The document examiner had both fax machines delivered to his office and he duplicated the scenario of the original facsimile by sending a similar document from the sending machine to the receiving machine. He then photocopied the faxed document and enlarged it several times. The multigenerational photocopy of this test document resembled the copy examined by the opposing document examiner because the repeated photocopies lost their staggered appearance. Based upon this evidence, the district attorney dropped the charges of perjury against the business man.

PHOTOCOPIERS

The use of carbon paper to make copies on typewriters has been replaced by photocopies. Modern businesses use photocopiers to make duplicates of documents. Photocopiers produce documents using a method that is similar to the method used by laser printers making it difficult to distinguish between a laser-printed document and a photocopy; however, differences are discernible under magnification.

A principal drawback to photocopies is the ease in which they can be altered without detection. A document can be cut and pasted and recopied without leaving evidence that the document is a composite. This limits the observations that a document examiners can make about photocopies.

Another drawback is the deterioration that occurs when multigenerational copies are made on a photocopier. Each succeeding generation loses detail.

Observations on photocopies are reliable if the copy examined is an accurate reproduction of the original document.

TRASH MARKS

A document is placed on the glass of a photocopier and a light projects an image on the drum of the copier that is transferred to a sheet of paper. Occasionally there is lint or dirt on the glass that is copied onto the document. These specks of dirt are called trash marks. Trash marks also result when the drum of a photocopier is nicked or scratched. Trash marks can help identify a photocopier.

Trash marks that result from dirt on the glass will leave a mark on a photocopy in approximately the same location on subsequent pages that are copied during the same time period. Marks caused by the drum, however, will be repeated according to the diameter of the drum on each page. These marks are usually found about three and a half inches apart on a page and will be repeated vertically. Since trash marks are transient, they can assist an examiner in determining when a photocopy was made on a specific photocopier.

Document examiners have been able to date photocopies by comparing the trash marks with other photocopies maintained in the normal course of business. They have identified documents there were purportedly written over a several month or year period as having been written and copied at the same time.

Altered photocopies have been identified by their trashmarks as indicated in the case study.

CASE STUDY

A three-page photocopy was presented as an authentic contract. There was no original document. A document examiner was asked to inspect this contract to determine if it was a cut and paste document. The trash marks on the tops of all three pages were the same. The trash marks on the bottom of all three pages were different. Pages two and three both showed misalignment of the lower part of each page thus proving that the contract was a cut and paste document and not an authentic document.

SUMMARY

Document examiners study documents created with the assistance of modern office equipment. This equipment may have been used to construct fraudulent documents or to alter existing documents for fraudulent purposes. Document examiners study typewritten documents, computer-generated documents, faxed documents, and photocopies to determine the nature of the documents.

Document examiners also identify the type of office equipment used to produce a document. Typewriters, word processors, computers, facsimile machines, and photocopiers all leave evidence of their method of construction of a document.

Part IV

Detecting Fraud

11

Forgery and Fraud

TYPES OF CASES

Document examiners handle cases that involve documents that are suspected of being fraudulent. The entire document or any part of it may be falsified. Cases include counterfeit and forged documents.

Many different kinds of documents are falsified from letters of credit to college diplomas. Types of cases include embezzlement, industrial espionage, threats, bank robbery notes, confessions, graffiti, medical malpractice cases, and false identification documents. Document examiners study altered medical records and raised checks; decipher sequences of writing, disguised writing, and indented writing; and identify insertions in contracts and fraudulent wills. Any document is vulnerable to fraud and may need a qualified document examiner to expose it's fraudulent nature.

In some cases it is sufficient to show that a questioned signature has been falsified. Unless the forger is highly skilled, this determination can be made fairly quickly, usually within a few hours. Document examiners may be asked to determine who wrote the fraudulent signature. This may be difficult to do if the writer attempted to imitate the genuine handwriting or the writer successfully disguised his handwriting. It takes much longer to identify the author of a fraudulent document than to demonstrate that the handwriting is not genuine.

This section deals with forgeries, how they are created and how they are uncovered by a document examiner. The following chapter deals with some of the other problems that concern fraudulent documents.

FORGERY

What is forgery? Forgery is the false making or the material alteration of a document with the intent to defraud. A person who, with the purpose of deceiving or injuring, makes, utters, or alters a writing in such a way as to convey a false impression concerning its authenticity, which imposes a legal liability, is guilty of forgery in its contemporary sense.

There are four elements needed to support a charge of forgery: falsemaking, legal liability, identity of the forger, and intent to defraud.

Document examiners are often asked to identify a fraudulent signature to determine if it is a forgery. Document examiners can identify fraudulent signatures but they cannot state that a fraudulent signature is a forgery. Document examiners can identify the person who wrote the fraudulent signature but cannot call the person a forger.

The court determines if a forgery has been committed, that is, if the suspect who attempted to pass a fraudulent document intended to defraud. Document examiners can only identify the handwriting as being nongenuine.

While forged checks are the most common type of forgery, many other documents are also forged. Wills and contracts constitute a large number of forgery cases.

FORGING METHODS

There are two types of forgery, simple and simulated. A simple forgery is one in which there has been no attempt to imitate a known signature. It can be a nonsimulated forgery of a particular person or a fictitious person. It is the easiest type of forgery to detect since the signature bears no resemblance to the victim's signature. If the forger has not disguised his handwriting, it may be possible to identify the author of simple forged signatures.

A simulated forgery resembles the signature of the victim. Until recently there were two basic methods of creating a simulated forgery, tracing and free-hand copying of a model signature.

Modern equipment makes it possible to create fraudulent signatures by scanning or cut and paste. It is more difficult to identify the maker of a simulated signature and in many cases it will not be possible to identify the forger.

TRACING

Forgers who lack skill in simulating a signature will trace a signature in order to duplicate it. It is difficult to replicate a signature by tracing it without leaving obvious signs of forgery. First, the forger must find a way to transfer the signature from one page to another. At times he uses carbon paper by placing it under the known signature over a sheet of paper. The forger then traces the outline of the signature with a sharp instrument such as a stylus or a pen. The forger removes the original and follows the lines of carbon with a broad point pen to hide the carbon line and to compensate for any deviations from the lines of the signature. See Figure 11.1.

Another tracing method uses a transmitted light source to replicate a signature. In this case, the forger places the genuine signature under a sheet of paper and using back lighting, traces the lines that show through the paper with a stylus. The light source could be a light box or a window. Some forgers use onion skin to trace signatures. The forger then goes over the indentations with a pen. The ink from the pen covers the indentations, however, it is difficult to keep within the lines and sometimes carbon traces or indentations in the paper may be seen along the writing line.

Some ingenious forgers are using pantographs or scribers to copy signatures. These devices enable one to copy a design and change the size of the design. The proportions remain the same but the signature is reduced or enlarged.

CUT AND PASTE

Forgers may take a genuine signature and copy it onto another document. This is accomplished by cutting out a genuine signature and pasting it onto another document. The document is photocopied and the original destroyed. The photocopy is presented as best evidence. A good photocopy of a cut and paste is difficult to detect. If the signature has not been properly aligned, a document examiner may be able to demonstrate its fraudulent nature by carefully measuring the vertical and horizontal alignment. Sometimes shadow lines are left where the paper was joined.

Figure 11.1
Evidence of Tracing Using Carbon Paper

SCANNING

The newest technique for creating fraudulent signatures is by scanning a genuine signature into a computer and printing it onto another document. This type of forgery can be exposed by the printing method used to create the fraudulent document. This can be identified under magnification. Ink from a pen usually spreads slightly and has an uneven edge. An ink jet printer leaves dots along the edge of the writing. A laser printer leaves a crisp edge and resembles photocopying. See Figure 11.2.

FREE-HAND SIMULATIONS

A free-hand simulation is the most difficult type of forgery to create. A good simulation is also the most difficult to detect. Few forgers are skilled enough to create good free-hand simulations.

A forger has to choose between speed and accuracy. The faster he writes, the harder it is to imitate another's writing style. If the forger slows down too much, he will loose good line quality and introduce tremor in the writing line. If he goes too fast, he will not have a good imitation of the model signature.

Some forgers write the signature upside down and backwards. This helps them eliminate their own writing characteristics. Backward writing can be detected under magnification by the crossing of the lines. The lines cross in the wrong direction. Pressure patterns are reversed in upside-down writing.

Another technique for simulation is to make each letter individually and blend them together. This can also be detected under magnification as the overlapping can be seen with a microscope or a high power magnifying glass.

Figure 11.2
Enlargement of a Scanned Signature

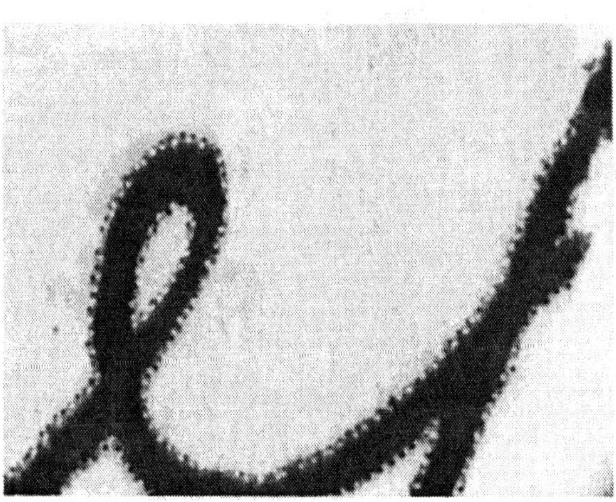

A skilled free-hand simulation may not be identifiable, especially if the victim has a simplified signature that is easily duplicated. A poorly executed signature may not be difficult for the forger to copy it.

TYPES OF FORGERS

Forgers are either professionals, amateurs, or opportunists. Professional forgers are generally skilled at copying other people's handwriting. They may concentrate on faking autographs of famous people or specialize in one person such as Clifford Irving who forged the autobiography of Howard Hughes. Professional forgers may concentrate on passing fraudulent checks or securities, using stolen checks and credit cards, or counterfeiting and forging documents.

Amateurs create most of the forgeries that can be quickly spotted as spurious documents. They also steal checks and credit cards but they are not adept at imitating someone else's signature. In most cases they make no attempt at imitation. They lack the skill or expertise of professional forgers so that their efforts are easily detected. They will go to considerable trouble to copy the capital letters in a signature and any outstanding idiosyncrasies while completely overlooking the subtle characteristics of the writer.

Opportunists are amateur forgers who take advantage of a situation. They are often caregivers of an elderly or infirm person who steal the individual's entire estate. They may be family members, neighbors, or home aids who see an opportunity to acquire a large amount of money with a minimum amount of effort or they may be embezzlers who are stealing money from their employers. They may cash a coworker's check and pocket the money figuring that they can disguise the endorsement and not get caught.

EASE OF FORGERY

The ability of the forger to duplicate a signature depends on the complexity of the signature being copied. Some signatures are easier to forge than others. The skill level of the genuine writer, the speed of the writing, and the method of connecting the letters determine the ease or difficulty of forging the model signature.

The skill level of writers varies significantly from highly skilled writers to those who are barely literate. Some writers have devoted much time and effort into mastering penmanship. They have achieved a high skill level that is difficult to duplicate by most writers. If the writer has a complex signature with frequent changes of direction and stylized letters, his signature will be difficult to imitate.

The poorly skilled writing refers to clumsy, illiterate, and halting writing and may contain hesitation due to weakness or disease. Between the two is the moderately skilled writer who displays better rhythm and coordination.

The act of forging is usually done slowly and deliberately. It is therefore more difficult to distinguish signatures that are imitations of poorly skilled signatures since the method used to create both types is similar.

Signatures that contain disconnected letters are easier to imitate since the forger can make one form at a time. Oversimplified signatures that consist of one or two letters and a squiggle can be duplicated without difficulty.

Therefore, the complexity of the signature affects the ability of the forger to create a signature that is difficult to detect. It is necessary to distinguish between easily-imitated signatures and ones that are difficult to copy.

SELF-FORGERY

Occasionally a person will disguise his own signature so that he can deny it later. A writer may draw a check on a closed account. He may be reluctant to sign a contract. Welfare recipients may cash their checks and then report the check lost in order to get an additional payment. Writers will also disguise request writing exemplars to avoid prosecution on a forgery charge.

Writers who want to deny their signatures frequently must sign their signatures in front of witnesses so that they have to be surreptitious in their methods of disguise. Even when they sign a document without witnesses they need to have it resemble their known signature so that it will be accepted, yet different enough so that they can deny it later.

Self-disguise is frequently accomplished by writing more slowly. The writer introduces tremor into his writing which he uses to support the argument that his signature is forged.

Sometimes a writer will alter his capital letters as a method of disguise. A writer will use printed forms instead of cursive, cursive if he customarily prints, or attempt to reverse the line direction to support forgery.

A person who creates a self-forgery generally relies on these few efforts to enable him to deny his signature. The self-forger fails to recognize that some of the subtle habits of his handwriting are present in the handwriting he attempted to disguise. The self-forger is unaware of the characteristics that identify his signature from all others. A careful scrutiny of a self-forgery can reveal similarities in slant, proportions, baseline, alignment, spacing, letter forms, connecting strokes, and terminal strokes.

DETECTING FORGERIES

Most writers depart from the penmanship system they were taught in school. They stylize letter forms, individualize handwriting characteristics, and ignore many of the rules of penmanship. These deviations from the norm enable a handwriting to be identified. Since each individual customizes her handwriting differently from any other individual. Handwriting can be identified as belonging to a writer when sufficient similarities exist between questioned and known handwriting samples.

FACTS THAT ASSIST IN HANDWRITING IDENTIFICATION

- No two people write exactly alike. A person's writing is the expression of his particular habit of movement. Individual characteristics that are unique to a writer exist in everyone's handwriting distinguishing it from every other handwriting. Variation in writing is a personal factor; it is different for each person.
- Writing can be identified as belonging to an individual when there are sufficient similarities in the characteristics of writing and no basic structural differences. There is no established number of similarities needed to identify the writer. The diversity and uniqueness of the similarities determine authenticity. A single basic unexplainable structural difference eliminates a writer.
- There can be striking similarities between two different people's handwriting. This is most likely to show up in families or groups of people who share a common bond. It is often the result of imitation, especially in individual characteristics. There will always be some differences in handwriting characteristics if enough handwriting is available for comparison.
- It is beyond the capability of any person to see all the typical features of a script and to reproduce them all exactly. No one can duplicate all of the intricate subconscious writing habits of another while eliminating all of his own subconscious habits in any extended writing sample.
- A good writer can imitate some of the habits and may be able to create a signature that bears a close resemblance to the original writer's. If the original writer oversimplifies his signature, it can be easily duplicated. Squiggles may contain enough similarities to pass as genuine signatures.
- The more diverse and unusual the combination of mutual characteristics and individual handwriting habits, the more difficult they are to imitate. Extended writing samples are impossible to duplicate due to the fact that the average writer cannot sustain the intense concentration needed to maintain a disguise over a long period of time. The more the forger writes, the more the writing reverts back to his natural characteristics.
- Imitated writing intentionally bears resemblance to the writing from which it is copied. Forgers concentrate on the pictorial effect and neglect the minute details. They imitate the outstanding features of a signature. Capital letters and letters containing flourishes are most likely to be copied. Middle zone letters and endings tend to be slurred. The subtle habits of the writer are ignored.
- No one can duplicate all of the intricate subconscious writing habits of another. It is these subconscious writing habits that the document examiner studies to determine the authenticity or spuriousness of handwriting.

SIGNS OF FORGERY

Obvious signs of forgery include patched writing, hesitation as revealed by ink blobs, plus breaks in the line of writing, unnatural pauses in the writing, tremor which causes poor line quality, erasures, and backward writing. Blunt initial and/or terminal strokes can indicate forgery but the presence of blunt strokes is not proof of forgery.

Presence of any of the signs of forgery does not necessarily indicate that the document in question is not genuine since any of the signs could be part of the writer's normal habits. Similarly, a lack of any sign of forgery does not indicate genuineness.

Freehand simulations by a skilled writer can be difficult to detect. Obvious signs of forgery are usually not present in good freehand simulations. It is the lack of similarity in the subtle habits of the writer that reveals the spurious nature of the freehand simulation.

A tracing can generally be identified from the model signature. A tracing doesn't have to be an exact copy of the model from which it was traced. It typically has less detail than the model signature as the writer fails to capture all the subtleties of the original. A tracing may deviate from the model due to slippage of the tracing paper or the deliberate moving of the paper to distort the copy. The forger generally presents the model signature for comparison to support the authenticity of the signature.

Forgers make mistakes and it is these mistakes that help identify them. They may copy the handwriting of an individual from the wrong time period. They may overlook important details that affect a handwriting. Their writing may be more skilled than the person they are attempting to imitate. Their attention may wander and they revert back to their normal writing habits.

Some forgeries are successful because they are never questioned. Close scrutiny would reveal the spuriousness of many documents that have been accepted as genuine. The forger depends on a cursory examination of a fraudulent document in order to ply his trade. He knows that under detailed examination his treachery will be discovered.

A document examiner must be able to differentiate between the natural variation of a writer and the writing of another person. It takes several years of experience examining thousands of handwriting samples to identify these differences.

Only a small percentage of all forgeries are created by highly skilled forgers. Most fraudulent signatures are created by amateurs who see an opportunity to take advantage of others. Most of these amateur forgers are not good at imitating handwriting and leave obvious signs of forgery in their attempts to defraud.

TREMOR

Tremor, the result of slow writing, is the most obvious sign of forgery. Writing can be compared to riding a bicycle. When the bike rider slows down, his wheels will wobble. If he leaves a path in the dirt, it will resemble a corrugated line. The same thing happens to the writing line when the writer slows down to copy or trace a line. The writing line will exhibit tremor. A fine tremor results in corrugation in the writing line, tiny side to side motions that can be seen under magnification. See Figure 11.3.

Fine line tremor that is often found in forged signatures is known as criminal tremor. This deterioration of the writing line produces poor line quality. Line quality relates to the smoothness of the writing. Forgers sacrifice line quality when copying another's handwriting. Poor line quality is most evident in traced signatures but may be present in freehand simulations as well.

Criminal tremor can be distinguished from the tremor produced by infirm and elderly writers. Criminal tremor consists of very fine osculations while the tremor of the infirm and elderly is erratic and much more obvious.

Some forgers attempt to imitate writing that contains tremor. This is much harder to duplicate than normal writing. When faking tremor the writer has a tendency to develop a rhythmic to and fro movement. The writer will usually not place tremor on curves but will execute a smoother stroke than the known writer could make.

There may be other signs of forgery present with tremor. Patching, retracing, erasures, blobs of ink, or other signs of hesitation can help identify a forgery.

PRESSURE PATTERNS

Forged writing that is slowly traced or copied looks as though it has been drawn instead of written — and it has. Simulated and forged writing usually lacks the normal pressure patterns of the writer being imitated. Most writers have varied pressure; their downstrokes are heavier than their upstrokes. Forged drawn writing doesn't resemble natural writing. The pressure of a forgery is too uniform. There is no change between upstroke pressure and downstroke pressure.

Pressure patterns are subtle but highly significant characteristics of writing. Some writing instruments, especially ballpoint pens, make it difficult to distinguish pressure patterns. Some writing surfaces affect pressure as well. Careful study of the handwriting by the document examiner with the aid of magnification should reveal the pressure patterns of the writer.

Pressure patterns may be valuable clues to the identity of the writer as it is difficult to consciously control pen pressure. The author of questioned writing might be identified by comparing changes in pressure of his genuine writing with the questioned writing.

Figure 11.3
Examples of Slowly Drawn Signatures

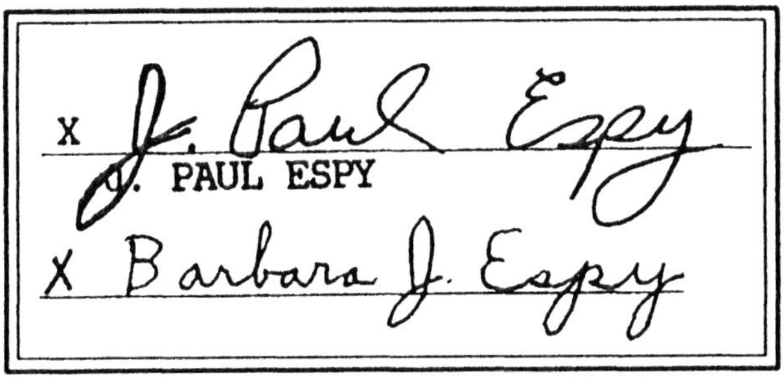

Depth of pressure is an important consideration although writing surfaces and writing instruments can distort the depth perception of pressure. Indentations are created in the paper by the writing instrument forming ridges on the back of the paper. The heavier the pressure, the deeper the indentations. The depth is heavier on a soft writing surface. The hard surface restricts the formation of indentations.

The type of grip pressure used to hold the writing instrument will be a clue to identity. If the writer held the writing instrument too tightly, the writing will appear cramped and rigid. If the writer's grip is too light the pen will slide around and leave air strokes and stray marks on the paper. Unskilled writers tend to grip the pen too tightly, limiting their control of the instrument.

PATCHING OR RETRACING

Forgers are rarely satisfied with the quality of their work. They are always trying to improve the appearance of their forgeries by touching up their work by patching letters and retracing strokes. Occasionally these strokes can be detected with the naked eye. Magnification makes them more obvious. What often appears to be a genuine signature will be exposed as spurious when magnification reveals patches and touched up lines.

Sometimes forgers will misspell a name and attempt to correct their mistake by patching or overwriting the incorrect letter. People rarely misspell their own names. Occasionally a writer will leave out a letter and insert it later but this is rare and this type of insertion is obvious. Most people sign their name and never even glance at their executed signature. They do not go back and try to make it look better.

There is a clear distinction between corrections in the pen line and careful retouching and patching. A writer may go back and touch up a stroke but it will be obvious. Forgers try to blend their strokes to hide their alterations. Any lifting and replacing of the pen may show a break in the writing line. There will be a heavier deposit of ink at the point of overlap.

BLOBS OF INK OR SIGNS OF HESITATION

When the writer pauses with his pen on the paper, the ink continues to flow from the pen and leaves a blob of ink on the writing line. Forgers will stop to check their progress and leave these telltale signs on the signature they are copying. Normal pauses occur in appropriate places but forgers stop at awkward spots. They hesitate in the middle of a circle or along a line where there is no reason for a pause.

These blobs of ink are sometimes confused with gooping caused by a ballpoint pen going around a curve. When a ballpoint pen changes direction, some of the ink adheres to the housing and is deposited on the paper when the pen changes direction again. These blobs of ink will be seen immediately after curved letters and are not signs of hesitation.

PEN LIFTS IN UNNATURAL PLACES

Forgers sometimes lift their pen to check their progress. When they return the pen to the paper they may leave a gap or they may overlap the writing. While all writers lift their pen at the end of a word, forgers tend to have pen lifts in unusual places. They interrupt the normal flow of the line with a pen lift. Writers normally do not lift the pen in the middle of a letter, particularly on a curved line but forgers will.

A more highly-skilled forger will make each letter individually and will blend the letters together to make it appear that the writing is continuous. This type of forgery can be detected under magnification.

BLUNT BEGINNINGS AND ENDINGS

Blunt initial and/or terminal strokes can indicate forgery. The blunt initial stroke is made when the writer places the writing instrument on the paper before she begins to write. If the writer stops her pen before lifting it from the paper, she will leave a blunt ending on her words.

The act of simulation lends itself to blunt beginnings and endings just as tracing does. The writer places the pen on the paper, checks her model and begins the simulation, pausing periodically to check the model as she continues writing. If the writer is a highly-skilled forger, she may complete each name without referring to the model. The forger generally stops the pen on the paper and checks her work before lifting the pen. This leaves a blunt ending with a bulb called a hesitation stroke.

UNDUE ATTENTION TO UNIMPORTANT DETAILS

Forgers pay undue attention to unimportant details. They will cross a "t" too carefully, dot an "i" too exactly, and sometimes even form the letters too precisely. Writing is a habit to which most of us pay little attention. When close attention enters the writing act, we are dealing with a probable forgery, especially when the known writing does not show the same care.

CLOSE SIMILARITY OR EXACT IDENTITY

Close similarity or exact duplication of words or combinations of letters indicates that the writer had one form in mind when imitating the writing. The forger doesn't recognize the need for natural variation and makes the words and letters as close to a model signature as possible. This is obvious when the forger attempts to copy extended writing. The writer will exactly duplicate the letter form, crossing the "t" at the same angle and in the same place, placing the i-dot in the same location, forming the design of the letter exactly like the model. This gives the writing a rubber stamp look. See Figure 11.4.

Figure 11.4
Handwritten Words That Are Too Similar

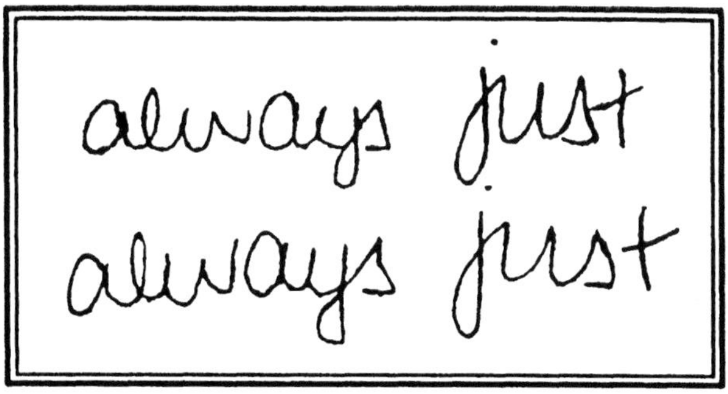

Reasonable variation is evident in genuine writing. Imitation conforms closely to a fixed letter form and lacks natural variation.

Some forgers cut a genuine signature from a document and paste it onto a fraudulent one. They recopy the photocopy and try to pass the document as authentic. If the original document is located, it is easy to recognize the duplication of the model signature. Even without the source document, the document examiner may be able to identify a cut and paste from misalignment or trash marks. Multiple copies of the same signature are evidence that the signatures are not genuine.

Identical original signatures can only be obtained by tracing the original signature, using a signature stamp, or creating a robot signature using a writing machine such as an autopen. Scanned signatures can also be printed onto a document and appear to be original genuine signatures to the naked eye. The fact that these signatures have been printed onto a document is obvious under magnification.

DISSIMILARITIES

A simple forgery is one in which there has been no attempt to imitate the genuine writing. The forger will leave some of her own characteristics in the simple forgery. This is one of the easiest types of forgeries to identify since there are significant differences between the known and the questioned writing. There will also be similarities between the questioned document and the suspect. Simple forgeries may not contain any other signs of forgery.

DISSIMILAR LETTER CONSTRUCTION

Since forgers concentrate on the appearance of the writing, they overlook the method of construction of the individual letter forms. While the letters resemble the known writing in appearance, the method of construction is not the same.

Forgers copy the obvious unusual letter forms, particularly capital letters but they don't usually pay as much attention to lowercase letters. In some cases they slur the letters instead of imitating them.

Forgers expect their handiwork to be given only a cursory glance. They know that their fraudulent signatures will not pass close scrutiny.

BACKWARD WRITING

Some forgers turn the model signature upside-down and copy it backward in an attempt to suppress their own handwriting characteristics. Upside-down writing will have altered pressure patterns with the upstrokes having heavier pressure than the downstrokes or the pressure may be even as a result of drawing instead of writing.

Backward writing can be identified by the intersecting lines which cross in the wrong direction, that is, the wrong stroke will be on top. Ballpoint pens reveal direction from their circle formations. Spur striations radiate outward on circle formations. The gooping common to ballpoint pens will also assist in line direction. Ballpoint pens leave blobs of ink immediately after the pen makes a curve.

SPEED VERSUS ACCURACY

Forgers must choose between speed and accuracy. Fast writing produces good line quality at the expense of adhering to the model signature. If the forger wants to duplicate the model signature more accurately, he must write more slowly. Slow writing looks drawn and tremulous.

ADHERENCE TO THE RULES OF PENMANSHIP

Forgers adhere more closely to the rules of penmanship than the writers they are copying, especially with letter formations, connecting strokes, and initial and terminal strokes of writing. Usually forgers form the letters more clearer than the writer he is imitating. Forgers fail to copy stylized letters. They usually ignore a writer's baseline placement and revert to their own style or write evenly on the baseline.

IDENTIFYING FORGED DOCUMENTS

While a simple forgery is easily identified because it does not resemble the known writer's signature, determining the lack of genuineness of a simulated forgery generally depends on more than one indicator.

Any of the signs of forgery may be present in the forged writing. Slight differences in subtle characteristics may be found. The forger may have penned signatures from a different time period; for example, a smooth signature when a person was unable to write smoothly due to age or illness, or a shaky signature that should have been smooth.

Forgers may overlook a handicap that limits a person's writing. A blind writer cannot place his signature carefully into a small box manipulating his writing around letters sharing that box. A person who suffered a trauma, such as damage to his writing arm, may not have been able to write at the time a document was executed.

Writers who are consistent in the method in which they pen their names, may have their signatures forged in a different style. For example, a writer who never uses a middle initial suddenly is confronted with a document bearing his signature containing a middle initial or a writer who never uses a nickname now finds a fraudulent signature containing his nickname.

Some writers have more than one signature. They may use one for checks and another for more formal documents. The forger may imitate the wrong signature.

If two or more original signatures are identical or almost identical, one or both of them is not genuine unless they are made from a signature stamp.

OBVIOUS FORGERIES

Some forgeries are so obvious that they will stand on their own merit as being forged. It is not always necessary to have signatures for comparison. The signs of forgery can identify a fraudulent signature. Signatures that are poorly formed with obvious tremor and which are badly patched reveal their fraudulent nature.

NO SIGNS OF FORGERY

Handwriting that shows no obvious signs of forgery is not necessarily genuine. Some writers are capable of copying another's writing with enough proficiency to mask the noticeable indications of fraudulent writing, especially when the genuine writing has a low form level. Identification is generally made in these cases on the subtle differences in the construction of the writing.

IDENTIFYING TRACED SIGNATURES

Traced forgeries are the easiest type of forgery to identify. The forger generally presents the model signature as a exemplar. Since no one ever writes his name exactly the same way, the document examiner can easily spot a model and the forgery.

Since there are several ways to create a traced forgery, document examiners consider the various methods used to trace signatures on questioned documents. If the forger used carbon paper to transfer an impression onto the paper, there will be a residue of carbon along the inked lines. If the forger used a stylus, there will be indentations along the inked lines where he deviated from the intended course. The document examiner utilizes sidelighting to locate the indentations or she can use an ESDA. The document can also be photographed using sidelighting.

Tracing requires that the forger slowly draw a signature instead of writing it. It is easy for a document examiner to recognize a slowly drawn signature. Drawings lack the normal shading of writing, that is, the pressure patterns with light upstrokes and heavier downstrokes found in normal writing. Frequently there is tremor in slow writing. There may be pen lifts or blobs of ink where the writer paused to check his progress or there may be retracing present where the forger touched up the writing line.

Forgers who trace signatures tend to miss subtle details. They follow the outline of the signature but eliminate the less obvious characteristics. They generally deviate slightly from the model signature.

More astute forgers will copy parts from several signatures, tracing them from different documents and presenting them as a single genuine signature. If the signatures used for models are presented as proof of genuineness, the document examiner may be able to match the signatures as the parts copied will overlay the traced signature.

A tracing doesn't have to be an exact copy of the original. It may deviate from the original due to slippage of the tracing paper or the deliberate moving of the papers to distort the spacing. The forger may move the signature slightly after copying the first few letters or the first name, which prevents the material from aligning exactly. One forger used a model tremulous signature to trace four other signatures of an elderly writer. The forger deliberately deviated slightly from the line to make the writing appear tremulous, however, every letter overlaid, including the i-dot and the period after the middle initial.

Tracings generally have blunt initial and terminal strokes due to the nature of the tracing act. The writer places the pen on the starting point before he starts tracing and stops moving the pen when he finishes tracing before lifting it from the paper.

HOLISTIC FORGERIES

While a forger may successfully imitate a small sample of handwriting, it is impossible to maintain a successful simulation of a lengthy document. It requires a strong sense of concentration to duplicate handwriting. Most people cannot maintain total concentration for the sustained period of time required to duplicate a holistic document. As they tire, their attention wanders and they return to their normal writing characteristics. Therefore, the longer the document, the more the writing reverts to the natural characteristics of the writer.

Holistic forgeries can be identified by their lack of internal consistency. Forgers of holistic documents grow careless as their writing progresses and they revert back to their normal writing. The writing at the end of the holistic document will more likely resemble the natural writing of the forger.

Holistic simulated forgeries can also be identified by their lack of normal variation when the forger adheres too closely to the model handwriting. The forger is intent on imitating a specific form and fails to recognize the need for natural variation that occurs in everyone's handwriting. The same word will look exactly the same every time it occurs in a holistic forgery.

In most cases, document examiners will be comparing a questioned document with known writing. Careful comparison of the habits of the known writer enable them to identify the spuriousness of a document. By focusing attention on the subtle influences that are most likely to escape the attention of the writer the document examiner will be able to identify the author of a spurious document.

HABITS OF THE FORGER

While forgers are concentrating on imitating another's writing, their own habits will creep into the writing. It is not possible to concentrate on all the handwriting characteristicsthat make up another's handwriting. Some forgers can concentrate on as many as five different characteristics of a writer but most can only copy one or two. Thus, many of the more subtle characteristics of the forger will be present, particularly those characteristics that lack conscious awareness.

IDENTIFYING THE FORGER

Since amateurs commit most forgeries, they not only fail to copy all of the writing habits of the victim, they include some of their own characteristics in the writing as well. They can be identified if there are enough handwriting characteristics that match.

Skilled simulated forgeries may not contain handwriting characteristics that identify the writer. Since a tracing is drawn, not written, the forger can generally suppress his habits so that they cannot be identified.

SUMMARY

The signs of forgery include patching, ink blobs, pen lifts, tremor, erasures, and blunt beginning and ending strokes. See Table 11.1. The presence of these signs is not proof of forgery and it is not necessary for any of the signs of forgery to be present in a forged instrument. Traced signatures generally contain most of the signs of forgery.

Table 11.1
Signs of Forgery

	Present	Absent
A. Traced Forgeries		
1. Exact match or composite	________	________
2. Loss of line value	________	________
3. Poor line quality	________	________
4. Patching	________	________
5. Erasures	________	________
6. Tremors	________	________
7. Blobs of ink	________	________
8. Hesitation	________	________
9. Traces of carbon	________	________
10. Indentation or overwrite	________	________
11. Outlining	________	________
B. Simulated Forgeries		
1. Skill of the writer		
________Better than known writer		
________Equal to known writer		
________Less than known writer	________	________
2. Poor line quality	________	________
3. Retracing	________	________
4. Erasures	________	________
5. Additions	________	________
6. Patching	________	________
7. Hesitation	________	________
8. Penlifts	________	________
9. Tremor	________	________
10. Dissimilarities to know writing	________	________
11. Misspelling	________	________
12. Habits of forger	________	________
C. Signs of Disguise in Handwriting		
1. Change of slant (usually back slant)	________	________
2. Slant reverts back to original	________	________
3. Change of size	________	________
4. Substitute letter forms	________	________
5. Block printing	________	________
6. Opposite-hand writing	________	________
7. Grotesque letter forms	________	________
8. Handprinting	________	________
9. Lack of internal consistency	________	________
10. Unnecessarily corrected letter forms	________	________

12

Detecting Fraudulent Documents

While the majority of cases that a document examiner handles involve forged handwriting or signatures, there are other problems that arise concerning documents that fall within the document examiner's purview. Document examiners make determinations on many types of fraudulent documents, including documents that have been altered through erasure or have had material inserted.

ALTERED DOCUMENTS

There are many types of alterations that can be made to a document. Material can be erased or overwritten; important information may be covered with whiteout; significant facts may be changed; terms and conditions of a contract can be altered and initialed; insertions can be made into contracts after they have been signed; and pages can be substituted in multipage documents. Document examiners have been trained to discover these alterations and to recover the original information.

ERASURES

Alterations usually include erasures of material from documents. There are two methods of removing material from documents: abrasion or chemical eradication. Some types of documents are easier to erase than others. Determining that an alteration or substitution has taken place and deciphering the material that has been altered or erased falls within the range of the document examiner's abilities.

Erasures are suspicious and can indicate forgery. Erasures may be used to cover mistakes or to raise the value of a check or other negotiable instrument. While all erasures are not suspect, signs of eradication on a document bear close scrutiny.

ABRASION

Abrasive erasures are accomplished with commercial erasers such as gum erasers, ink erasers, and pencil and typewriter erasers. Abrasive erasing can also be accomplished using a knife, a razor blade, or other sharp instrument. Some material is easier to remove than others. Some paper surfaces aid in erasing material, particularly erasable bond paper.

Abrasion disturbs the paper fibers and destroys finishes on paper leaving the surface rough and irregular, making the paper more porous unless it is erasable paper. It is difficult to write on the rough surface when the finish has been removed. Any ink that is applied over the erasure is readily absorbed into the paper and appears feathery.

Not all abrasion is easily detected. Abrasion can be detected visually using strong lighting and magnification. It can also be detected by dusting the surface of the paper with a powder compound. The compound adheres to the rough surface of the paper. It can then be brushed off the paper. Transmitted light will show that the paper is thinner where abrasion has removed the finish.

CHEMICAL ERASURES

Chemical erasures are accomplished by applying a liquid such as chlorine bleach to ink to remove the color. Chemical agents leave a residue on the paper which generally stains the paper. These erasures can be detected under strong lighting and magnification. Chemical erasures may also be detected with ultraviolet light.

Any liquid applied to the paper causes the paper to swell. When the paper dries it does not shrink back to its original size and the paper remains wrinkled.

Safety paper has been specially treated so that any alterations are obvious. It is designed to reveal attempted alterations with ink eradicators. It changes color when chemicals are applied to the paper or it releases fugitive inks that say void. The design of the paper is affected by the chemicals. Chemicals applied to safety paper delete the colored background leaving the area blank.

OBLITERATIONS

Sometimes alterations are made on a document by covering material with an opaque substance. This substance is usually color coordinated with the paper or it may be black to obliterate everything below it. An opaque substance can be liquid such as liquid paper or it can be a powder such as dry line. Material is sometimes marked with dark ink such as felt tip pens or magic markers.

IDENTIFYING OBLITERATIONS

Document examiners have been trained to decipher material under opaque substances. There are several nondestructive methods used to read under obliterated materials. One method for reading under whiteout is accomplished by a special photocopying technique. A procedure for reading under black-out involves placing evidence tape over the material to be read. The evidence tape can be removed for about east ten minutes after it has been applied without damaging the document.

Ultraviolet and infrared illumination can be employed to decipher writing that has been covered over with either dark ink or whiteout. It will not be possible to decipher all material that has been covered using these methods but document examiners prefer to use these nondestructive testing techniques.

INSERTIONS

Insertions of information are sometimes made on an existing document. A contract may be changed after the parties have come to an agreement and signed it; a page may be substituted or print may be added that alters the meaning of the contract; a check may be raised to a higher amount; the date on a document may be changed; or doctors may add notes to their patients' medical charts after a lawsuit has been filed.

Document examiners should be able to recognize typed insertions by their misalignment if the material was added to the document after it was signed. They can identify raised numbers and altered dates, and they can usually detect differences in initials fraudulently added to changes on documents. Document examiners can pinpoint insertions by irregular placement or crowding of the text.

SEQUENCE OF WRITING

Sometimes the question arises as to the sequence of placing material on a document as in the cases mentioned previously when material is added after signatures have been applied. If there is a commingling of the suspect material with the signature, a document examiner can determine which line is placed on the document first. This is not always a simple process as darker lines always appear to be on top. However, with strong lighting and magnification, a document examiner generally can determine sequence.

OVERWRITING

In some cases, documents are altered by overwriting existing material. This type of alteration is frequently used to raise the amount of a check. Alterations of this type can usually be detected by examining the instrument under close scrutiny. Sometimes it is necessary to use special lighting to identify additions to the document. Infrared or ultraviolet lighting may be needed to identify a different ink. Thin layer chromatography can be used to differentiate inks but it involves destructive testing.

Document examiners are using computer technology to detect overwrites. Documents are scanned into the computer and special software enables the examiner to eliminate the overwrite.

PAGE SUBSTITUTIONS

Pages substituted or inserted into a multipage document can sometimes be detected using ultraviolet lighting if pages fluoresce differently. Substituted pages may contain watermarks that differ from the original pages. Original pages may have more staple holes than added pages, the type may be different, or a different pen may have been used.

If a document has been altered, evidence of that alteration can be detected by subjecting the document to close scrutiny under strong light and magnification. And, if necessary, destructive testing will reveal the fraudulent nature of the document.

DISGUISED DOCUMENTS

Writers who do not wish to be identified by their handwriting resort to disguised writing. Disguised writing is found on anonymous letters, hate mail, extortion notes, threatening letters, graffiti, and hold-up notes. It is sometimes used to sign or endorse forged checks or credit cards.

Originality in disguise is rare. Most disguised writing is relatively simple in nature as the writer tends to focus on changing the pictorial effect of the writing while overlooking the less obvious habits.

Document examiners can identify disguised writing because it lacks internal consistency and it frequently appears to be drawn or slowly executed instead of written fluently. It may involve the use of grotesque letter forms.

Change of slant is the most frequently used method of creating disguised writing. Change of size, or speed, opposite hand writing, or block print are other methods of disguise that are frequently utilized.

People who disguise their handwriting do not realize that their writing habits are so ingrained that they cannot alter them sufficiently to avoid detection. While the writer is concentrating on one or two changes to his handwriting, he leaves behind many of his handwriting characteristics which can be identified.

CASE STUDY

An employee in a company was receiving threatening anonymous letters on his desk in his workplace. The building was secure and visitors could not enter the building unescorted. The company hired a document examiner to identify the culprit. Several letters had been received over a period of several months. The writer twisted the loops and wavered his lines to avoid revealing his normal writing habits.

Employees records including the victim's were compared with the questioned documents. The examination of the questioned material revealed that some of the anonymous writing was not disguised. The writer had failed to maintain his disguise completely and natural writing was extracted from the disguised material. Indented handprinting was discovered on one page of the questioned material. Side-lighting revealed the numerous indentations. The indented material was the result of notes having been made on a previous page and it contained the natural handwriting of the victim who was identified as the author of the notes and terminated from his place of employment.

IDENTITY THEFT

Thieves are stealing peoples' identity and ruining their reputations. They obtain financial information about an individual in a variety of ways. Once they have a social security number and basic information about a person's credit, thieves apply for a credit card or a line of credit in the victim's name by stealing solicitations from the victim's mailbox. The thieves may rent a private mailbox to retrieve the credit card or they will steal the card from the victim's mailbox. The victim is unaware of the theft until he either receives a bill or discovers that his financial reputation is ruined and his credit report indicates large unpaid bills.

Identity thieves who raid mailboxes may also take a returned check from a victim's bank statement and use that check to have similar checks printed. Since they have received the statement, they know how much money the victim has in his account. The thieves generally return the statement to the mailbox. The victim is unaware that his account has been accessed until his checks bounce or he receives a subsequent statement.

ASSUMING IDENTITIES

People sometimes assume the identify of others in order to hide their own identity. Drivers may give the police officer a false identity when stopped for a traffic violation. Criminals are using false identification when caught in unlawful activities and innocent people are having their reputations ruined with convictions for crimes in their names that they did not commit. People assume new identities in order to commit more serious crimes such as bigamy or extortion. Inmates have been known to forge confessions from comrades in crime in order to exonerate themselves. One woman sent a threatening letter to a judge and signed her ex-boyfriend's name for revenge. The boyfriend was arrested and charged with making the threat.

COUNTERFEIT DOCUMENTS

Document examiners evaluate counterfeit documents to identify their spurious nature. Counterfeiting refers to the fabrication of a copy of a document without the authority or right to do so. Counterfeiting commonly refers to the criminal manufacture or duplication of money or securities. It can also include stocks, bonds, or fraudulent checks. Counterfeiting identification documents is another large arena of fraud. Counterfeit birth certificates, drivers licenses, passports, and other identification documents are being produced all over the world.

Counterfeit documents are being created on personal computers and color photocopiers. Modern computers enable the unscrupulous to scan genuine documents into their computers, manipulate the information, and produce counterfeit documents that are difficult to detect. Any kind of negotiable instrument can be counterfeited with the most common being forged checks.

Color photocopiers are also tools of the trade for would-be fraud artists. Refund checks are duplicated and cashed as originals. Documents are being cut and pasted electronically to create new documents. Colored photocopies are passing for originals.

DESKTOP FORGERIES

Until the recent proliferation of computer equipment a forger was a highly skilled professional who needed specialized knowledge and skill to create expert forgeries and counterfeit documents. Knowledge of chemicals, papers, and inks was essential, as well as skill in printing, engraving techniques, and lithography.

A variety of mechanical devices used to be needed for an individual to forge and counterfeit various documents. Typewriters, checkwriters, protectographs, rubber stamps, date stamps, and professional printing equipment were necessary tools of the trade. Forging and counterfeiting required a considerable investment of expensive equipment; it also required a lot of time.

In the past twenty years, computer equipment has simplified the creation of spurious documents. The personal computer is a powerful publishing tool when coupled with the right software and a high resolution printer. It can produce and store logos as well as fonts in all sizes and styles. As resolution is increased and printing techniques continue to improve, it is becoming easier to create bogus documents that pass as genuine. Desktop publishing is making it easier for forgers to create fraudulent instruments from letters of credit to spurious checks.

Fraudulent documents are being created on personal computers with a scanner and a laser printer in a relatively short period of time. For as little as $2,000 a criminal can purchase computer equipment that enables him to duplicate many different kinds of documents. For a few dollars more white collar criminals can purchase a print cartridge that uses magnetic ink. Forgers can pop the magnetic ink cartridge into their printer to encode the bottom of their forged checks with magnetic strips. What used to be available to only a few skilled and unscrupulous people is now within the price range of many would-be forgers.

What can be fabricated on a modern home computer system? Business records such as job recommendations, expense account receipts, letterheads with phony names, and many other documents used in business transactions are easily duplicated by modern day forgers. Bank records including cashier's checks, certified checks, letters of credit, and similar financial instruments are being counterfeited. Other documents such as property records, wills, insurance claims, passports, birth records, and college transcripts are subject to forgery. In fact, any legal or financial document can be counterfeited or forged.

In one case, a last will and testament was scanned into a computer and bequeaths to beneficiaries were altered. The will was printed on a color printer and presented to the register of wills office for probate. The witnesses recognized their signatures and attested that they had witnessed the deceased's will. An examination under magnification enabled the document examiner to identify the fraudulent manner in which the will had been created.

SCANNED SIGNATURES

Modern technology enables the unscrupulous to scan genuine signatures into a computer and print them onto contracts and other legal documents. The signatures are printed with colored ink onto promissory notes, contracts, and many other negotiable instruments and passed as original genuine signatures. To the naked eye, these signatures appear to be original pen and ink signatures.

Scanned signatures can be detected under magnification. A six power magnifying glass enables one to see the row of dots along the edge of the ink line created by an ink jet printer or the sharp crisp edge of a laser printer. As printers continue to improve, it will become increasingly difficult to distinguish between a printer and fluid ink from a pen.

Forgers sometimes place more than one scanned signature on a fraudulent document. They are frequently caught when they exactly duplicate a single signature because individuals do not duplicate signatures exactly when they sign documents. The overwhelming similarity of multiple signatures is an indication of their spurious nature.

COUNTERFEIT CHECKS

Since the proliferation of personal computers, the majority of forged checks are now computer generated. With bank safety paper purchased at stationery stores, anyone can create counterfeit checks that defy detection. Forged bank documents cost the banking industry billions of dollars a year. Even imitation documents that are not perfect escape detection long enough for con artists to deposit bogus checks into fictitious accounts and collect against them.

There are checking account kits that enable companies to create their own checks on their personal computers. Since the technology for creating checks is the same whether the checks are genuine or bogus, it may be impossible to determine from examining the checks if they are counterfeit.

Bank stationers are using more safety features to thwart check forgers. Most checks contain microprinting, which is very small print that cannot be scanned or photocopied. Most computers can create small print as seen in Figure 12.1.

Figure 12.1
Example of Microprint

However, microprint is an irregular font that appears as clusters when it is photocopied. Microprint is used to create the signature line on checking accounts and can be identified by the MP at the end of the line.

Strips of magnetic foil are used to create a logo that cannot be duplicated by a scanner or printer. A warning band is also placed across checks stating that the check has these special features and if any are missing the check is bogus. Some checks contain fugitive inks that print the word, void, on photocopies. These, of course, can be eradicated by a good print program.

How does a document examiner spot a computer forgery? Preferably, a genuine check should be available for comparison with the suspect checks. A document examiner will check out the alignment, cut edges, and perforations. Forgers don't usually perforate their phony checks and genuine checks will contain perforations along at least one side of the check except for government-issued checks. Document examiners hold the check up to the light to see if the routing number across the bottom of the check reflects light. A routing number imprinted with magnetic ink will not reflect light while regular print will.

Many counterfeit checks are poorly constructed. The counterfeiter usually doesn't use safety paper or any other security measure found on genuine checks; the printing may be misaligned; the bank logo may be missing; or the numbers on the check may not match the numbers on the routing line.

The American Banking Association assigned routing numbers to each state and major city. This number precedes the bank's assigned number found in the numerator on the right side near the top of the check. The first two numbers of the denominator on the check represent the federal reserve district containing the clearing house for the check. The country is divided into twelve federal reserve districts.

The routing numbers are repeated in magnetic ink on the bottom of the check; the numbers on the top and bottom should match. Counterfeiters will deliberately put the wrong routing number on a check to delay discovery of its fraudulent nature since the check will be sent to the wrong clearinghouse and it will take longer to get back to the bank on which it was drawn.

The modern technology that enables forgers to create better forgeries is the same technology used in the detection of these forgeries. Document examiners keep pace with technology to be able to identify forging and counterfeiting methods.

FRAUDULENT CHECKS

Forged and fictitious checks result in billions of dollars of loss per year. In addition to counterfeit checks, many checks are stolen and cashed. Traveler's checks and cashier checks are preferred by thieves as these are more easily cashed than personal checks. Blank checks are lifted from the back of checkbooks with the thief filling in the information and cashing the checks.

Checks may contain alterations of the dates, the payee, or the amount. Routing numbers may be changed to delay discovery of fraud. Checks are being photocopied or scanned into computers and duplicates printed. The method of completing a check will be of importance to the document examiner. The document examiner should consider the following:

1. What safety features does the check contain?
   - Safety paper?
   - Microprint on signature line?
   - Warning band describing the special features of the check?
   - Holograms, embossing, or foil emblems?
2. How is the date on the check written?
   - All numbers, abbreviated month, or month written out?
   - Dashes between numbers/slashes between numbers?
   - Are the numbers consistent?
   - How are cents indicated?
3. Is the amount written with capitals or all small letters?
   - Any misspelled words on the check?
   - Are there any signs of erasures or alterations on the check?
     - Has the amount been raised?
     - Has the date been changed?
4. Do the signatures start in the same place on the signature line?
5. Is the entire check including the signature written in the same hand?
6. Is the amount of the check consistent with the payee (for example, weekly checks of $1000 for housekeeping services)?
7. Is the check properly endorsed?
   - Has the check been cashed or deposited?
   - Are the bank markings proper?
   - Does the endorsement match the signature on the face of the check?
8. Could the check be counterfeit?
   - Are the checks properly numbered and dated?
   - Are the magnetic numbers opaque?
   - Is the correct bank number on the checks at the top and on the routing line?
   - Are there perforations on the check that correspond with a bank book?
   - Could the check be a colored photocopy?

OTHER TYPES OF FRAUD

In addition to forged and counterfeit documents, examiners are concerned with self-destructing documents and cases involving disappearing ink.

Disappearing ink can be restored and photographed though sometimes it requires the services of an ink chemist to do so. Most document examiners can refer a client to a specialist who handles multifarious problems.

Document examiners may review photographs, drawings, sketches, walls, locker doors, even geese decoys that contain marks of identification. Examiners are often asked to identify the writer of graffiti or anonymous letters. Document examiners may be asked to find an embezzler from his handwriting or an industrial spy who is selling trade secrets.

EMBEZZLEMENT

Embezzlement generally revolves around the manipulation of financial data. The embezzler creates fraudulent accounts and invoices the employer for fictitious supplies. The bookkeeper alters records to cover for money she has pocketed.

Most people do not disguise the way they write numbers. A writer can be identified by his numbers if there are sufficient numbers available for comparison, both questioned and known. Unusual number formations make it easier to identify a writer.

MEDICAL MALPRACTICE

Doctors have been known to create fictitious records or alter existing records to make it appear that they have completed all the proper procedures in the care of their patients. It is possible to identify documents that have been created all at one time instead of over a period of time and to determine how much writing was created at one sitting based upon the consistency of the writing.

Ink dating can be used to determine if the documents have been penned within the last three and one/half years. Ink dating requires destructive testing since some ink must be removed from the document in order to perform the necessary tests.

Alterations in medical records can also be detected. Inserted items may have to be fit into a small area resulting in the crowding of the letters. When additions are made to a record after the fact, the insertion can be detected if it intersects writing already on the document by determining the sequence of writing.

SUMMARY

Document examiners analyze many types of suspect documents, including forged and counterfeit documents and documents that have been altered or contain substitutions or indentations. Alterations may be accomplished by chemical means, abrasion, obliterations, or overwriting. Genuine signatures may be cut and pasted onto fraudulent documents or scanned into a computer and printed onto a contract or will.

Part V

Testimony

13

Opinions, Reports, and Exhibits

PREPARATION

Preparation for court begins when an attorney contacts an expert about a case. Preparation also includes the information and instructions given to the document examiner. What is the document examiner being asked to do? What documents are being supplied to the examiner? Where are the original documents and when will they be available? What background information about the case is being given to the examiner?

The examiner should keep the attorney informed of the progress of the case. The examiner should let the attorney know if more information or documents are needed. She should provide the attorney with an oral opinion before putting anything in writing. The examiner should ask the attorney if he wants a written letter of opinion or an affidavit. A copy of the examiner's curriculum vitae should be attached to any written opinion. In federal cases, a detailed report needs to be completed by the examiner; other cases may also require a detailed report. It may be necessary for the examiner to prepare exhibits with the report.

A document examiner should maintain records of any action taken in the case such as laboratory tests she performed and provide feedback on the case as it progresses. She should inform the attorney of the strengths and weaknesses of the case as soon as they are detected.

The examiner can also supply information about any opposing experts and their reports. The expert should identify flaws in an opposing expert's opinion or report; assist in preparing for depositions of opposing experts and provide feedback on the depositions; assist in preparing strategy in a case and help draw up cross-examinations questions; and prepare exhibits and jury books.

If you have never handled a questioned document case, you may want your expert to give you a crash course in document examination, especially in the area you are litigating.

OPINIONS

After a document examiner completes her examination of documents, standard procedure dictates that she give an oral opinion. The attorney then has the option of requesting a written opinion. The written opinion is generally in the form of a letter of opinion. Occasionally the client will request an affidavit. An attestation clause can be attached to the end of the letter of opinion.

LETTER OF OPINION

A document examiner's opinion letter should contain the following features:

1. The question that the examiner has been asked to address.
2. The documents that the examiner examined designated as known or questioned.
3. The opinion that the examiner reached.

The list of documents examined should include a description of each document so that it can be easily identified and distinguished from all other documents. The date of the document and the number of pages should be noted. The examiner should indicate the nature of the documents examined. Did she look at original documents, photocopies, carbon copies, photographs, or faxed copies? The designation assigned by the examiner such as K-1, Q-1, should also be added.

The opinion should state that the handwriting or signatures are genuine or not genuine, written in the same hand as the exemplars or not written in the same hand as the exemplars. It should not state that any writing is a forgery since the examiner doesn't know the intent of the writer.

The letter might also contain a generic sentence stating that an identification is based on sufficient similarities to identify a writer with no unexplainable fundamental differences between the known and the questioned handwriting.

Letters of opinion do not explain how or why an examiner reached her opinion. Most attorneys prefer a letter of opinion that is brief and succinct. Reasons for an examiner's opinion are usually left for deposition or court testimony. Exhibits may also be included. An example of a letter of opinion can be found on Figure 13.1.

A copy of the examiner's curriculum vitae is sent with the letter to demonstrate that the examiner has the training and experience to render an opinion in a case involving questioned documents.

AFFIDAVIT

An attestation clause can be added to a letter of opinion. Some lawyers prefer that a document examiner submit an affidavit instead of a letter.

Figure 13.1
Letter of Opinion

Dave Lawyer
123 Main Street
Anytown, USA
RE: Goldie Finch

Dear Mr. Lawyer:

I have reviewed the documents you sent to my office. At your request I have examined and compared the signatures of Goldie Finch on the following documents. You have asked me to determine if the signatures on the document captioned as the Questioned Document are genuine.

QUESTIONED DOCUMENT:

Q-1: Lease agreement on a birdhouse located at 456 Mockingbird Lane bearing the questioned signature of Goldie Finch dated 6/21/99. Original.

EXEMPLARS:

K-1: Check #1010 drawn on Maryland National Bank on the Account of Goldie Finch dated 6/21/99. Original.

K-2: Lease agreement for 1236 Blackbird Lane, Apartment 301A dated 5/14/98. Original.

CONCLUSION:

Based on the documents submitted, it is my professional opinion that the signature of Goldie Finch that appears on the Questioned Document is not genuine.

COMMENTS:

In order to establish that a questioned signature was written by a particular person, an examination with known genuine signatures must show substantial agreement in sufficient handwriting characteristics to identify the maker and eliminate the possibility of any other writer. Any significant unexplainable differences will be sufficient to eliminate the writer. There are significant differences between the questioned signatures and the exemplars.

Please notify me as soon as you have obtained a court date so I can place that date on my court schedule. At that time, I will prepare exhibits with enlargements to graphically demonstrate how I came to my opinion as stated above.

If you have any questions, please do not hesitate to contact me and I shall be prepared to go into greater detail.

Sincerely,

Forensic Document Examiner

DETAILED REPORT

In some cases a detailed report is necessary. This report should list the reasons the document examiner came to her opinion and describes the outstanding characteristics.

Exhibits should accompany the report and these generally consist of enlargements of the documents and a side-by-side comparison of comparable material. Exhibits are made from photographs or photocopies and are used in court to support an expert's opinion.

Standardized Handwriting Opinion Terminology

When the examiner gives an opinion, she may wish to qualify or limit her opinion. The following standardized terminology is usually used when an opinion is given.

Identification

Definite identification, highest degree of confidence in one's opinion that the handwriting belongs to the identified party. It is an unqualified opinion and says, "It is my professional opinion that the handwriting in the documents examined is genuine."

Strong Probability

Highly probable, very probable. May be qualified such as "Subject to examination of the original." or "It is highly probable that the document is genuine."

Probability

Evidence indicates that the questioned and known may have been written by the same person but it is not conclusive. "It is my professional opinion that the document probably is genuine." It is based on the fact that there are similarities between the questioned and the known but not enough to make a positive identification.

Indications

There are some indications of similarity but not enough to identify conclusively. "There is evidence suggesting that the handwriting samples compared were written by the same person but not enough material to support a definite conclusion."

No Conclusion

Totally inconclusive, unable to make a determination. The zero point, a neutral position. "It is not possible to reach a conclusion based upon the materials submitted."

Indications/Did Not

Equivalent to the more positive "Indications," but on the negative side. "I found indications that the material does not match."

Probably Did Not

Evidence more strongly against the questioned and known having been executed in the same hand. "It is my professional opinion that the document was probably not written in the same hand."

Strong Probability

Evidence indicates that the writing very probably is not done in the same hand, almost certainty that it is not the same, a qualified opinion. "It is highly probable that the handwriting of the known writing is not the same."

Did Not/Elimination

Definite conclusion that the questioned and known writing are not in the same hand. Highest degree of confidence. "It is my professional opinion that the writer of the questioned and known are not the same."

The degree of probability or improbability is based on the quality of the evidence available and/or the amount of writing. When adequate material containing sufficient handwriting characteristics is compared, document examiners are usually able to come to definite conclusions, which is identification or elimination as the writer of the questioned material. When less material is available, document examiners must weigh the evidence available and limit their opinions to a degree of probability. The less suitable material for comparison, the less confidence there is in the opinion.

An inconclusive opinion is a valid opinion that can be argued in a questioned document case. If an examiner gives an opinion based on insufficient evidence, an opposing examiner can testify to the lack of suitable material in which to give an opinion. An opinion of "no conclusion" indicates that there is insufficient evidence to either identify or eliminate a suspect as the writer of questioned material.

A QUALIFIED OPINION

In addition to the various degrees of probability, it is prudent for document examiners to qualify their opinions under certain conditions. There are four major reasons to qualify opinions. They are: (1) no original documents, (2) lack of sufficient suitable exemplars for comparison purposes, (3) inability to conduct tests, and (4) prior testing destroyed evidence.

A lack of sufficient exemplars for comparison can prevent the expert from giving a definite opinion. Since handwriting identification involves the comparison of handwriting characteristics, it is imperative that enough comparable material be available. Comparable material is material that is similar to the questioned material. Handprinting should be compared with handprinting and handwriting with handwriting; signatures should be compared with signatures. Documents should be dated around the same time and should have been written under similar conditions. However, it may be possible to compare handwriting with handprinting and handwriting with signatures if the material is similar. The principal reason for giving conditional opinions is a lack of sufficient suitable comparable characteristics for handwriting comparison.

If the original questioned document is not available for examination, the document examiner should give a qualified opinion. If a photocopy is an accurate reproduction of the original, the opinion will be accurate. However, a photocopy is easily doctored. A qualified opinion is necessary to allow for the possibility that the photocopy is not representative of the original. If the only available documents consists of poor quality material, the document examiner will be hampered in rendering an opinion and will have to qualify the opinion.

Examination may not be possible on some documents. Documents may have been altered or damaged by careless handling. The original may not be available for testing or permission may be withheld. Poor quality photocopies eliminate many subtle characteristics.

Sometimes material is subjected to testing so that the original is damaged or destroyed before the examiner has had the opportunity to do his analysis. Under these circumstances, a definite conclusion cannot be given. Even a conditional opinion may not be possible. Document examiners must have the opportunity to examine originals before they are subjected to any destructive testing.

The document examiner must indicate the limitations of his ability to make a positive identification due to a lack of sufficient identifying individual characteristics.

It is not always possible to determine the author of spurious writing. A "no conclusion" is a valid opinion. It can be defended in court. A document examiner may have occasion to testify that the suspect writing could have been created by someone other than your client based on the lack of identifying characteristics or lack of sufficient material for comparison purposes.

A good forger will copy obvious idiosyncracies so that it isn't always possible to identify a questioned document by the obvious individual characteristics. Even if all the characteristics of a particular writing are evident in the suspect handwriting, the document examiner must be able to prove that no one else could have executed that handwriting sample in order to give a definite conclusion. If it isn't possible to eliminate all other writers, then the document's authorship cannot be determined.

The document examiner should limit his opinion of photocopies with a statement: "Subject to examination of the original documents."

Even with original documents a stipulation should be made that: "This opinion is based upon the documents submitted."

AFFIDAVITS

An affidavit can be given in place of a letter of opinion. The affidavit usually starts with a paragraph that states that the document examiner is over the age of twenty-one and is a certified document examiner capable of rendering opinions in questioned document cases. A description of the problem posed and the documents provided follow with an opinion and an attestation clause. A copy of the document examiner's curriculum vitae is attached to the affidavit.

Sometimes an affidavit clause is attached to a letter of opinion.

DEMONSTRATIVE EVIDENCE

Demonstrative evidence consists of exhibits made from questioned documents and exemplars that support an expert's opinion. Properly designed, they graphically portray the reasons for the opinion. Models, diagrams, charts, photographs, videos, maps, transparencies, and slides can be used as demonstrative evidence.

A forensic document examiner should not give an unsupported oral opinion in court. The reasons for the opinion must be given and must be demonstrated so that the trier-of-fact can see for himself. Handwriting comparisons can be illustrated with visual aids. Document examiners can and should support their findings with suitable graphics.

Jurors retain facts longer, maintain attention, and understand information better when it is presented both verbally and visually. Properly formulated and designed visual exhibits are among the materials most easily understood and best remembered by jurors. In fact, good exhibits demonstrate the facts more clearly than any other testimony.

EXHIBITS

Exhibits should be used whenever an expert witness wants to demonstrate his findings. Most handwriting cases can benefit from demonstrative evidence. Ordway Hilton says that, "Virtually every document case should be illustrated to make the testimony clearer and more effective" (p. 391). Albert Osborn concurred when he wrote, "Appropriate illustrations enable court and jury to see for themselves and understand that upon which a judgment must be based" (p. 637).

As a general rule, exhibits should be used whenever an expert witness testifies about any complex handwriting matter. The expert should give reasons for his opinion with demonstrations so that the trier-of-fact can see for himself/themselves.

Exhibits are usually generated by the expert or under his supervision. They should be designed to inform and educate, to persuade and justify, as well as focus attention on critical issues of the case. They should enhance the expert's verbal testimony and assist the trier-of-fact in understanding the evidence.

TYPES OF EXHIBITS

Exhibits can range from a simple photocopied page to elaborate computer generated graphics and videotaped demonstrations. Most fall somewhere between the very simple and the highly complicated. Exhibits can be made from photocopies, photographs, or the material can be scanned into a computer to create an exhibit. Exhibits can take the form of large charts or handheld pages, bound into jury books or made into a slide presentation. Sometimes videos and live demonstrations are utilized as well. While various types of exhibits can be used to illustrate document problems, there are some attributes that all exhibits must have.

Exhibits must meet court standards in order to be entered into evidence. These exhibits must be accurate representations of the material in the case. They must be clearly marked, factually portray the evidence, and be easily identified.

DOCUMENT IDENTIFICATION DESIGNATIONS

Questioned and known documents should be marked with a document identification designation for easy verification of the source documents. Document examiners identify questioned and known documents with designated letter and number combinations. For example, questioned documents are marked Q-1, Q-2, Q-3, known documents are given designations of K-1, K-2, K-3 for Known , S-1, S-2, S-3 for Standards, or E-1, E-2, E-3 for Exemplars. Some document examiners prefer to use letters of the alphabet for identification.

Multiple page documents should have each page clearly identified so that the document identification designation reads Page 1 of Q-1 or K-1. If signatures are being identified and a page contains more than one signature, further delineation is needed. Signatures can be marked K-1A and K-1B or K-1A on Page 1 to distinguish a particular signature. They may also be marked A-1, A-2, A-3.

If handwriting is the issue, lines on the page of the source documents are numbered. In cases where the same word appears in a sentence on the same line, the individual word needs to be numbered as well.

Once the source documents are clearly marked, the exhibits can also be marked to show the source of each word on the exhibit in the location of that particular signature or handwritten word. The trier-of-fact needs to be able to locate the source of the illustrated item on the exhibit.

If a word is used from a document, the line number must be included with the document identification designation on an exhibit to facilitate locating that word on the source document. If individual letters are used, the word must be identified as well as the location of that word.

The location of the letters or words illustrated should be marked for easy reference. The document identification designation identifies the document as K-1, K-2, Q-1, Q-2, and so on, plus the page and line from which the material is taken are listed as "Page 1, Line 5." When individual letters are used, the word and its location should also be identified such as "K-1, P. 1, Line 1 word." Arrows may be used to highlight points of specific features of the exhibited material.

PLANNING EXHIBITS

There are several facts the expert needs in order to prepare suitable exhibits. The expert needs to know whether the trier-of-fact will be the judge, a jury, or a panel. If it is a jury trial, how many jurors and alternates will be present? If a panel, she will need to know how many sit on the panel.

What is the layout of the courtroom in which the case is going to be heard? The witness needs to know what type of exhibits will be most effective for the courtroom environment. Some courtrooms cannot be darkened while others are especially arranged to handle overheads or slides. Some judges have preferences which determine the type of demonstrative evidence that can be used.

The purpose of exhibits is generally to show enlargements of samples of handwriting so that details can be more clearly seen. Some exhibits show a side by side comparison between known and questioned writing to demonstrate similarities or differences between questioned and known writing. These features can be recognized more clearly when placed side by side on a comparison chart.

Enlargements should be sufficient so that the details are obvious. The degree of enlargement can vary depending upon the characteristics being featured. A 200 percent enlargement works well on signatures. Fine detail may need further enlargement. Individual letters may benefit from 400 percent enlargement, while a feature of an individual letter may need to be enlarged 1,000 percent. Demonstrating the sequence of writing usually requires 400 percent to 1,000 percent enlargements.

The amount of enlargement should be marked on the exhibit. Comparable material should be enlarged by the same percentage. That is, if the questioned document is enlarged 200 percent, the known should also be enlarged 200 percent.

Each exhibit should illustrate a single point. Clutter distracts and background noise obscures the lines of writing. Extraneous material should be removed so an exhibit can be easily understood.

PHOTOCOPIES

The simplest exhibit is a photocopy. Photocopies are inexpensive and easy to obtain. They can be enlarged from 1 percent to poster size. Photocopies are ideal for small cases especially when they do not have to be enlarged more than about 400 percent. The most practical size enlargement for a photocopy is 200 percent. They lose detail when enlarged too much. Lines separate and begin to break apart leaving gaps. Subtle details are obscured when photocopies are enlarged such as ticks on letters, patching, overwrites, and tapered strokes.

Photocopies are becoming the first choice of many examiners for making exhibits. Care must be taken to accuratelyportray the evidence since photocopies can be easily distorted and doctored.

Photocopies can be produced more quickly and less expensively than photographs. They are especially useful for creating exhibits for comparison charts where individual letters or words are placed side by side, known handwriting next to questioned.

Colored photocopies make good exhibits, especially when enlarged. When documents from a case have different colored backgrounds and/or ink, the colored copies help distinguish the source documents.

A photocopy can be made of an enlarged photograph. A photocopy of an enlarged photograph will retain many of the subtle characteristics of the photograph.

Some problems cannot be illustrated with photocopies. For example, it is not possible to show line sequence or the direction of the writing line with a photocopy.

PHOTOGRAPHS

Photographs are more expensive than photocopies but reveal more details. Photographs should be large enough so that fine details can be clearly seen, at least 200 percent, which is a ratio of two to one.

The documents should be photographed with a measuring device to show the original size of the document since photographs can be printed in different sizes. The documents should also be photographed without the measuring device in case the judge objects to the measuring device. A one on one photocopy should also be made of questioned documents to show the original size.

Photographs should cover only a small portion of the document. A photograph of an entire page of a document reduces an 8½" x 11½" page to a piece of film which is approximately 1¼" square so everything is shrunk down by a factor of eight to one. It must then be enlarged back to an 8"x 10" print. The resulting detail is generally less than what can be obtained with a quality copier.

Most photographers bracket their shots, that is, they take one at the optimal settings of the aperture and one at settings once removed in both directions.

Photographs properly taken are better for comparison than photocopies.

SCANNED EXHIBITS

A more modern method of creating exhibits is now available. Scanners attached to computers enable document examiners to scan their exhibits into the computer, enlarge them, rearrange them, label them, and print them in one operation. This method is easy but labor intensive and requires special equipment. In addition to a computer and a scanner, one must have proper software to manipulate the data with a graphics program.

Once a document is scanned into the computer, it can be manipulated and enlarged. Extraneous material can be removed. Labels can be typed next to the scanned writing. Letters and words can be placed side by side for comparison. The graphics programs enable the document examiner to cut and paste and enlarge through the computer. Once she has arranged the material satisfactorily, it can be printed. Photographic paper may be used that will give the exhibit the appearance of a photograph. Some programs will also allow one to make slides from the computer screen as well. There are also software programs on the market that allow photographic negatives to be scanned into the computer and printed.

Computer generated exhibits can be printed on color printers or in black and white. Color can be added to black and white exhibits to draw attention to important points. Small removable colored arrows are available to call attention to specific features. Color should not be placed directly on the feature but next to it since the color might make the feature more difficult to see clearly.

FACSIMILE TRANSMISSIONS

Facsimile transmissions have been enlarged and presented as exhibits in court cases and courts have accepted them as evidence. However, the exhibits were not challenged by the opposing counsel. A challenge could lead to exclusion due to the distortion of the faxed copies. These early facsimiles were crude reproductions with large jagged lines. Modern facsimile machines can transmit a fine line with less distortion. As technology continues to improve the facsimile transmissions, the distortion will be eliminated and faxed copies will be equivalent to photocopies.

CHARTS AND DIAGRAMS

Side by side comparison charts and diagrams can be made from letters or words by cutting photocopies or photographs apart and aligning similar material next to each other. Most examiners will mark one side of the paper with the word, QUESTIONED, and the other side, KNOWN. See Figure 13.2. Sometimes a questioned signature is placed at the top and the known signatures are arranged under them. See Figure 13.3. Arrows are used to highlight specific features. Explanations of the features illustrated can be added to the exhibits or listed on a separate sheet and attached to the exhibit.

A group of related information can often be incorporated into a table and placed on a chart to demonstrate an important point in the expert's testimony. A chart can clarify the expert witness' testimony.

Charts and diagrams can be made in many different sizes. Charts designed for court contain greatly enlarged documents so that the evidence can be seen from a distance. Charts are generally two to three feet high with letters at least an inch tall. The chart will be placed on an easel in front of the jury. Posterboard or foamboard are materials used to support large charts. They can be transported in an artist's portfolio case.

Charts containing enlarged handwriting are a popular method of displaying evidence although they may not be as effective as other types of exhibits. Document examiners deal in small details, therefore, it is difficult to make the details large enough on a chart that they can be seen by the jury from the jury box. Most charts are not able to show the detail as effectively as handheld enlargements.

Figure 13.2
Example of Exhibit Layout

QUESTIONED	KNOWN

Figure 13.3
Another Example of Exhibit Layout

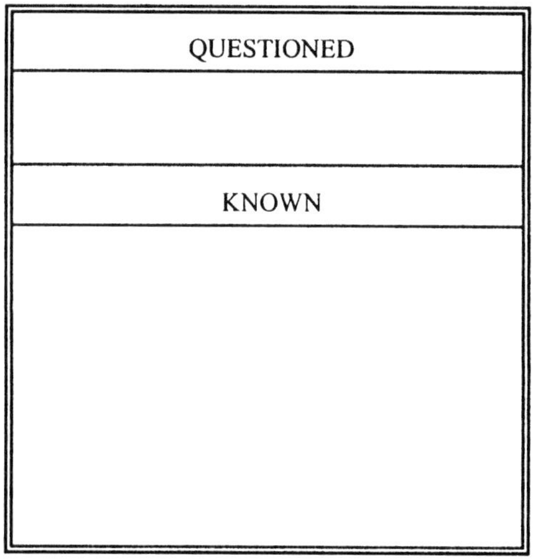

Jurors do not pay close attention to charts, especially when they cannot see the evidence clearly. The document examiner can use a pointer to show jurors the area being discussed. This may help the jury focus on the evidence while the witness is presenting his testimony but they may not be able to follow the reasoning of the expert witness without better exhibits.

Most charts cover too much material instead of just one concept. They are awkward. The line quality of photocopies will deteriorate when the material is enlarged. Photographs are easier to enlarge but they are much more expensive. Scanned documents are inexpensive and they don't lose line quality like photocopies. Scanning documents is time-consuming, not everyone has the time or the capability to create scanned exhibits.

JURY BOOKS

Enlarged signatures and side by side comparison charts can be placed into notebooks or folders so that they can be handled by the jury. These jury books can be stapled, spiral bound, or presented in a binder. They should contain a table of contents so documents can be easily located and each page of the book should be numbered. The source documents should be placed in the back of the books and referenced, or a separate book can be prepared for source documents.

There are various types of binders available for report writing that would accommodate exhibits. If the number of exhibits is large, a loose-leaf binder can be utilized to hold exhibits. Original documents can be placed in clear plastic sheets to protect them from damage. Dividers can be placed in the binders to make it easier to locate material.

The degree of enlargement should also be marked on the exhibit. If making a comparison chart, the documents should be enlarged the same amount. The exhibits should be detailed enough so that the jury can see the point the expert witness is making just by looking at the evidence.

The major disadvantage to jury books is that the trier-of-fact may not be able to follow the witness. A combination of large charts and jury books work well. The witness can point to a feature on the chart with a laser pointer and tell the jury where to find that feature in the jury book.

TRANSPARENCIES

Transparencies can be made from any exhibit. These transparencies can be distributed with handheld exhibits so that they can be placed over other signatures or used with an overhead projector. They can be printed in black and white or colored ink. Transparencies can be made by photocopying exhibit material or by scanning and printing the material onto clear acetate sheets. Cardboard frames can be glued in place and notes can be made on the frame that will not be seen on the projection. Transparencies are most useful in cases involving traced forgeries or cut and paste documents.

When an overhead projector is required in the courtroom, it should be set up during a break in the proceedings or before the court convenes. The material should be viewed ahead of time to make sure that it can be seen clearly by the judge or jury. A laser pointer can be handled by the witness from the witness box to point to details being discussed.

LIVE DEMONSTRATIONS

Some techniques are best illustrated with a live demonstration in the courtroom. For example, a document examiner can show juries how traced copies are created by creating a traced signature in front of the jury. She may show the jury how to "see" indented writing with sidelighting. The expert witness may also illustrate points on a blackboard or large chart.

The witness needs to be comfortable when conducting a live demonstration. She should have practiced until she felt competent when conducting her demonstration.

Closed circuit television can be used for close-up demonstrations on the witness stand. This type of demonstration must be planned in advance so that the equipment is available and easy to set up.

Videotapes can also be used instead of live demonstrations. There are several advantages to video taping. First, the video camera is able to handle close-ups so that the jury can see exactly what is being demonstrated. Second, segments can be retaped until a suitable tape is prepared and finally, there is no danger of the experiment failing which can occur with a live demonstration.

A good exhibit is a stand-alone document that will continue testifying after your expert has left the stand. See Table 13.1.

Table 13.1
Exhibits

Type	Advantages	Disadvantages
Chart	All can follow	Everyone can't see detail
Slides	Colorful	Dark room — lose attention
Overheads	All can follow	May not be able to darken room
Booklets	Easily seen	Jurors may lose their place
Videos	Entertaining	Difficult and expensive to prepare

EXTEMPORANEOUS EXHIBITS

Avoid "on the spot" exhibits unless your expert is requested by the court to demonstrate a point. Extemporaneous exhibits are less effective and lack the impact of prepared demonstrative evidence. An illustration on a blackboard or drawing pad will not be as accurate or as clear as a planned exhibit. In most cases, extemporaneous exhibits will not be taken into the jury room or if taken, may not be as clear and concise as other exhibits.

If a spontaneous exhibit is used, it should be placed on a drawing pad so that it is preserved as opposed to a blackboard that will be erased. It may be advisable to photograph the exhibit to preserve it.

CONSTRUCTING EXHIBITS

It is important to emphasize the most convincing and obvious similarities or differences when preparing exhibits. The exhibits should tell a story. Anyone should be able to look at an exhibit and understand its message.

Whatever method is used: charts, transparencies, jury books, slides, or a combination, start with the original document and enlarge it to the appropriate size. Eliminate extraneous material that distracts from the features being highlighted. This may require using a scanner to eliminate a noisy background or cutting out a signature to minimize the background.

Keep each exhibit simple. Use one idea per page or per chart as too much material on an exhibit creates clutter and causes confusion. The exhibits should be self-explanatory. Text can be added to feature important attributes. Arrows can also be placed on strategic points.

POINTS TO REMEMBER

1. Keep exhibits uncluttered and easy to read.
2. Concentrate on one concept at a time.
3. Make your point obvious and easily discernible.
4. Make your exhibits support your reasons.
5. Limit exhibits to important issues in the case.

SUMMARY

Document examiners give opinions regarding questioned documents. These opinions may be verbal or written. Letters of opinion and/or affidavits are used to convey a written opinion. Detailed reports can be prepared on request. Federal courts require experts to prepare detailed written reports of their findings. Opinions can be positive or probable. The degree of probability is based on the number and quality of a characteristics being compared.

14

Preparation for Court and Deposition

PRETRIAL MEETING

The attorney should set up a pretrial meeting shortly before the trial to review the case and plan strategy. The attorney needs to understand the document examiner's opinion and the foundation for that opinion. The expert needs to understand how the expert's testimony will be brought out by the attorney's direct examination.

The attorney will want to know:

- What are the important points of the expert's testimony?
- How will they be emphasized?
- How can the strengths of the case be highlighted?
- How can the weaknesses be minimized?
- Are there any documents that the expert has not had a chance to examine yet?
- Are there any questions about the document that you still need answers to?
- What type of exhibits are being used?
  Has the expert supplied you with all of the information needed to litigate this case?

You need to be aware of the strengths and weaknesses of the case.

The expert witness needs to know:

- Will this be a jury trial or a bench trial?
- If it is a jury trial, how many people will be on the jury and how many alternates?
- Will the expert be on call for court?
- When will she testify?
- Will she be sequestered?
- Will she be excused after she testifies or will she have to wait in case of rebuttal?
- Will the expert assist the attorney during cross-examination of the opposing expert?
- Will she sit at the counsel table during the examination of the opposing expert?

The document examiner needs to let you know what documents were examined and which documents she intends to use in her court presentation.

- Can the documents examined be admitted into court or will there be difficulty in proving their authenticity?
- Are all of the documents internally consistent, that is, are all the exemplars written by the person who is supposed to have written them?
- Are all of the known documents created by one person or have several people created them?
- How will these documents be introduced during the trial?
- How will the authenticity of the exemplars be verified in court?
- What is the strategy if some of the documents cannot be authenticated?

EXHIBITS

The expert should have prepared exhibits. These could be enlarged photographs or photocopies on charts or in exhibit books.

- Has the expert prepared exhibits to graphically illustrate her findings?
- Has she supplied you with a copy of these exhibits in a timely manner?
- Are the exhibits clearly marked and easily understood?
- Do the exhibits tell a story?
- Do the exhibits contain enlargements of questioned material as well as the source documents from which they were taken?
- Are the exhibits marked so that anyone can locate the source material on the original documents?
- Are the exhibits bound together so that they can be easily marked for identification in court?
- Are the exhibits organized for easy retrieval?

QUALIFYING QUESTIONS

The document examiner should supply you with a list of qualifying questions to help qualify your witness as an expert in court. Let the expert know what other questions will be asked. Different circumstances may require additional questions. A list of suggested questions will be covered in the next section.

DEPOSITION

If the expert has been deposed, make sure that she receives a copy of the deposition before the court trial. The expert needs to thoroughly review her deposition so that she is familiar with the contents. The expert should look for any areas that could lead to impeachment and should prepare suitable answers to questions about these areas. The attorney may have to assist the expert in this process if the expert is not highly experienced.

TELEPHONE CONFERENCE

While ideally you should meet with your expert in person, this is not always possible. A telephone conference should be scheduled if you cannot meet face to face. Be sure that the document examiner supplies you with exhibits prior to your conference call.

GOING TO COURT

Most attorneys will put an expert witness on call rather than have the witness sit in court for an extended period of time. The witness should have an idea of your scheduling so that she can be available when needed. If the witness is on call, you need to know how much time it will take her to get to court once she is notified.

To avoid any problems, you should know if the witness has ever testified in this court district. Has she ever appeared before this judge? How many similar cases has the witness handled? How many cases has she testified in? What was the outcome of any of these other cases? Has the witness ever failed to qualify as an expert in court?

Has the witness ever worked with the opposing attorney? Are there any biases or prejudices that the witness has? How does the witness present her evidence? What concerns does the witness have? How will her testimony fit into the strategy of your case? Is it consistent with the testimony of your other witnesses? How will the witness handle cross-examination?

Has your expert supplied you with all of the information that you will need to litigate this case? Are there any questions about the documents that are still unanswered?

COURT TESTIMONY

Jury surveys reveal that a witness appears more credible when she is allowed to testify in the narrative. It is best to keep your direct examination to a few general questions.

The expert needs to teach the trier-of-fact about handwriting identification. What can be determined from handwriting? What are handwriting characteristics? What are the signs of forgery?

Once the expert has laid the foundation, she is ready to discuss the important factors in this case. Exhibits need to be introduced at the proper time to graphically illustrate verbal testimony. Any problems or weaknesses in the case should be brought out in direct testimony so that they lose their impact in cross-examination.

If possible, the expert should get out of the witness box and stand before a jury during direct examination. Juries respond favorably to an expert who leaves the witness box and demonstrates evidence.

Direct examination should go smoothly for an experienced expert witness. Experts who lack court experience may need coaching and more detailed questions in direct examination.

Experienced experts should be asked if they have any additional comments about the case on completion of their direct examination and especially in redirect after cross-examination.

CROSS-EXAMINATION

A witness who is well prepared should not have difficulty with cross-examination. Most attorneys feel obligated to cross-examine expert witnesses. An experienced witness will use cross-examination to enhance and reinforce her testimony. She should be prepared to handle any problem areas of her testimony and turn them to the expert's advantage.

REDIRECT

If the expert has difficulty with a question in cross, the attorney must be ready to handle the problem in redirect. When a witness is not allowed to explain his answers in cross, she should be given the opportunity to explain in redirect. An open-ended question will cover all bases. Simply ask the expert if there is anything that she wishes to clarify from her cross-examination and follow that question with, "Anything else?"

REBUTTAL

Occasionally it is good strategy to have an expert rebut testimony from an opposing expert. Some experts only testify as rebuttal witnesses. Rebuttal strategy is used to show that the opposing expert is incorrect because he didn't have enough suitable material for comparison or he or she didn't interpret the material correctly. Some opinions are based on limited samples of handwriting. It is necessary to have your expert point out that there is not sufficient material to draw a conclusion of identity or elimination. Other opinions are based on drawing a conclusion that is not compatible with your case.

Experts can also rebut testimony from other witnesses in the case in matters concerning handwriting. For example, a witness testified that she held the writer's wrist to steady her hand. The expert testified in rebuttal that holding one's wrist impedes writing.

SUMMARY

Pretrial preparation is essential in court cases. After the document examiner has provided a report, she should prepare exhibits to graphically demonstrate his findings. A pretrial meeting should be arranged in order to review the strategy of the case and the testimony of the expert.

15

Deposition Testimony

DEPOSITION TESTIMONY

An attorney questions an expert witness in a deposition to learn as much as possible about the strengths and weaknesses of the case before it goes to court. What does the expert know about the case and what is her opinion? The examining attorney wants to elicit as much information as he can from the witness. What can be done to discredit the expert?

PREPARATION

Preparation for a deposition actually begins when the document examiner fields the first inquiry into a case. The examiner should maintain records of the attorney's initial contact as part of her file. The examiner should have a log of her activities and the amount of time spent on each one. She should keep an accurate billing record and accounts receivable.

The expert's records should indicate the date various documents were received into her office and the tests that were conducted on those documents. The examiner should have photographs and photocopies of the relevant documents and should have documents arranged for easy retrieval. If original documents were transferred to different parties, there should be a chain of custody form in the document examiner's files as well as a copy accompanying the documents.

An expert should notify you if she receives a subpoena for a deposition. The examiner should verify the date, time, and location of the deposition and indicate if that is going to be convenient. She should send an estimated bill for the deposition.

Expert witnesses usually collect their fee in advance. Most expert witnesses collect their fee on arrival at the deposition. Some experts prefer to receive a check prior to the day of the deposition.

It is important to spend time with your expert prior to the deposition. Some witnesses are more comfortable giving testimony than others. You should assess your expert's vulnerabilities prior to a deposition.

If you are deposing an opposing document examiner, you may want your own witness to assist with deposition questions, and attend the deposition so that she can assess the opposing expert and offer any additional suggestions for questions or strategy. The examiner can also review the deposition and assist you in preparing questions for court.

Make sure that your expert receives a copy of the transcript when it is ready after the deposition. The expert needs to be familiar with her testimony so that it is consistent when she testifies in court.

The following list of questions has been prepared to assist you in phrasing your questions for a deposition of a forensic document examiner.

GENERAL QUESTIONS

The first set of questions pertains to the percentage of time a document examiner has worked in the field and the type of office the document examiner maintains:

1. What is your profession?
2. Are you a full-time document examiner?
3. Is that your only source of income?
4. If not, what percentage of income comes from document examination?
5. Are you currently self-employed, or are you employed by someone else?
6. Have you always been self-employed as a forensic document examiner?
7. Have you ever worked for any police department?
8. How much of your time is spent on document examination per day? Per week?
9. What services do you offer as a forensic document examiner?
10. Where is your office located?
11. Is that office located in your home?
12. Do you have a separate room for your office?
13. Do you have a laboratory?
14. Is that laboratory in a separate room from your office?
15. Do you have anyone else working in your office with you?

Advertising Methods

The second set of questions relates to the methods the document examiner uses to attract business:

1. How do you get your clients?
2. Do you advertise your services to the public?
3. What services do you advertise?
4. Where do you advertise?

5. Do you advertise in the yellow pages? Which ones?
6. Do you advertise on the Internet?
7. Where is your webpage?
8. Where else do you advertise?
9. How much do you spend on advertising a year?
10. To whom is your advertising directed?
11. Do you have a brochure describing your services as a forensic document examiner?
12. Do you have a curriculum vitae or a resume that you give to prospective clients?
13. Is this your most up-to-date curriculum vitae?
14. When was your curriculum vitae last updated?
15. Who are your clients?

Education

The next section covers the background and education of the deponent:

1. How did you become a document examiner?
2. Do you have a college degree?
3. What type of degree do you have?
4. Can you obtain a degree in document examination?
5. What college courses have you taken that assist you in your work as a document examiner?
6. Have you taken any college courses in document examination?
7. Have you taken any college courses in forensic science?
8. Have you taken any other courses in document examination?
9. Did you take any correspondence courses in document examination?
10. Have your taken the course offered by the National Questioned Document Association?
11. Have you taken courses from Andrew Bradley?
12. Have you taken any courses from the American Institute of Applied Science?
13. Did you take the FBI course at Quantico?
14. Have you taken any training from the Secret Service?
15. How long did the courses last?
16. How long have you been studying handwriting?
17. How much training have you had in handwriting identification?
18. How much training have you had in ink analysis?
19. How much training have you had in the sequence of writing?
20. Did you have any training in document dating?
21. How much training have you had in insertions or deletions of material from documents?
22. How much time have you spent studying handwriting versus other areas of document examination?
23. Did you serve an apprenticeship under a qualified document examiner?
24. If so, how long did you apprentice?
25. To whom did you apprentice?
26. Did you meet with your mentor on a daily basis?
27. If not, how often did you meet?
28. Did you work in your mentor's laboratory?

29. What did you learn from your mentor?
30. What are the qualifications of your mentor?
31. What equipment did you use during your training?
32. What training did you have on the equipment that you are using now?
33. During your apprenticeship did you study the effects that illnesses have on handwriting?
34. Did you study the effects of substance abuse on handwriting?
35. Have you studied the effects of drugs and medication on handwriting?
36. Have you studied the effects of learning disabilities on handwriting?
37. Did you study the effects of personality on handwriting?
38. Have you studied the effects of aging on handwriting?
39. Have you studied the effects of emotions on handwriting?
40. What happens to handwriting when the writer is depressed?
41. What happens to writing when the writer is angry?
42. Have you studied the effects of trauma on handwriting?
43. Have you studied the effects of body positions on writing?
44. Have you studied the development of writing in young children?
45. Have you studied the effects of various writing surfaces on handwriting?
46. What seminars have you attended in connection with your area of expertise?
47. What seminars have you attended in the past ten years?
48. When did you last attend a seminar?
49. What are the names of the organizations who sponsored the seminars?
50. What topics were covered in those seminars?
51. Were you tested on the topics covered?
52. How did you fare on the tests?
53. How many credit hours did you receive for your training seminars?
54. Who were the instructors of these seminars?
55. What are the credentials of these instructors?
56. How do you keep current with new developments in the field of questioned documents?
57. Have you done anything else to increase your knowledge in the field of document examination?
58. Have you taken any training on how to testify as an expert witness?
59. If so, from whom did you take this training?
60. Have you ever attended conferences sponsored by the National Forensic Center?
61. Are you a member of the National Forensic Center?

Familiarity with Relevant Books and Journals

It is helpful to know what books and journals the document examiner considers to be important in the field:

1. What books do you have in your library?
2. What books have you read pertaining to document examination?
3. Did you read the books or just skim them?
4. Have you read the entire book?
5. Who do you consider to be an authority in the field of document examination?
6. Who is considered the "Father of Document Examination"?

7. What book is considered "the Bible"?
8. Do you agree that Albert Osborn is a leading authority in document examination?
9. Is there anything in *Questioned Documents* that you disagree with?
10. When did you read *Questioned Documents* by Albert Osborn?
11. When was the last time you referenced it?
12. Why did you refer to it?
13. What other books do you believe to be authorities in the field of questioned documents?
14. Are you familiar with the book, *Suspect Documents*?
15. Do you know who wrote *Suspect Documents*?
16. Would you agree that Wilson Harrison wrote *Suspect Documents*?
17. Is he an authority in the field of questioned documents?
18. Are you familiar with the book, *Scientific Examination of Questioned Documents*?
19. Do you know who wrote it?
20. Would you agree that Ordway Hilton wrote *Scientific Examination of Questioned Documents*?
21. Who was Ordway Hilton?
22. Have you read anything else written by Ordway Hilton?
23. Are you familiar with Ordway Hilton's book, *Detecting and Deciphering Erased Pencil Writing*?
24. Are you familiar with the book, *Scientific Examination of Documents*?
25. Do you know who wrote it?
26. Do you agree that David Ellen wrote *Scientific Examination of Documents*?
27. Are you familiar with Bradford and Bradford's *Introduction to Handwriting Examination and Identification*?
28. Have you read *Law of Disputed and Forged Documents* by J. Newton Baker?
29. Did you read *Evidential Documents* by James Conway?
30. Are you familiar with *Forging History* by Kenneth Rendell?
31. Have you read *Experiments with Handwriting* by Robert Saudek?
32. Have you read *Handwriting Identification: Facts and Fundamentals* by Huber and Headrick?
33. Do you subscribe to the *International Journal of Forensic Document Examiners*?
34. What trade journals do you subscribe to?
35. What journals do you read?
36. Are you familiar with any of the following journals?
    - *Forensic Science International*
    - *Journal of Forensic Document Examination*
    - *Journal of Forensic Sciences*
    - *Journal of the National Association of Document Examiners?*
    - *WADE Journal or the Wade Exchange*
    - *IAQDE Journal*
37. What books have you read covering the history of handwriting?
38. Do you reference *Drugs and Handwriting* by Patricia Wellingham-Jones?
39. Do you use Marcel Matley's *QDE Index*?
40. What other books do you consider to be important in your field?
41. What books do you reference?
42. What books did you reference in this case?
43. What did you look up in this reference book?

44. Have you read any books on how to testify as an expert witness?
45. If so, what are the names of the books?

Membership/Certification by Relevant Organizations

The next section covers the organizations that the document examiner belongs to and whether or not she is certified by any of these organizations:

1. What professional scientific associations are you currently a dues paying member of?
2. What organizations of document examiners do you belong to?
3. Are you a member of any of the following organizations?
   - National Association of Document Examiners (NADE)
   - National Questioned Document Association (NQDA)
   - Independent Association of Questioned Document Examiners (IAQDE)
   - Association of Forensic Document Examiners (AFDE)
   - American Society of Questioned Document Examiners (ASQDE)
   - World Association of Document Examiners (WADE)
4. Are you a member of the questioned document section of the following organizations?
   - American Academy of Forensic Science (AAFS)
   - International Association for Identification (IAI)
   - American Board of Forensic Examiners (ABFE)
5. Are you a member of any of the regional chapters?
   - Southwest Association of Forensic Scientists
   - Southern Association of Forensic Scientists
   - Northeast Association of Forensic Scientists
   - Mid-Atlantic Association of Forensic Scientists
   - Mid-Western Association of Forensic Scientists
6. Are you a member of the American Board of Forensic Document Examiners (ABFDE)?
7. Are you a member of Fraud Investigators Association of Texas (FIAT)?
8. Are you a member of the Certified Fraud Examiners?
9. Have you ever applied for membership in any of these organizations?
10. What are the requirements for membership in these associations?
11. Have you ever been a member of any of these associations?
12. Have you ever applied for membership in any of these organizations and been refused?
13. If so, why were you refused membership?
14. What are the requirements for membership in these associations?
15. Do you meet the requirements for these associations?
16. If you do not, why don't you meet the requirements?
17. Have you ever held any position in any of these organizations?
18. Have you received any special awards from this organization or any other organization?
19. Have you attended any meetings of these organizations?
20. How frequently do you attend meetings?
21. Are you a member of any other professional associations?

Graphology

Graphology is the study of handwriting to determine personality features of the writer. Some document examiners are also graphologists:

1. Are you a graphologist or a graphoanalyst?
2. Have you studied graphology?
3. What is graphology?
4. What is the difference between a forensic document examiner and a graphologist?
5. Do you use graphology in document examination?
6. Are you certified as a graphologist?
7. Did you use graphology in this case?

Levels of Achievement

The next set of questions refers to the level of achievement the expert has reached:

1. What is a certified document examiner?
2. Are you a certified document examiner?
3. Are you certified by any of these document examiners' organizations?
    - National Association of Document Examiners (NADE)
    - National Questioned Document Association (NQDA)
    - Independent Association of Questioned Document Examiners (IAQDE)
    - Association of Forensic Document Examiners (AFDE)
    - American Society of Questioned Document Examiners (ASQDE)
    - World Association of Document Examiners (WADE)
    - International Association for Identification (IAI)
    - American Board of Forensic Examiners (ABFE)
4. When were you certified?
5. What is involved in the certification process?
6. Are there any educational requirements that you had to meet in order to apply for certification?
7. What type of testing did you undergo?
8. Can you describe the type of test that members of your organization must take to become certified?
9. Were you required to review questioned handwriting or signatures and make a determination as to their genuineness or nongenuineness as part of the testing process?
10. Has anyone failed the certification test?
11. Who presided over the testing?
12. Did you participate in mock trials?
13. Did you have a judge preside over a mock trial?
14. Were you grandfathered into the certifying organization?
15. Is certification the highest level of your field?
16. What is a diplomate?
17. Are you a diplomate in any organization?
18. What is a fellow?

19. Are you a fellow in any organization?
20. Does your organization require recertification?
21. What is involved in the recertification process?
22. How often do you have to be recertified?
23. Are there any continuing education requirements associated with your certification?

Certification by the ABFDE

Some document examiners are certified by the American Board of Forensic Document Examiners (ABFDE):

1. What are the requirements to become a member of the American Board of Forensic Document Examiners?
2. (If member) What did you do to become a member?
3. Were you grandfathered into the American Board of Forensic Document Examiners?
4. Did you take a written test to be certified?
5. Is the American Board of Forensic Document Examiners recognized by the courts as the only organization of document examiners that can certify members as handwriting experts?
6. How many members are there in the American Board of Forensic Document Examiners?
7. How many members were grandfathered into the organization?
8. How many members would not meet the requirements if they applied for membership now?
9. Can a document examiner with a background in graphology be certified by the American Board of Forensic Document Examiners?
10. Do you have to be certified to work for the government?
11. What other organizations certify document examiners?

If the expert is not certified, you may want to ask him the following questions:

12. Have you ever applied for certification?
13. Are you qualified for certification?
14. Why aren't you certified?
15. Did you take any tests for certification?
16. Did you pass any tests that you took for certification?
17. Since there is no license for document examiners, isn't it important to be certified by a professional organization in order to prove that you are qualified as a document examiner?

Proficiency Testing

If the forensic document examiner participates in proficiency testing, you may want to investigate to determine the type of testing:

1. Do you participate in proficiency testing?
2. What is the agency that you use for proficiency testing?

3. How long have you been participating in proficiency testing?
4. What is your percentage of accuracy?
5. Are you familiar with Collaborative Testing Services?
6. Have you taken any tests with Collaborative Testing Services?
7. Are you familiar with any other proficiency testing agencies?
8. If so, which ones?
9. If no testing, why don't you participate in proficiency testing?
10. How do you measure your progress?
11. How do you know that you are correct in your opinions?
12. What kind of feedback do you get to verify your findings?

Publication Contributions

Document examiners should contribute to their field by publishing articles and books about questioned documents:

1. What articles have you written in the field of forensic document examination?
2. Where were these articles published?
3. Is that a peer review publication?
4. When were these articles published?
5. What books have you written on the subject of forensic document examination?
6. Who published these books?
7. How many copies have you sold?
8. Who buys your books?
9. If I wanted to purchase your books, how would I do it?
10. Are your books available in bookstores?
11. Do you have any books or articles that you have written that have not been published yet?

Participation in Seminars

Document examiners should also participate in seminars:

1. Have you participated in any seminars on document examination?
2. What topics have you presented?
3. For what organization were you a presenter?
4. How long did your presentations last?
5. Who sponsored your presentation?
6. Have you been the featured speaker at any of the seminars in which you presented?
7. How many attendees were there at these seminars?
8. Did you distribute handouts?
9. Do you have copies of any of those handouts?
10. Were you compensated for your time?

Research and Scientific Papers

Document examiners should conduct research and present scientific papers:

1. Have you conducted any research in the field of questioned documents?
2. Where has your research been published?
3. Are you planning to publish any research papers in the future?
4. Have you presented any scientific papers?
5. For whom did you present your papers?
6. Were any of your papers published?
7. (If no papers or presentations) Isn't it customary for an expert to publish papers in his field of expertise?

Training Apprentices

Some document examiners train others in the field of questioned documents:

1. Have you trained any apprentices?
2. How many and who are they?
3. How long did the apprentices study with you?
4. How many hours of training have you provided?

Laboratory Equipment

An investigation of the document examiner's laboratory and equipment can be helpful:

1. What equipment do you have in your laboratory?
2. Do you have an approved laboratory?
3. What type of microscope do you have?
4. What magnification capabilities do you have through your microscope?
5. What power of magnification is most useful to a document examiner?
6. What is a stereoscopic microscope?
7. What is the advantage of the stereoscopic microscope?
8. What is a comparator microscope?
9. How is the comparator microscope used?
10. Do you use reticles?
11. What kind of magnifiers do you use?
12. What type of measuring devices do you have in your laboratory?
13. Do you use the measuring devices?
14. What do you measure?
15. What kind of gauges do you use?
16. What type of grids do you use?
17. Do you have any typewriter grids in your laboratory?
18. Do you use grids on handwriting?
19. If so, how do you use grids on handwriting?
20. Do you use infrared or ultraviolet lighting in your work?
21. Do you know what an ESDA is?
22. What do you use the Electrostatic Detection Apparatus for?
23. Is that the only way to reveal indented writing?
24. What is TLC?
25. Do you use thin layer chromatography in your work?

26. When does a document examiner need to use thin layer chromatography?
27. What is a Video Spectral Comparator (VSC)?
28. What is a Video Spectral Comparator used for?
29. Do you use a Video Spectral Comparator?
30. Do you have access to one?
31. Do you use calipers?
32. How do you use them?
33. Do you use protractors? When do you use them?
34. Why would you use a micrometer?
35. Do you use a micrometer?
36. Do you know how to use them?
37. If the deponent works for a government agency and operates a private business on the side, ask him if he maintains a separate laboratory.

If the document examiner says she doesn't measure, refer her to Albert Osborn's *Questioned Documents*' section on measurements and if the document examiner says she eyeballs the documents, refer her to Wilson Harrison's *Suspect Documents* who says in his introduction that eyeballing a document is not scientific.

1. Albert Osborn recommends measuring, why don't you measure?
2. Do you eyeball the documents?
3. Do you use a light box?
4. How do you use a light box?
5. Do you use photography equipment?
6. What type of camera do you have?
7. What type of film do you use?
8. How frequently do you photograph documents in your work?
9. Do you develop your own film?

Experience

One of the most important qualifications of a document examiner is her experience in looking at handwriting. The more handwriting that a document examiner observes, the better a document examiner is able to identify the frequency of occurrence of individual characteristics. These questions relate to a document examiner's experience.

1. How long have you been a forensic document examiner?
2. How long have you been examining handwriting?
3. How many handwriting samples have your examined since you have been a forensic document examiner?
4. How many questioned document cases have you handled?
5. How many cases have you handled involving handwriting matters?
6. If the document examiner doesn't know, ask if he keeps accurate records of his cases?

Cases

1. How many cases do you average in a year?
2. How many cases have you handled so far this year?
3. What percentage of those are handwriting cases?
4. How many cases have you gotten in the past month?
5. What are some of the types of cases that you have handled?
6. What are some of the types of cases that you are working on at present?
7. How many cases are you working on at present?
8. In what percentage of those cases are you able to make a positive identification?
9. What percentage of the cases result in an opinion of inconclusive?
10. In what percentage of cases do you find against your client?

Case History

1. Do you know what outcome your clients are looking for when you are hired to work on a case?
2. Do you ask your clients for their position on a case before you conduct your examination?
3. What information do you think is important to obtain from your clients in order to come to a conclusion on a case?
4. What background information do you get from your clients when contacted for a case?
5. Do you inquire about the writer's health or age?
6. Do you ask about any extenuating physical factors such as body position?

Testimony and Court Qualifications

It is helpful to find out how frequently the document examiner testifies and in what courts he has been qualified.

1. In what percentage of your questioned document cases do you testify?
2. In what courts have you had occasion to testify?
3. How many times have you testified?
4. How many times have you given testimony in a deposition?

If the expert doesn't know how many times she has testified in court or deposition, ask:

5. Do you testify in federal court?
6. Do you not have to maintain an accurate record of the number of times that you have testified in court and deposition for the last four years for federal cases?
7. How many times have you testified in the past year?
8. If you do not know, give me an estimate of the number of times that you have testified?
9. How many times have you testified in court and deposition in the past year?
10. How many times have you testified in court and deposition in the past month?
11. When was the last time that you testified?
12. Where did you testify?

13. What other courts have you had occasion to testify in?
14. How many times are you opposed by another document examiner?
15. Do you work on civil or criminal cases or both?
16. What percentage of your cases are civil?
17. What percentage are criminal?
18. How frequently do you testify for the plaintiff?
19. How frequently do you testify for the defense?
20. Have you ever had opposing counsel stipulate to your qualifications?
21. Have you ever failed to qualify as an expert in any court?
22. If you have failed to qualify, why did you fail?
23. How frequently are you opposed by another document examiner in court?
24. Are some document examiners more skilled than others?
25. Do document examiners ever disagree?
26. Why do document examiners disagree?
27. Have you ever had opposing counsel stipulate to your findings?
28. Have you ever been proven to be wrong in your opinion?
29. How frequently does the outcome of the case reflect your opinion?
30. In what percentage of cases does your client prevail?
31. Could you be mistaken in this case?

Fees for Service

You may want to ask the deponent about his fees for services.

1. What is your normal fee?
2. Do you require a retainer? If so, how much is that?
3. Have you collected your retainer fee in this case?
4. Do you charge an hourly rate?
5. If so, how much do you charge per hour?
6. How much have you been paid in this case?
7. How many hours have you worked on this case so far?
8. Is that your standard rate or did you make a special agreement with your client or your client's attorney?
9. Is your rate for deposition higher than your rate for services to your client?
10. Do you charge a different rate for court appearances?

Level of Knowledge

There are many questions that can be asked of the expert to determine his level of knowledge in the field of document examination. Appropriate responses are listed in italics.

The Writing Act

1. What conditions must come together in order for an individual to be able to write fluidly?
   - *When the sound of the letter evokes its graphic image.*
   - *When we are comfortable with the language.*

- *When we do not have to pay attention to the act of writing because it is automatic.*

2. What is graphic maturity in a writer?
   The level reached in handwriting when all movement is made from habituated neuromuscular patterns.
3. When does a writer reach graphic maturity?
   When the writer writes with perfect ease, usually around puberty, according to Saudek although in many writers, graphic maturity occurs when the person reaches adulthood.
4. Don't you agree that a person must reach graphic maturity in order to write fluidly?
5. What is the earliest age of a writer whose handwriting you can identify?
   When sufficient individual characteristics are present in the writing which can be any time after a writer begins to write.

Principles

1. Is handwriting identification an exact science?
   It is based on scientific principles.
2. What is the criteria for determining that two writings are written by the same person?
   Writing can be identified as belonging to a writer when there are sufficient similar individual characteristics of writing when compared with known writing and no unexplainable significant differences according to the FBI who quoted Osborn.
3. What are the basic principles of Document Examination?
   - *No two people write exactly alike.*
   - *There is natural variation in everyone's handwriting.*

Exemplars

1. What is an exemplar?
   A known handwriting sample.
2. How many exemplars do you need to make an identification of a signature?
   Usually ten to twenty-five signatures, sometimes more, sometimes less.
3. What would be the minimum number of exemplars that you would need to make an identification?
   None if you match the handwriting to another writer or have more than one copy traced from a model. In some cases, one signature would be sufficient in a simple forgery.
4. How many exemplars do you need to eliminate a writer?
   You need samples of all of the different ways a writer can write.
5. How many samples of writing do you need when you are comparing handwriting?
   Document examiners usually need about four to five pages of handwriting.
6. Are some exemplars better than others?
   Yes. Exemplars dated close to the questioned document and similar in style are best.
7. How many types of exemplars are there?
   There are two types, formal and informal.
8. What are the various types of exemplars?
   Informal or normal course of business documents and formal, also known as request writing exemplars.
9. What are the advantages of using informal exemplars?

They are contemporary with questioned writing and there is less conscious-awareness of the writing act by the writer who penned the exemplars.

10. What are the disadvantages of using informal exemplars?
One may not be able to find similar handwriting for comparison.
11. What is another name for formal exemplars?
Request writing standards.
12. What are the advantages of using formal exemplars?
It is possible to duplicate the writing scenario of the questioned material.
13. What are the disadvantages to request writing samples?
They may not be close enough in time to the questioned documents or the writer may disguise his handwriting.
14. What type of exemplars are most suitable?
Exemplars written in the normal course of business near the date of the questioned material and written under similar circumstances.

Penmanship

1. What styles of penmanship are currently being taught in the school systems of the United States?
The most popular are Palmer, Zaner-Bloser, and D'Nealian.
2. How many styles of penmanship are you familiar with?
Over fifty styles have been taught in the twentieth century in the United States.
3. What styles of penmanship have you studied?
4. What are the primary differences between Palmer and Zaner-Bloser Penmanship Systems?
The Palmer "d" has a looped stem and additional forms for "r" and "t."
5. What is the distinguishing feature of the D'Nealian system?
The ease of transition from printing to cursive.
6. When do children learn to write?
Usually at the end of second grade or the beginning of the third grade.

Characteristics of Writing

1. How do you distinguish a genuine signature from a spurious signature?
By the characteristicsof writing.
2. How do you determine the authenticity of a signature?
With sufficient similarities and no fundamental unexplainable differences in handwriting characteristics.
3. How many points of similarity must you have to make an identification of genuineness?
The process is always a twofold process. First there must be sufficient similarities with no fundamental unexplainable differences. There is not an exact number of similarities needed.
4. What do you mean by sufficient similarities?
There must be enough individual characteristics of writing present in the writing that the chance of two different writers using the same characteristics is beyond reasonable probability.
5. How many kinds of characteristics are there?
Two kinds: class characteristics and individual characteristics.
6. What are class characteristics in handwriting?

Class characteristics are those shared by a large number of people. They include the rules of penmanship systems that were taught to children when they learned to write. They also include characteristics that many people adopt such as substituting printed capital letters for cursive forms.

7. What are individual characteristics of writing?
Individual characteristicsare those features that deviate from the rules of penmanship and from forms commonly used. They are unusual habitual movements developed by a writer. An example would be hooks and ticks in the writing.
8. What are hooks and ticks?
Hooks are spontaneous small curves usually found at the beginning or ending of letters. Ticks are abrupt changes in direction that form an angle to the writing line.
9. What characteristics of handwriting do you compare?
   - *Line quality or line value*
   - *Size and proportions*
   - *Alignment including baseline*
   - *Initial and terminal strokes*
   - *Connecting strokes*
   - *Speed of the writing*
   - *Method of construction*
   - *Finger, hand or arm movement*
   - *Embellishments*
   - *Pressure patterns*
   - *Rhythm*
   - *Slant*
   - *Spacing*
   - *Letter forms*
   - *Skill level*
   - *Legibility*
   - *Penscope*
10. What is line quality?
Line quality refers to the smoothness of the line. Since writing is normally executed rapidly, good line quality is smooth and even, without tremor or corrugation. Poor line quality is the result of slow writing which may indicate forgery. When creating a forgery, the forger draws the signature. The art of drawing is slow and laborious resulting in tremulous strokes of writing.
11. How important is line quality?
In many cases it is the most important criteria of identification.
12. What is pressure in handwriting?
There are two kinds of pressure. One is grip pressure and refers to how tightly the writer holds the writing instrument. The other pressure is the amount of force applied to the writing instrument when pushing it across the paper during the act of writing.
13. What are pressure patterns?
Variations in the pressure between upstrokes and downstrokes of writing.
14. How important are pressure patterns?
They are highly significant when they are obvious in handwriting.
15. What is rhythm in handwriting?
It is the even return to the baseline.
16. What types of connecting strokes are there?
Garlands, angles, arcades, and thready strokes or no connecting strokes.
17. What type of connecting strokes did the writer use in this case?
18. What are embellishments in handwriting?
Embellishments are ornamentation not necessary to the design of letters. They consist of flourishes, ticks, hooks, or rubrics.
19. How do you determine spuriousness?
You must have significant differences when compared with known writing.
20. What constitutes a significant difference?

A basic fundamental difference in any of the handwriting characteristics between the questioned and the known writing.

21. Does a different pressure pattern indicate a significant difference? *Yes.*
22. Do different letter forms constitute a significant difference?
Not always. They may represent an attempt of the writer to disguise his writing.
23. Does a different level of skill indicate a different writer?
Usually. A person cannot write better than he can write.
24. How do you determine the speed of the writing?
By the indications of fast or slow writing. (See next two questions).
25. What are some of the indications of fast writing?
Speed is indicated by good line quality, smooth strokes, illegibility, slurred endings to words, and a rightward slant.
26. What are some of the indications of slow writing?
Carefully constructed letters, wavering strokes, frequent pauses in writing and readjustment of the writing instrument, and narrow letters with retracing.
27. What is penscope?
Penscope is the distance covered by the pen before the writer readjusts his hold.

Factors That Affect Handwriting

1. What are some of the human factors that affect handwriting?
Substance abuse, illness, trauma, emotions, medication.
2. What effect does substance abuse have on handwriting?
It causes writing to expand and become slurred.
3. What effect does medication have on handwriting?
There are variable effects.
4. What effect does the writing position have on a writer?
It alters the appearance of the writing.
5. What is an accidental?
A rare variation that occurs infrequently in handwriting.
6. How frequently do you find accidentals in handwriting?
Rarely.
7. How frequently do they occur, according to Ordway Hilton?
According to Hilton (p. 174) "Once in 100 to 200 specimens."
8. Is it possible to gauge someone's age group through their handwriting, such as children, adolescents, adults, elderly? *Yes.*
9. What are some of the mechanical features that affect handwriting?
They are the writing instrument, the paper and the writing surface as well as lighting, temperature, and position of the writer whether standing, sitting, or lying down.

Disguised Handwriting

1. What are the different ways that people disguise their handwriting?
Change of slant, change of size, or speed, opposite hand writing, block print, introduction of unusual letter forms into the writing.
2. Can people successfully disguise their handwriting?
Not in an extended handwriting sample.
3. Why can't people successfully disguise their handwriting in an extended sample?
It takes too much concentration to maintain a disguise and attention will wane.

4. How can disguise be recognized?
   By its lack of consistency.

Forgeries

1. How many kinds of forgeries are there?
   There are two kinds of forgery; simple and simulated.
2. What is a simple forgery?
   One in which there has been no attempt to imitate a genuine signature.
3. What is a simulated forgery?
   It is an imitated signature.
4. What are the different methods that a forger uses to create a simulated forgery?
   Freehand simulation or tracing a known signature.
5. How can you identify a forgery?
   A forgery deviates from the original. There are significant differences in the handwriting characteristics.
6. Did you see any signs of forgery in the questioned signature?
7. What are the obvious signs of forgery?
   - *Poor line quality*
   - *Tremor*
   - *Patching*
   - *Pen lifts*
   - *Hesitation*
   - *Ink blobs*
   - *Blunt beginning or ending strokes*
   - *Carbon residue or indented line along writing line.*
8. What other signs of forgery can you describe?
   Other signs of forgery are:
   - *No resemblance to the genuine known signature.*
   - *Undue attention to unimportant details.*
   - *Backward writing.*
   - *One or more signatures identical to another (model) signature.*
   - *Close attention to the rules of penmanship.*
   - *The lack of natural variation.*
9. Is it possible to have a forged document that does not contain any of the obvious signs of forgery?
   Yes, forgers must choose between slowly copying a signature with poor line quality or writing more rapidly and not adhering to the features of the writing.
10. What is the significance of a duplicate signature on a document?
    One or both of the duplicate signatures is not genuine.
11. What are the various ways in which duplicate signatures are created?
    Tracing, cut and paste, scanning it into a computer, a signature stamp, or autopen.
12. Albert Osborn says that a simulated signature is the most difficult to detect. Do you agree?
13. Is there such a thing as a perfect forgery?

Miscellaneous

1. How do you distinguish between natural variation and a different writer?
2. What is paleography?
   The study of ancient handwriting.
3. What is a serif?

Additional lines at the bottoms of letters or at the end of curves on some letters having nothing to do with the basic letter formations.

4. What is a rubric or a paraph?
A flourish under or after a name.

Questions about Other Experts

1. Who was Charles Hamilton?
He was a well-known autograph dealer who wrote numerous books on the subject. He also examined the Hitler Diaries and determined that they were not genuine.
2. Who is Kenneth Rendell?
He is a rare books dealer who examined the Hitler Diaries, the Jack the Ripper Diaries, and the Mormon Papers and determined that they were not genuine.
3. What was Kenneth Rendell's opinion on the Hitler Diaries?
He said they were not genuine.

Types of Office Machines

If your case involves typed or printed documents, it is necessary to question the expert about his knowledge of the various types of office machines.

1. Is it possible to identify the typewriter used to type a document? *Yes.*
2. How is it possible to identify the typewriter used to type a document?
Through the individual characteristics of the typewriter.
3. What are the characteristics that distinguish an individual typewriter?
Letters may be off their feet, they may contain broken serifs or clogged ink.
4. What are the various types of typewriters?
Manual typewriters, electric typewriters, and electronic typewriters.
5. Is there another name for an electronic typewriter?
Yes, it is also called a word processor.
6. Can the printer used to create a document be identified?
The type of printer can be identified but not an individual printer.
7. Why can't the printer used to create a document be identified?
There are no individual characteristics on printers.
8. What are the various types of printers on the market?
Dot matrix, ink jet, and laser printers.
9. What is a font?
A full set of printing type of the same size and face. It consists of letters, numbers, and symbols.
10. What does the term, "san serif" mean?
It means without serifs. Serifs are ornamental strokes at the ends of letters.
11. What is proportional spacing?
It is a system that spaces letters according to their width instead of same spacing for all letters.
12. What does flush right mean?
That the type will be flush with the right margin.
13. What can you tell about a typewriter ribbon?
The type of ribbon whether it is film or fabric.
14. Is it possible to read a typewriter ribbon?

If the ribbon is nonreusable type, the imprint from the letters will remain and can be read.

15. What are trash marks on photocopies?
    Marks left on photocopies by a photocopier from dirt on the glass or a nick on the drum.

SPECIFIC QUESTIONS ABOUT THE CASE

Once general questions have been asked about the expert's knowledge of the various phases of document examination, specific questions about the case being litigated are discussed.

1. What did you do to prepare for deposition today?
2. Did you discuss this case with anyone?
3. Did you discuss this case with your client's attorney?
4. What did you bring with you to the deposition today?
5. What were you asked to bring to the deposition in this case?
6. How long does it take you to make a determination about a questioned signature?
7. How much time did you spend working on this case?
8. How much time do you usually spend working on a case?
9. How much time did you spend preparing for deposition?
10. When were you first contacted in this case?
11. Who made the first contact?
12. Did you know the attorney who contacted you about this case?
13. Have you had any other cases with this attorney or other attorneys in this law firm?
14. What did the client asked you to do when he first contacted you?
15. What did your client tell you about the case when he contacted you?
16. Was the information given to your orally or in writing?
17. Were you advised at that time whether your client believed that the documents were genuine or not?
18. Who hired you?
19. How did you receive the documents in this case?
20. When did you receive the documents in this case?
21. From whom did you receive the documents in this case?
22. Do you have the original documents?
23. Have the documents been under your control at all times since you received them?
24. Did anyone else look at the documents while they were under your control?
25. Do you have a completed chain of custody form?
26. How did you maintain the chain of custody?

Testing Conducted

1. What equipment did you use to examine the questioned documents?
2. Did you use your microscope?
3. What magnification did you use?
4. What measurements did you take?
5. What tests did you conduct?
6. What reference books did you consult?

Exemplars

1. What exemplars did you compare the questioned documents to?
2. How many exemplars did you use for comparison purposes?
3. How did you obtain these exemplars?
4. Did you have enough exemplars?
5. Did you ask for more exemplars?
6. Why didn't you ask for more exemplars?
7. Did you verify the authenticity of the exemplars?
8. How did you verify the authenticity of the exemplars?
9. Did you do a comparison of the exemplars to determine if they were consistent?
10. Are any of the exemplars post litem motam signatures or handwriting?
11. Did you take request writing samples from your client?
12. Did you take request writing samples from anyone else?
13. Did anyone else take request writing samples?
14. Describe the procedure you used for taking request writing?
15. Did the writer make any attempt to disguise his writing?

Same Exemplars

The examiner should have examined the same exemplars as your expert. If he did not, you should pose the following questions.

1. Don't document examiners disagree on some cases because they examined different material?
2. Could you give an opinion about another examiner's opinion without looking at the same documents that the opposing examiner examined?
3. If, for example, a document examiner gave an opinion based upon a first generation photocopy and you compared a second or third generation photocopy, couldn't the differences you find be due to the photocopying process?
4. You didn't examine the same documents that opposing expert examined in this case, did you?
5. You didn't ask to see the documents that the opposing expert examined in this case, did you?

Originals versus Photocopies

If the examiner didn't examine originals, you may want to discuss photocopies versus original documents.

1. Did you examine original documents?
2. Did you ask to examine the original documents?
3. If not, why not?
4. Isn't it important to examine originals?
5. Did you examine photocopies, scanned or faxed documents in this case?
6. You can get more information from originals than copies, can't you?
7. Is a photocopy as useful as an original in determining characteristics of handwriting? *Photocopies have drop-out and loss of line quality.*
8. Aren't there some things you cannot determine from copies?

9. Can you tell line quality from a photocopy?
10. Can you tell pressure patterns from a photocopy?
11. Can you tell which line crosses on top from a photocopy?
12. Can you tell if a signature has been cut and pasted onto a photocopy?
 If you have two or more identical signatures you may be dealing with a cut and paste.
13. Aren't details lost on photocopies?
14. Doesn't the photocopying process distort the documents?
15. Did you find any significant trash marks on the photocopies?
16. Don't faxed copies contain distortions?

Poor Photocopies

If the examiner reviewed poor photocopies and didn't ask for better copies, emphasize this with the following questions.

1. When working on a questioned document, isn't it important to use the earliest generation photocopy when no original is available?
2. Isn't there a problem with drop out on multigenerational photocopies?
3. Isn't there a problem with distortion on multigenerational photocopies?
4. You did not examine the earliest generation photocopy in this case?
5. Wouldn't the best evidence be necessary in order to render a valid opinion?
6. You didn't ask to examine the earliest generation photocopy in this case?

Photographs versus Photocopies

Since photographs show more detail than photocopies, you may want to ask the expert why he didn't use photographs.

1. Do photographs show evidence more clearly than photocopies?
2. Can enlarged photographs reveal details that photocopies drop out?
3. In fact, photocopying techniques do not record the same degree of detail as properly made photographs?
4. Did you photograph the questioned document?
5. Did you photograph the original documents?
6. How many photographs did you take?
7. What specifically did you photograph on the documents?
8. Why did you take those particular photographs?
9. What type of camera did you use?
10. What type of film? Black and white or color?
11. Do you develop your own film?
12. Did you develop these photographs?
13. Did you bring all of the photographs with you today?
14. Did you bring all of the negatives with you today?
15. Did you make any enlargements of the photographs?
16. Do you plan to make enlargements in this case?

Expert's Exhibits

The expert's exhibits should be examined and discussed.

1. Did you prepare exhibits in this case?
2. Did you prepare these exhibits yourself or did you supervise the preparation of these exhibits?
3. How were the exhibits prepared?
4. Are they accurate reproductions of the originals?
5. Would you explain your exhibits?
6. Why did you choose to illustrate the features that are on your exhibits?

Questions about Conclusions

1. What were your conclusions in this case?
2. How did you arrive at your conclusions?
3. Were you able to come to a positive opinion in this case?
4. How strong is your conclusion?
5. In what percentage of cases are you able to make a positive identification of handwriting?
6. Is your opinion qualified in this case?
7. If yes, what are the reasons for you qualifying your answer?
8. Are there any documents that you have not seen that you would like to see in this case?
9. If you had additional material, would you be able to come to a more positive opinion?
10. If you had looked at the original documents, would you be able to come to a more positive opinion?
11. What level of conclusions do your normally give?
12. Have you prepared a written report in this case?
13. Have you ever made a mistake?
14. Could you be mistaken in this case?

Future Work

Any future work the examiner intends to prepare should be covered.

1. Do you plan to do any further work on this case?
2. If you do any additional work, do you plan to provide a written report?
3. When do you intend to prepare an additional report?
4. Do you plan to prepare additional exhibits for trial in this case?
5. If so, when do you intend to prepare them?

PROBLEMS ASSOCIATED WITH DOCUMENTS

Document examiners work on many different types of cases. Some of these different types of problems are addressed in this section.

Altered Documents

1. Has the questioned document been altered in any way?
2. How has the questioned document been altered?
3. How can you determine that the document has been altered?
4. Has anything been obliterated from the document?
5. Can you determine what has been obliterated?
6. How can you reconstruct what has been obliterated from the document?
7. Has material been added to the document?

Additions and Deletions

1. How can you tell that material has been added to the document?
2. What material has been added to the questioned document?
3. Have pages been substituted in a multi-page document?
4. If so, what pages have been substituted?

Sequence of Writing

1. How can you determine the sequence of writing?
2. When two different inks intersect, how can you determine which one is on top?
3. How can you determine the sequence of writing when ink and typewriting intersect?
4. How can you determine the sequence of writing when pencil and ink cross?
5. How can you tell if the writing was placed on a document before or after it was folded?
6. How do you determine what writing is done at one time as opposed to different times?
7. How can you tell when matter has been inserted into an existing document?
8. How can you determine that a set of notes has been rewritten?
9. Does the paper contain watermarks?
10. What did you determine about the watermarks?
11. Did you examine the ink that was used to complete the document?

Substitutions

Some multi-page questioned documents may contain substituted pages.

1. How can you identify different types of paper if there is no watermark?
2. How can you identify different printed material?
3. How do you distinguish the type of equipment that was used to create the questioned document?
4. Can you determine if a document has had the staples removed and reinserted?
5. How can you distinguish different inks on a document?
6. Was there more than one kind of paper on multipage documents?
7. Are the watermarks the same?
8. Do the watermarks face the same direction?
9. Is all of the paper the same size, thickness, and color?
10. Are there any indications that pages were clipped together with paper clips?
11. Are there any holes where the paper may have been stapled?
12. Are the holes consistent for each page?

Erasures

1. How can you determine if something has been erased or eradicated from a document?
2. How can you determine what has been erased or eradicated?
3. Can you determine what was used to make the erasure?
4. What did you discover in your examination of erasures in this case?
5. What was erased or removed from the questioned document?

Indented Writing

1. What is indented writing?
2. How does indented writing get on a document?
3. How can you determine what the indented writing says?
4. How can you restore indented writing?
5. Did you perform the necessary tests to determine what the indented writing says?
6. What does the indented writing say?

Read Under Whiteout or Blacked Out Material

Sometimes it is necessary for the document examiner to read under whiteout or material that has been blacked out with a felt tip pen.

1. How can you determine what is written under whiteout?
2. What method is used to read under material that has been blacked out?
3. What does the document read without the whiteout (or blackout)?

Signs of Forgery

1. Did you find any significant differences between the questioned and known writing?
2. Did you find any signs of forgery on the questioned documents?
   - Did you find any tremor on the handwriting?
   - Did you find any pen lifts on the writing line?
   - Were there any blobs of ink on the writing line?
   - Was there any patching along the writing line?
   - Was the signature written backward?
   - Was there any undue attention to unimportant details on the questioned documents?
   - Did the questioned writing contain blunt beginning strokes or ending strokes?
3. Did the writing look drawn instead of being written fluidly?
4. Was the signature executed slowly?
5. Do the questioned signatures lack natural variation?
6. Has the questioned signature been copied from a model signature?
7. Could the signature be a cut and paste?
8. Could the signature be a scanned signature?

Identical Signatures

When you encounter identical signatures on different documents, one or all of the signatures are not authentic since no one can exactly duplicate his signature. The expert should be questioned about the fact that the signatures are identical.

1. Is the signature an exact duplicate of another signature?
2. What do the experts say about two signatures that are exactly alike?
   There is natural variation in everyone's handwriting. No one can duplicate exactly anything he has written. When one encounters two identical signatures, at least one of those signatures is not genuine.
3. Isn't it true that no one signs his name exactly the same way twice?
4. How do you account for the fact that each of the questioned signatures can be superimposed and all of the letters are in the same location?
5. How are identical signatures affixed to different documents?
   - *A genuine signature can be cut and pasted from one document to another and photocopied.*
   - *Signatures can also be scanned into a computer and placed on another document via a printer.*
   - *Signatures can be duplicated by a autopen.*
   - *Signatures can be traced from one document to the next.*
6. Do you agree with Albert Osborn's statement on page 342 of *Questioned Documents* that, "A tracing may also differ slightly from the model?"
7. Why does a tracing differ slightly from the model?
   Because of slippage or the forger will deliberately move the paper slightly so that he doesn't create an exact duplicate.
8. Did you find any indications of tracing when you examined the original?
   - Was there any carbon residue along the writing line as a result of tracing?
   - Were there indentations along the writing line indicating tracing?

Self-disguise

Sometimes writers disguise their own signatures so that they can deny them later.

1. Are there any signs of disguise?
2. Could the writer have disguised his signature so that he could deny it later?
3. How can you determine that a signature is disguised?
4. How can you identify disguise in handwriting?
5. How do you distinguish between disguise and a different writer?
6. How can you differentiate between disguise and forgery?
7. What are some of the methods of disguise that are frequently employed?
8. Can a person successfully disguise his handwriting?
9. What elements of disguise did you find in the handwriting?

Genuineness of Signatures

It may be necessary or more effective to ask the witness specific detailed questions about the case. The following questions are suitable for court or deposition concerning the genuineness of signatures.

1. Are the signatures genuine?
2. Are there any problems with the signatures?
3. Are the signatures correct according to the date on the document?
4. What style of penmanship does the writer use?
5. Are the signatures of the witnesses genuine?
6. Are the signatures properly notarized?

Handwriting

1. Is all of the handwriting written by the same person?
2. If not, how many writers wrote on each page?
3. What section of handwriting is attributed to each writer?
4. Was the writing placed upon the document sequentially?
5. When was the writing placed upon the document?
6. Was the writing placed upon the document all at the same time?
7. Was the writing placed upon the document at different times?
8. Is the body of the document written in the same hand as the signature?
9. Was the signature written last?
10. Could anything have been added to the document after it was signed?

Writing Materials

The next series of questions covers the materials used to create documents.

Paper

1. What kind of paper was used?
2. Is there a watermark on the paper?
3. Are there lines on the paper?
4. Are there any marks on the paper?
5. Was the paper torn or damaged?
   - Can you match the tears?
   - Did it come from a pad?
   - Is the paper soiled?
   - Is the paper crumbled?
   - Is the paper faded?
   - Has the paper been cut by hand?
6. Are there any discolorations or stains on the paper?
7. What caused the stains?
8. Did ink from another page bleed through?
9. Is there any indented writing on the paper?
10. If so, can the indented writing be deciphered?
11. Can the indented writing be photographed with side lighting or raised on an ESDA machine?

12. Are there any signs of erasure through abrasion or the application of chemicals?
13. Are the margins on the paper all the same?
14. Are they the standard one inch on each side of a typed document?

Writing Instruments

1. What kind of writing instrument was used on the document?
2. Was the same writing instrument used for the handwriting and signature?
3. Was the same writing instrument used for all of the signatures?
4. Was that writing instrument in existence on the date the document was executed?
5. Was that the type of writing instrument the writer would have used?

Ink Pens

1. Was the same pen used throughout the writing and the signature?
2. Was there more than one type of ink used on the document?
3. What type of pen was used? Ballpoint pen? Roller ball pen? Fountain pen? Fiber tip/felt pen?
4. What type of ink was used?
5. Was there more than one type of ink used on the document?

Pencil Writing

1. Did the writer use pencil to execute the document?
2. What type of pencil was used? Graphite pencil? Mechanical pencil? Colored pencils?

Envelopes

1. Is there a postmark on the envelope?
2. What is the postmark on the envelope?
3. Is the cancellation consistent with the date on the enclosed document?
4. Is the proper amount of postage on the envelope?
5. How was the envelope opened?
6. Was the envelope resealed?
7. Was the envelope properly addressed?
8. Was the envelope written in the same hand as the enclosed letter?
9. Does the letter fit into the envelope?

Stamps

1. Was the document stamped with any kind of rubber stamp?
2. Did the stamp contain any flaws?
3. Is the stamp the appropriate stamp for that document?

Fasteners

1. Was the document fastened together in any way?
2. Was it stapled?
3. Were there holes where staples had been inserted and removed from the document?
4. Were the holes consistent on each page?

Typewritten Documents

1. What kind of typewriter was used? Manual typewriter? Electric typewriter? Electronic typewriter?
2. Do you know what make and model the typewriter was?
3. Was the typewriter available when the document was prepared?
4. What type element did the typewriter use? Typebar? Typeball? Daisy wheel?
5. What type of spacing is there between each letter? Pica type, that is 10 characters per inch? Elite type, that is 12 characters per inch? Proportional? Other type of spacing?
6. Was each sheet written continuously without the paper being removed and replaced in the typewriter?
7. If removed and replaced, how many times and what was written each time?
8. Is the date of the document consistent with the age of the typewriter?
9. Is the style consistent?
   - Are the paragraphs indented?
   - Was proper punctuation used?
   - Are there corrections and how were they made?
   - Were the corrections made with a liquid whiteout?
   - Was a correction ribbon used?
   - Did the typewriter use lift-off tape to correct mistakes?
   - Was a typewriter eraser used?
   - Did the typist overwrite another letter?
10. Is the spacing uniform?
11. Was the document typed by an experienced typist?
12. Is there a carbon copy and is it identical?

Computers and Printers

1. Was the document prepared on a computer and printed on a printer?
2. What type of printer was used? Daisy wheel printer? Dot matrix printer? Ink jet printer? Laser printer?
3. Does the printer print in color or black and white?
4. What type font was used to complete the document?

Ribbons

1. What kind of ribbon was used on the typewriter? Cloth ribbon? Mylar film ribbon?
2. Can the ribbon be read?
3. What can be determined from the ribbon?

Last Will and Testament

1. Is each page of the will signed or initialed by the testator and the witnesses?
2. Does each page form a continuous pattern?
3. Could a page have been substituted?
   - Are the sheets of paper the same type of paper?
   - Is the watermark consistent throughout all the pages?
   - Is the type font the same throughout the document?
   - Is the text continuous throughout the document?

4. Are the signatures of the witnesses genuine?
5. Is the will properly notarized?
6. What is the date on the will?
   - Are the paper and ink proper for the date?
   - Were the watermarks available on the date of the signing of the will?
   - Were the writing instruments on the market on that date?
7. Are there any corrections or changes on the will?
   - Are there any erasures and substitutions?
   - Are there any staple marks or other holes indicating that the document was taken apart and put back together?
8. Are the folds in the paper consistent among all of the pages?

Contracts

Ask the same questions as for wills including the following:

1. Are all the signatures on the contract genuine?
   - Are the signatures consistent?
   - Are the signatures witnessed?
   - Are the signatures properly notarized?
2. Is the contract properly dated?
   - Are the ink and paper consistent with the date?
   - Are the signatures consistent with the date?
3. Are all copies of the contract exactly the same?

Dating a Document

1. Is the document dated correctly?
2. Is the paper consistent with the date on the document?
   - Was the paper manufactured when the document is dated?
   - Does the paper contain a watermark?
   - Was the watermark in use at that time?
3. Was the writing instrument available at the time the document was created?
4. Was the proper machine used to create the printed material in existence?
   - Was the document written on a typewriter?
   - Was a computer used to create the document?
   - Was the document printed on a printer attached to a computer?
5. If the document is a preprinted form, is there a date of origin on the form?
6. Does the document show normal wear and tear consistent with its age?
7. Has the document been artificially aged?
   - Has the document been aged chemically? If so, with what chemicals?
   - Has the document been heated in an attempt to age it?
   - Was the document heated with an iron or in an oven?

OPPOSING EXAMINER

1. Are you familiar with the opposing expert?

2. Have you opposed the opposing expert in any other cases?
3. How frequently have you opposed the opposing expert?
4. How frequently are you opposed in other questioned document cases?
5. Have you read the opposing expert's report in this case?
6. What is your opinion regarding the opposing expert's report?

ORGANIZATIONS

If a witness testifies that an organization such as NADE or WADE is a graphology organization:

1. Are you a member of NADE?
2. Have you ever been a member of NADE?
3. Have you ever applied for membership in NADE?
4. Have you attended any NADE Conferences?
5. Have you read the NADE by-laws?
6. Have you read any publications by NADE?
7. Where did you get your knowledge of the type of organization that NADE is?
8. What is graphology?
   Graph = to write, ology = to study — the study of writing. Common usage generally refers to the study of handwriting to identify the personality of the writer.

After you have thoroughly covered all of the opinions of the expert, the following question should be used to sum up the information that you have obtained.

1. Have you given me all of your opinions in this case?

SUMMARY

Attorneys question expert witnesses in deposition to learn as much as possible about the witness and the witness' opinion. The questions in this chapter and the next two chapters are designed to cover as many possible scenarios as possible.

16

Presenting a Document Case

QUALIFYING AN EXPERT IN COURT

An expert is a person qualified by experience, special training, or board certification who is capable of forming accurate opinions of his own that represent a division of science, branch of art, or department of trade in matters not generally known without specializededucation. The expert witness is allowed to testify in a trial in order to assist the trier-of-fact on matters related to the witness' expertise.

A list of qualifying questions will help you to elicit information that will enable your witness to be qualified as an expert in his specialized area. Failure to ask the proper questions in this area could be disastrous since an expert cannot testify unless the court accepts her qualifications.

Each document examiner's background will vary according to training and special study. Information relating to his education, training, extent of experience, accomplishments, and membership in professional societies are all important areas that need to be emphasized when qualifying an expert for court.

Suggested questions and possible answers are discussed to enable you to tailor your questions to emphasize your expert's strengths.

PROFESSIONAL EXPERIENCE

The first set of questions pertains directly to the expert's professional experience in his field. How long has the expert worked in the field of document examination and how much work does the expert do on a regular basis?

1. What is your profession?
2. Is this your full-time profession?
3. What does a forensic document examiner do?
4. How did you become a forensic document examiner?

5. Where is your office located?
6. How long have you been working as a forensic document examiner?
7. Approximately how many questioned document cases have your handled?

Level of Achievement

The next set of questions refers to the level of achievement the expert has reached. It should only be used if your client is certified.

1. Are you a Certified Document Examiner?
2. By whom are you certified?
3. How did you become certified?
4. What is involved in the certification process?

Specialized Training in the Field of Document Examination

1. Do you have a college degree?
2. What type of degree is it? (The actual degree should only be mentioned if it pertains to the field of document examination.)
3. Have you taken any courses on Document Examination? If so, where?
4. Have you taken any college courses related to document examination?
5. Did you serve an apprenticeship? If so, how long did your apprenticeship last?
6. How do you keep current with new developments in the field of questioned documents?
7. What seminars have you attended in connection with your area of expertise?

Authors and Books in Field of Questioned Documents

1. Are you familiar with the works of other document examiners?
2. What books have you read on the subject of document examination?
3. What trade journals do you read?
4. How frequently do you read them?

Proficiency Testing

If the expert participates in proficiency testing you may want to emphasize it.

1. Are you familiar with proficiency testing?
2. What is proficiency testing?
3. Do you participate in proficiency testing?
4. What is your accuracy rate?

Professional Organizations for Document Examiners

1. What professional organizations of document examiners are you affiliated with?
2. How long have you been a member?
3. Have you held any offices in these organizations?
4. Have you received any awards or honors from a document examiners' association?

Publications and Lectures

A document examiner should have published books or articles and lectured or presented papers on topics related to the field of document examination.

1. What books have you written in the field of questioned documents?
2. What articles have you written in the field of questioned documents and where have they been published?
3. What seminars have you conducted in the field of questioned documents for your colleagues?
4. When did you last participate in a seminar?
5. What did your participating involve?
6. What papers have you presented related to your field of expertise?
7. What research have you conducted?

Laboratory Equipment

A document examiner should maintain a laboratory equipped with equipment that measures and magnifies.

1. Do you maintain a laboratory?
2. What equipment do you have in your laboratory?
3. What type of microscope do you use?
4. What type of magnification does your microscope have?
5. What type of measuring devices do you use?
6. What equipment did you use in this case?

Types of Cases

Types of cases handled by the document examiner should be discussed, as well as court appearances. A document examiner should be an impartial witness who testifies for both the plaintiff and the defendant.

1. How long have you been studying handwriting?
2. How long have you been a forensic document examiner?
3. How many cases have you handled?
4. How many active cases are you working on at present?
5. What are the various types of cases that you handle?
6. How many times have you testified in court?
7. In what courts have you been qualified as an expert?
8. Have you ever not qualified as an expert?
9. How often do you testify for the plaintiff? For the defendant?
10. How often do you find against your client?

Minimizing Obstacles

Sometimes it is wise to ask a question in direct to avoid it in cross. If your witness has any weaknesses that the opposing party plans to exploit in cross-examination, they can often be minimized by bringing them up in direct testimony. You may want to ask the expert the following questions:

1. How much are you being paid?
2. Why do document examiners disagree?

Graphology

If your expert has been trained in graphology or graphoanalysis, you should ask the following questions in direct examination to inform the court that your expert has only used the principles of handwriting identification to make a determination in this case.

1. Are you a graphologist?
2. Have you studied graphology?
3. What is graphology?
4. Do you use graphology in document examination?
5. Are you certified as a graphologist?
6. Did you use graphology in this case?

Curriculum Vitae

Some attorneys like to present their expert's curriculum vitae to the court and will do so at this time. Usually the attorney will ask his expert if this is the most recent version of his curriculum vitae.

DOCUMENT EXAMINATION

Once an expert has been qualified, you are ready to ask questions about document examination.

1. Do document examiners use a particular theory to evaluate handwriting specimens?
2. Has that theory been tested?
3. What is the result of the testing?
4. Has that theory been subjected to peer review in publications?
5. Is that theory generally accepted by a majority of experts in the field of forensic document examination?
6. What are the basic principles of handwriting identification?
7. Why don't people write alike?
8. What is a questioned document?
9. What is an exemplar?
10. How does a document examiner make a determination about the authenticity of a signature?

11. What handwriting characteristics do you compare?

THE CASE AT HAND

Specific questions about the case at hand should be addressed.

1. Who hired you?
2. What were you asked to do in this case?
3. Did you prepare a written report?
4. What documents did you examine and compare?
5. What equipment did you use?
6. Did you verify that the known handwriting samples are internally consistent?

The expert's exhibits should be introduced before the expert goes into his explanation of the case so that the trier-of-fact can look at the evidence as it is being described.

1. Did you prepare exhibits for the court?
2. How did you prepare the exhibits?
3. Are they accurate reproductions of the originals?
4. Would you explain your exhibits to the court?
5. Did you come to an opinion to a reasonable degree of scientific certainty in this case?
6. What is your opinion?
7. Would you please tell the court how you arrived at your opinion?
8. How positive are you of your opinion?
9. What degree of certainty do you have?
10. If the answer is probable, ask what would be needed to give a definite opinion? The answer is generally, *more comparable material.*

JURIES

Jury surveys indicate that jurors place more trust in a witness who testifies in the narrative. Experience shows that it is easier for a witness to testify in the narrative than to answer questions, especially if the questions are not in order. It may be necessary to assist your expert with more detailed questions about the case or the expert may forget a point that should be covered. Since this information was discussed in the pretrial conference, the attorney is prepared to ask about any area that the expert failed to cover.

SUMMARY

An expert is a person qualified by experience, special training or board certification who is capable of forming accurate opinions representing a division of science, branch of art or department of trade in matters requiring specialized knowledge.

Qualifying questions are asked of the expert to introduce the expert's credentials to the court. Once the expert is qualified by the court, the expert will be allowed to express an opinion regarding a matter before the court.

Additional questions can be found in Chapters 15 and 17.

17

Cross-Examination

CROSS-EXAMINATION OF OPPOSING EXPERT

A competent witness will use cross-examination to strengthen her case. The expert will reinforce his direct testimony and may be able to introduce additional points that were not covered in direct. However, a vulnerable witness can be successfully cross-examined.

A detailed list of questions can be found in the Chapter 15 on deposition testimony. There are additional questions in this chapter that are not listed elsewhere.

The first set of questions pertains directly to the expert's professional experience in her field. How long has the expert worked in the field of document examination and how much work does the expert do on a regular basis?

Professional Experience

1. What is your full-time profession?
2. Why do you consider yourself to be an expert?
3. What qualifies you to be a document examiner?
4. How long have you been working as a professional handwriting expert?
5. How many hours per week do you spending working as a handwriting expert?
6. How much of your income comes from your work as a document examiner?
7. Approximately how many questioned document cases have you handled?
8. What type of work do you do as a document examiner?
9. Have you done any work for the state or federal government?

Level of Achievement

The next set of questions refers to the level of achievement the expert has reached.

1. Are you a certified document examiner?
2. By whom are you certified?
3. How did you become certified?
4. Is certification the highest level of achievement in your field?
5. What is involved in the certification process?

If not certified:

1. Since there is no license for document examiners, isn't is important to be certified by a professional organization in order to prove that you are qualified as a document examiner?
2. Do you qualify for certification?
3. Have you ever applied for certification?

Training in the field of document examination should also be covered.

1. Do you have a college degree? If yes, in what subject?
2. Does your degree relate to document examination?
3. Have you taken any college courses related to document examination?
4. Have you taken any college courses in forensic science?
5. Have you taken any courses on document examination?
6. How much training have you had as a document examiner in handwriting identification?
7. Did you serve an apprenticeship? If so, for how long?
8. To whom did you apprentice?
9. When did you last attend a seminar?

Books Read

1. Are you familiar with the works of other document examiners?
2. What books do you have in your library pertaining to document examination?
3. What books have you read on the subject?
4. Was the author an authority in the field of questioned documents?
5. Who do you consider to be an authority in the field of questioned documents?
6. How do you keep current with new developments in the field of questioned documents?

Professional Organizations

1. With what professional organizations of document examiners are you affiliated?
2. In what professional scientific organizations are you currently an active dues paying member?
3. When was the last time you attended a seminar of the document examiner's organization?
4. Are you a member of the Certified Fraud Examiners?
5. Have you been refused membership in any document examiners' organizations?
6. If so, what organizations?
7. Have you attended seminars of any other document examiner's organizations?

Books and Articles Published

A document examiner should have published books or articles and/or lectured and presented papers on topics related to the field of document examination.

1. What books have you written in the field of questioned documents?
2. What articles have you written in the field of questioned documents and where have they been published?
3. What seminars have you conducted in the field of questioned documents?
4. When did you last participate in a seminar?
5. What papers have you presented?
6. Don't experts generally publish papers and articles about their field?
7. Have you ever conducted any studies on the characteristics of handwriting?
8. Have you trained any document examiners?

Office and Laboratory

A document examiner should maintain a laboratory equipped with instruments that measure and magnify.

1. Do you maintain an office and a laboratory? or, Do you maintain a private office and a laboratory separate from the police crime laboratory?
2. What equipment do you have in your laboratory?

Types of Cases and Court Appearances

Types of cases handled by the document examiner and court appearances can be discussed.

1. How many cases are you working on at present?
2. How much time have you spent studying handwriting identification as opposed to the other aspects of document examining such as paper and ink analysis?
3. What are the various types of cases that you handle?
4. In what percentage of cases are you able to make a positive identification of handwriting?
5. In what percentage of cases do you testify?
6. When was the last time you testified? Where?
7. In how many court cases was there an expert on the other side?
8. How many times have you testified in deposition?
9. How frequently do you testify for the plaintiff or defendant?
10. Have you ever not been qualified as an expert in court? If not, why not?

Prejudice or Bias

Does the expert have any prejudices or biases that may impact his opinion.

1. What percentage of clients are plaintiffs? Defendants?

2. How often do you find in favor of your client?
3. How often do you find against your client? What percentage?
4. Are some document examiners more skilled than others?
5. Do document examiners ever disagree?
6. Why do document examiners disagree?

Proficiency Testing

Proficiency testing is another means of checking the accuracy of one's work. Some document examiners participate in proficiency testing.

1. Have you ever heard of Collaborative Testing Services?
2. Have you participated in proficiency testing through Collaborative Testing Services?
3. Do you participate in any other proficiency testing?
4. What is your error rate?
5. How do you know that you are correct in your findings?

FINDINGS AND OPINIONS

After covering the expertise and knowledge of the document examiner, the cross-examining attorney will want to discuss what the examiner did in this case and what his findings were in this case. In addition to the questions listed in Chapter 15 on depositions, you may want to ask the following questions.

1. What equipment did you use in examining the documents in this case?
2. Did you use an ESDA machine? Microscope? Measuring Devices? Infrared Lighting? Ultraviolet Illumination?
3. Did you take any measurements?
4. Why didn't you use (ESDA, microscope, measuring devices)?
5. How much time did you spend examining the documents in this case?
6. How many exemplars did you have for comparison purposes?
7. Did you have enough exemplars for comparison?
8. How did you obtain the exemplars that you used?
9. How did you verify the authenticity of the exemplars?
10. Did you take any request writing?

The Habits of the Writer

1. What type of pressure patterns does the writer have?
   a. Does the writer have heavy downstrokes with light upstrokes?
   b. Does the writer use light downstrokes with heavy upstrokes?
   c. Does the writer have erratic pressure patterns?
   d. Is the pressure even throughout the writing?
   e. Does the writer use light pressure, moderate pressure, or heavy pressure?
2. What is the writer's skill level?
   a. Does the writer possess a high skill level evidenced by smooth flowing lines?
   b. Does the writer exhibit low skill level with erratic line quality?

3. What type of penstroke does the writer use?
   a. Does the writer use finger strokes?
   b. Does the writer use hand and wrist movements?
   c. Does the writer make arm strokes?
4. What type of connecting strokes does the writer use?
   a. Does the writer connect his letters with garlands?
   b. Does the writer use arcade connections?
   c. Does the writer join his letters with angular formations?
   d. Are connecting strokes thready and ill-formed?
   e. Does the writer leave some or all of his letters disconnected?
5. What letter forms does the writer use?
   a. Does the writer adhere to copybook style writing?
   b. Does the writer slightly modify his letter forms from copybook style?
   c. Are the letters highly stylized?
   d. Does the writer use flourishes and embellishments with his letters?
   e. Have the letter forms been simplified?
   f. Are the letters deteriorated or ill-formed?
   g. Does the writer use handprinted forms?
6. Does the writing exhibit good rhythm?
   a. Does the writer have good rhythm as evidenced by a regular return to the baseline?
   b. Is there some variation in the return to the baseline?
   c. Does the writing display poor rhythm with an erratic return to the baseline?
7. What is the overall size of the letters?
   a. What size are the loops, both upper and lower extenders?
      (1) Are the loops narrow, moderate, or wide?
      (2) Are the loops retraced?
      (3) Is there a single line instead of loop?
      (4) Are the loops short or long
   b. Are the circle letters narrow, oval, round, or full?
   c. Are the middle zone letters narrow, retraced, average, or wide?
8. What is the relationship of the size of the letters to each other?
   a. How do the zonal proportions relate to the other letters?
   b. How do the middle zone letters relate to the capital and upperzone letters?
   c. How do the capital letters relate to the lowercase letters?
   d. What is the relationship of the height of the letters to their width?
   e. Are any of the letters larger or smaller than they should be?
9. How does the writing relate to the baseline?
   a. Does the writing sit on the baseline?
   b. Does the writing sit above the baseline or below it?
   c. Does the writing vary above, through, or below the baseline?
   d. Is the writing arched on the baseline?
   e. Does the writing slant uphill or downhill?
10. What type of margins does the writer make on the writing page?
    a. Are the margins on left, right, top or bottom, wide or narrow?
    b. Do the margins increase or decrease in size along the left or right margin?
11. Where does the writer place his signature on the line?
    a. Does the writing start at the beginning of the signature line?

b. Is the writing centrally placed?
c. Does the writer start to the left of the beginning of the line?

12. How much space is there between letters, words, and lines of writing?
    a. Is the spacing narrow, average, wide, or erratic?
    b. Does the writing adjust to fit comfortably in the available space?
13. How does the writing slant?
    a. Does the writing slant rightward?
    b. Is the writing vertical?
    c. Does the writer slant his writing to the left?
    d. Is the slant variable?
14. How are the initial and terminal strokes formed?
    a. Are the writer's lead-in strokes straight, curved, short, long, or missing?
    b. Are there hooks or ticks on the lead-in strokes?
    c. Are there eyelets on the lead-in strokes?
    d. Are the terminal strokes long or short, straight or curved, high or low, or absent?
    e. Are there hooks or ticks on the terminal strokes?
15. What type of letter designs does the writer make?
    a. What type of t-bars does the writer make?
        (1) Is the shape of the t-bar straight, curved, or arched?
        (2) How high is the t-bar on the stem of the "t?"
        (3) Is the t-bar on the top of the stem, in the middle or lower?
        (4) Does the t-bar occur at various places on the stem?
        (5) Is the length of t-bar short, average, or long?
        (6) In what direction was the t-bar made?
        (7) Does the t-bar slant down, or up?
        (8) Does the t-bar miss the t-stem completely or partially?
        (9) Does the t-bar occur before or after the stem of the "t?"
        (10) Are there other variations of t-bars such as the Palmer "t" or star-shaped t?
        (11) Is the t-bar connected to the next letter?
        (12) Is the t-stem looped, retraced, a single stroke, or an inverted v-formation?
    b. How is the i-dot placed in relation to the i-stem?
        (1) Is the i-dot immediately over the stem of letter, "i?"
        (2) Does the i-dot appear before the stem of the letter, "i?"
        (3) Is the i-dot made after stem of "i?"
        (4) How high is the i-dot above the stem of the "i?"
        (5) Is the i-dot missing?
        (6) What shape is the i-dot?
            (a) Is the i-dot static or dynamic?
            (b) Is the i-dot dashed up, down, or diagonally?
            (c) Is the i-dot hooked, curved, or circular?
    c. Describe the circle letters.
        (1) Are the circles uncontaminated, clear circles?
        (2) Are there loops inside the circles?
        (3) Where do the circles start and finish: at the top, to the right, or to the left?
        (4) Is the perimeter of the circle incomplete?
        (5) In what direction was the circle made, clockwise or counterclockwise?
    d. Are the letters rounded or pointed on top?
        (1) Are the "h," "n," and "m" rounded on the top or pointed?

(2) Are the looped letters rounded on top or pointed?
(3) How is the letter, "r," constructed?

e. Are the letters flat-topped?
f. Are there any specific letter forms such as a Greek "E" or a figure-eight "s" or "g?"

16. How legible is the writing?
    a. How easily can the writing be read?
    b. Are the letters clearly defined?
    c. Are word endings slurred?
    d. Was the writing done very quickly or very slowly?
17. What was the skill level of the writer?
    a. Was the writer a highly skilled writer?
    b. Did the writer exhibit low skill level?
18. Did you find any grammatical errors?
    a. Was punctuation correctly placed?
    b. Was punctuation used incorrectly?
    c. Was punctuation missing?
    d. Did the writer use contractions improperly?
    e. Were there any spelling errors?
    f. Were easy words misspelled while difficult ones were spelled correctly?
    g. How were sentences structured?
    h. Did the writer use well-structured sentences?
    i. Were all of the sentences short or did they ramble?
    j. Were sentences properly organized into paragraphs?
19. Did the writer have a wide range of writing?
    a. Was the writer a consistent writer?
    b. Was the writing highly stylized?
20. What key characteristics did the writing possess?
    a. What individual characteristics did the writer use?
    b. Were there any stylized formations in the writing?
21. Did the characteristics of the questioned writing match the exemplars?

Disguised Writing

The opposing expert may state that differences in the writing are attributed to disguise.

1. How can you identify disguise in a handwriting?
2. How do you distinguish between disguise and a different writer?
3. What is the foremost indication of disguise?
   Lack of internal consistency of the handwriting.
4. Why is disguise difficult to maintain?
   Our handwriting is an ingrained habit that cannot be easily changed.
5. What are the principal methods used to disguise handwriting?
   Change of slant, block printing, change of size, change of speed, alternate-hand writing.
6. When a person attempts to disguise her handwriting, what characteristics is she most likely to disguise?

According to Hilton (p. 169) the prominent features such as capital letters and slant generally undergo the most marked change, while the smaller less prominent identifying features remain.

7. What method of disguise was used in this case?
8. What characteristics of the writer do you see in this handwriting?
9. Isn't it just as possible that we are dealing with a different writer in this case?

Challenging the Findings of the Witness

You may want to challenge the witness regarding his findings.

1. How many points of agreement do you need to make an identification? or How many points of agreement do you need to exonerate a writer as the author?
2. Isn't it a fact that any two sets of specimens, no matter how similar in appearance, will contain many points of dissimilarity? or Isn't it a fact that any two sets of specimens, no matter how dissimilar in appearance, will contain many points of similarity?
3. Isn't it true that a forger usually uses a model signature? or Isn't it true that someone who simulates another's signature attempts to make the simulation look like the genuine signature?
4. Isn't it true that imitation tends to conform closely to a fixed form and does not display the unconscious abandon that in genuine writing produces natural variation?
5. Isn't it true that a fraudulent signature contains characteristics not found in genuine signatures?
6. How do you account for the tremulous lines in the questioned signature when the known signatures are smoothly written?
   or
   How do you account for the poor line quality in the questioned signature when the known signature exhibits good line quality?
7. How do you explain the difference in (slant, proportions, line quality, writing speed, writing skill, pressure patterns) between the questioned signature and the known signatures?
8. Isn't that a significant difference?
9. If the examiner says it not significant, ask what is.
10. How do you account for the fact that the questioned signatures has ——— while none of the known signatures have ———?
11. How did you reach the conclusion that the signature in question is genuine? or How did you reach the conclusion that the signature in question is not genuine?
12. That's just your opinion, isn't it?
13. Is document examination a science?
14. Is the science of handwriting identification an exact science?
15. Did you examine the handwriting of any other suspects in this case?

Challenging the Expert

If the expert did not do a thorough examination of the documents, she may be challenged on that area.

1. Have you done everything that you should have in this case?
2. Why didn't you take measurements?
3. You didn't do everything that you should have, did you?

The witness may be challenged on her veracity.

1. How much are you being paid for your testimony?
2. Do you always tell the truth?
3. Have you ever been proven to be wrong?
4. Could you be mistaken in this case?

REDIRECT TESTIMONY

It may be necessary to rehabilitate your witness with redirect examination questions. This is important in cases in which the witness was not allowed to offer a complete answer to questions directed to her. Often an attorney will ask the expert witness to compare letter forms since these are the most obvious characteristics of writing. The attorney will point out similarities while trying to prove identity and dissimilarities when trying to prove the handwriting was completed in a different hand. Any misconceptions created by opposing counsel need to be addressed in redirect.

1. When comparing handwriting characteristics, can you rely on letter forms to draw conclusions about handwriting?
   They are not as reliable as other characteristics of writing.
2. Why aren't letter forms as reliable as other characteristics?
   Anyone who copies another person's handwriting is going to make the letter forms similar.
3. Can you rely on any one characteristic of writing to make an identification or elimination?
   No, it is not any one characteristic but the combination of characteristics that make an opinion possible.
4. What are the most important characteristics of handwriting for making an identification or elimination of a writer?
   The subtle characteristics of writing are the most important because they are executed without conscious awareness by the writer.
5. Can you give me an example of subtle differences?
6. How many characteristics of handwriting do you compare?
7. Did you compare similarities and dissimilarities when you made your examination?
8. Did you take the similarities and differences into consideration when you came to your conclusion?
9. How do you account for the similarities?
   There will be some common characteristics in the handwriting of different individuals. A few common characteristics do not make an identification.
   or
   How do you account for the dissimilarities?
   There is natural variation in everyone's handwriting.

10. Since there is natural variation in everyone's handwriting, how do you identify handwriting?
It is a twofold process. First there must be significant similarities between the known and the questioned writing in the subtle characteristics, and second, there can be no significant unexplainable differences.
11. What do you mean by significant differences?
Significant differences are structural differences; basic disparities in handwriting characteristics that are incompatible with the exemplars.
12. What do you mean by unexplainable differences?
Unexplainable conditions would be those for which there is no reason for the change.
13. What would cause differences to occur in a person's handwriting?
Differences can be caused by various factors such as attempted disguise, a sudden change in health, substance abuse, or mechanical factors such as poor lighting or a faulty pen.
14. Did you determine if any of the various factors caused the differences in the handwriting you examined?
15. Did you determine if there was an attempt to disguise in the handwriting you examined?
16. Your opinions are based on the principles of handwriting identification, are they not?
17. How do you account for the fact that the questioned writing contains a different letter form than the known writing?
Writers often use more than one letter design when writing their letters.

You may want to have your expert witness compare other forms among the known writing that show dissimilarities so that you can emphasize that dissimilarities among some letter forms are common in handwriting.

REBUTTAL TESTIMONY

Some expert witnesses are held for rebuttal testimony to counter evidence presented by an opposing expert. After the expert is qualified, the following questions can be asked.

1. Have you examined the documents in this case?
2. What documents have you examined?
3. Are these the same documents examined by the opposing expert?
4. Have you heard the testimony of the opposing expert?
5. Based on the documents that you examined, do you agree with the testimony of the opposing expert?
6. Why don't you agree with the opposing expert?
7. What is the basis for your opinion?

Insufficient Material

If the expert finds that the material examined was insufficient to draw any conclusion, the following questions could be used.

1. How do you determine the authenticity or non-genuineness of questioned handwriting?
   By comparing the characteristics of handwriting.
2. Did you have enough comparable material for comparison with the questioned documents?
3. Why wasn't the material sufficient for drawing conclusions about the questioned handwriting?
   There were not enough distinguishing characteristics to make an identification or an elimination.
4. What would you need in order to draw a conclusion about the questioned material?
5. Why didn't you obtain enough material?
6. Did you take any request writing? If not, why not?

Material of Poor Quality

If the material consisted of poor quality photocopies, any opinion given should be qualified or of a low probability. Questions can be posed to bring out the nature of these documents.

1. Did you examine the material in this case?
2. What documents did you examine?
3. Based on the quality of the documents, were you able to give an opinion?
4. Why couldn't you give an opinion in this case?

SUMMARY

The questions in Chapter 15 on depositions and the questions in this Chapter on Cross-Examination will assist an attorney in cross-examining a forensic document examiner.

18

Court Citations Pertaining to Handwriting

FEDERAL COURT CASES

There are many case citations related to handwriting exemplars and testimony by handwriting experts. The cases discussed here are primarily federal cases that have had an impact on handwriting issues.

Cases relating to expert witnesses have had impact on document examiners. Prior to 1993, expert witnesses came under the Frye Rule, *Frye v. U.S.*, 54 App.D.C. 46, 293 F. 1013. The court opined that while it would go a long way in admitting expert testimony, deduced from a well-recognized scientific principle or discovery, the thing from which the deduction is made must be sufficiently established to have gained general acceptance in the particular field in which it belongs.

Daubert v. Merrell Dow Pharmaceuticals, Inc., Schuller v. Merrell Dow Pharmaceuticals, Inc., 727 FS 570 (S. D. CA 1989); affirmed, 951 F2 1128 (9 Cir 1991); vacated and remanded, 125 L Ed2 469, 113 S Ct 2786 (1993); affirmed 43 F3 1311 (9 Cir 1995); cert. denied, U.S., 116 S Ct 189, 133 L Ed2 126, changed the threshold for expert testimony. Factors affecting admissibility are:

- whether the theory can or has been tested;
- whether the theory has been subjected to peer review in publication;
- the known or potential rate of error;
- the extent of acceptance in the relevant scientific community;
- compliance with the hearsay exception; and
- the balance of probative value versus prejudicial effect.

In order to determine that the expert's declaration meets the requirement of reliability, the court considers factors such as:

- that the expert's testimony grew out of pre-litigation research; or
- that the expert's research has been subjected to scientific scrutiny through peer review and publication in scientific journals; or
- a precise explanation of how the experts reached their conclusions in sufficient detail to allow the district court to determine reliability of the research.

CHALLENGING HANDWRITING EXPERTS

There have been several different types of challenges on document examiners in various courts around the country. Some college professors have testified that document examination is not a valid science and they try to have document examiners disqualified or discredited. Other challenges attack specific document examiners as being unqualified.

Professors D. Michael Risinger, Mark P. Denbeaux, and Michael J. Saks published an article in the *University of Pennsylvania Law Review* entitled, "Exorcism of Ignorance as a Proxy for Rational Knowledge: The Lessons of Handwriting 'Identification Expertise'" in January 1989 (137:73–92). The authors claim that there is no verification that handwriting is distinctive and can be identified. According to the authors, they found no empirical studies when searching for information to validate handwriting identification. These professors have been holding themselves out as experts on experts.

The first challenge occurred in *U.S. v. Roberta and Eileen Starzecpyzel,* No. 93 Cr. 553 (LMM), 880 FS 1027 (S.D. N.Y. 1995). The court granted defendants' request for a *Daubert* hearing. Mary Wenderoth Kelly, a document examiner who also has a law degree, testified for the government in support of document examination as a valid science. She was unable to cite any research projects on handwriting identification. She also failed to identify the principles of handwriting identification.

Professor Michael Saks and Professor George Stelmach testified that they could find no supportive research to verify that anyone can identify handwriting. As a result of this hearing, Judge McKenna ruled that (1) forensic document examination expertise was outside scope of *Daubert* which, Judge McKenna said, addressed only scientific expert testimony; (2) forensic document examiner's testimony is admissible as nonscientific or "skilled" testimony; and (3) possible prejudice deriving from possible perception by jurors that forensic testimony met scientific standards of reliability did not require exclusion of testimony.

The Supreme Court determined in *Kumho Tire Co., Ltd., et al. v. Carmichael et al.*, reversing *Carmichael v. Samyang Tire, Inc.*, 131 F3 1433; 119 S Ct 1167 (1999), that all expert testimony is subject to meeting the Daubert standards or any reasonable set of standards.

Since the *Starzecpyzel* case, document examiners have been challenged by these professors even though they have no studies except their own to support their position. Experts on experts can be cross-examined as follows:

Questions for Experts on Experts

1. What training have you had in the study of document examiners?
2. What qualifies you as an expert on experts?
3. What studies have been conducted and published supporting and validating your expertise in critiquing handwriting experts?
4. Have you published any other articles than "Exorcism of Ignorance as a Proxy for Rational Knowledge: The Lessons of Handwriting Identification Expertise?"
5. Has anyone else published any similar articles?
6. What independent studies have been conducted that support your position?
7. What competency testing did you undergo in your specialty? (Name the subject in which the professor claims expertise.)
8. What studies support your opinion that handwriting cannot be identified?
9. What training have you had in handwriting identification?
10. What experience do you have in handwriting analysis?
11. What research have you conducted regarding the individuality of handwriting?
12. Have you conducted any research with document examiners to determine their ability to identify handwriting?
13. You have had no training or experience in this field and have not conducted any statistical research to support your position that you are an expert on experts, correct?

These professors have admitted that they are not handwriting experts and are not familiar with the principles of handwriting identification.

Professor Mark P. Denbeaux attempted to qualify as a defense expert in *United States of America; Government of the Virgin Islands v. Velasquez*, 64 F2 844, 33 V. Is. 265 (3 Cir 1995). The trial judge did not allow Denbeaux to present his testimony that handwriting analysis is not a valid field of scientific expertise. The case was appealed to the Third District and the court determined that, "The district court erred as a matter of law in refusing to permit Professor Denbeaux to testify as to the limitations of handwriting analysis." This court also determined that document examination was sufficiently reliable to be admissible when it said, "Following voir dire examination on the admissibility of Ms. Bonjour's testimony, the trial court rejected the defense's arguments that handwriting analysis did not constitute a valid field of scientific expertise. In so doing, the court relied, in part, on Ms. Bonjour's testimony regarding the standards and methodology of handwriting analysis" (33 V. Is. 265, 268–269).

In May of 1999, the Court of Appeals upheld the District Court's exclusion of Professor Denbeaux in *U.S. v. Sunonda G. Paul*, D.C. Docket No. 1:97–CR–-115–1–GET (N.D. GA 1997); 11 Cir No. 97–9302 (1999). That court concluded that "Denbeaux was not an expert on the limitations of handwriting analysis. Denbeaux's background did not qualify him as an expert, and his knowledge of the subject matter was so limited that it was not an abuse of discretion for the district court to exclude his testimony under rule 702."

Some defendants are challenging document examiners without the benefit of an "expert on experts" testifying in their behalf. *U.S. v. Kathleen Kremser Jones*,

880 FS 1027 (E.D. TN 1995); 1997 US Ap LEXIS 3696, 1997 Fed Ap 0082 p, 107 F3 1147 (6 Cir 1997); cert. denied, 117 S Ct 2527 (1997), is such a case. Jones asserted that the expert's testimony was inadmissible under *Daubert v. Merrell Dow Pharm., Inc.*, because it was not sufficiently reliable. The court disagreed. They stated that nonscientific experts are experientially (sic) qualified. Their experience largely is their expertise.

CITATIONS PREVENTING SOME EXPERTS FROM TESTIFYING

Some attorneys have filed motions in limine to prevent document examiners from qualifying in court as expert witnesses. They frequently target document examiners who have a background in graphology. A graphologist is only qualified to testify as a document examiner if she has been trained in document examination. The author has found no case which stated that the fact of having been a graphologist or Graphoanalyst disqualifies a proffered expert in questioned documents or handwriting identification. Only a failure to show positive qualifications in questioned document and handwriting has caused some proffered witnesses to be excluded, while most others have had no difficulty in qualifying as expert witnesses.

People v. Hester, 39 IL2 489, 237 NE2 466 (1968); cert. denied, 397 US 660, 90 S Ct 1408, 25 L Ed 2 642 (1970). A Graphoanalyst was offered to prove a murder victim was in a state of shock when writing the last two words of a note. At 237 NE2 466, 480, the Illinois Supreme Court states, "We believe that the trial court's refusal to allow this witness to give an opinion on the victim's emotional state of mind was well within the court's discretionary powers to exclude proffered testimony which is speculative and therefore incompetent." He had said "being in fear and being startled can possibly be determined by the examination of a particular piece of handwriting." There was no issue of questioned documents or handwriting, and the decision turned not on the witness' qualifications but on the admissibility of evidence deducing one's mental state from handwriting.

Daniels v. Cummins, 66 Misc 2 575, 321 NYS2 1009 (1971). Hanna F. Sulner was plaintiff's expert. She said decedent's signature on deed was genuine but showed "that at the time of signing the deed, she was not of sound mind and did not know what she was doing." Her testimony was not admitted by the trial judge, a ruling upheld upon appeal. There was sound scientific basis for her opinion, both in questioned documents literature and in medical literature, in fact her own book cites many cases allowing such testimony. Apparently, the attorney calling her failed to make a full record in support of admissibility.

Carroll v. State of Arkansas, 276 Ark. 160, 634 SW2d 99 (1982). John Scott was proffered as a defense witness. Admission of an expert witness is largely in the discretion of the trial court who may reject such a witness who is "unable to cite any training or experience that clearly qualified him as an expert with respect to the question at issue."

"Trial court ruled that a proffered defense witness, John Scott, was not qualified as a handwriting expert." Scott had stated he was a Certified Graphoanalyst. However, he was not disqualified for that reason, but because he had no qualification specifically in questioned documents.

People v. Tidwell, 706 P 2d 438 (Colorado App. 1985). The court held, "The trial court did not abuse its discretion in refusing to allow the defendant's proffered witness to testify as an expert concerning questioned document examination." The witness claimed to have "knowledge of graphoanalysis." The record did not show qualification specific to questioned document examination.

State v. Anderson, 379 NW2 70 (MN 1985). Quoted by the dissenting opinion in *Hooten v. State*, 492 S2 948, 958. "We hold the exclusion of a graphological personality assessment. . . was proper." However, the dissenting opinion used the citation to support a contention that a graphoanalyst ought not testify as a questioned documents examiner. *Anderson* was not concerned with questioned documents in any manner.

Arizona v. Livanos, 151 Arizona 13, 725 P. 2d 505 (Court of Appeals 1986). The court of Appeals held that"precluding witness proffered as handwriting expert . . .was not abuse of discretion." The witness "spent substantial amount of time working in area of graphology." This is another case which only stated the proffered witness lacked specific qualifications in questioned documents, though it is misconstrued as saying no graphologist may be a document examiner.

Graves v. State, 547 N.E. 2d 881 (Indiana Appeal 2 District 1989). This 1989 Indiana Court of Appeals affirmed defendant's conviction on forgery and fraud charges, holding that the trial court did not err in refusing to qualify defendant's expert in handwriting analysis. Defendant's witness testified that she was a graphoanalyst, a graduate of the International Graphoanalysis School in Chicago, a member of the International Graphoanalysis Society and the World Association of Document Examiners, and had previously testified as an expert on four occasions. At page 882 the Court states: "Therefore, notwithstanding her previous acceptance as an expert, we conclude the trial court did not abuse its discretion in excluding the proffered testimony based upon an inadequate foundation for the witness's expertise." The object lesson is that the attorney calling an expert witness must be sure to set forth qualifications in full. What the trial court does not hear, the trial court cannot consider as evidence.

Vinci v. Ceraolo, 607 N.E. 2d 1079 Ohio App 8 Dist (1992). The court ruled that the expert was not qualified to testify as an expert and stated: "The record plainly demonstrates that while McKanze received some training in preliminary document analysis and graphoanalysis, he has little, if any, formal training in examining forged signatures. In fact, when questioned by the trial judge, McKanze admitted that graphoanalysis does not involve determining whether a person's signature is genuine or not. Further, his only professional certification does not indicate an expertise in this field. Finally, McKanze was unable to identify any legal proceedings in which he has been permitted to testify as an expert.

Sosa v. State, 841 SW2 912 (TX Ct Ap 1992). Citing *Kelly v. State*, 792 SW2 579 (Ct Ap TX Fort Worth 1990; affirmed, 824 SW2 568 (Ct Cr Ap TX 1992), as to three criteria to prove novel scientific evidence is reliable by clear and convincing evidence, The Court of Appeals upheld the trial court's ruling not to permit a graphoanalyst to compare handwriting, since graphoanalysis is used to determine character traits. At page 916: "The witness, who is the mother of two of the three attorneys who tried this case for the two defendants, is an accountant." The record reflected no specific training or experience in questioned documents.

U.S. v. Bourgeois and Crowe, 950 F.2d 980 (5 Cir 1992). The court rejected the testimony of a proffered handwriting examiner because his training was completed through a correspondence school with its emphasis on graphoanalysis. "Judge Porter was in the position to assess Walker's credibility and to evaluate the conflicting evidence on Walker's qualifications." Contrariwise, using the same information and acting under essentially the same rules of evidence, the trial court found Walker qualified in *First Coppell Bank v. Smith*, 742 SW2 454 (Ct Ap TX Dallas 1987). The finding was upheld upon appeal.

CITATIONS ALLOWING EXPERTS TO TESTIFY

Heller v. Murray, 112 Misc2 745, 447 NYS2 348 (1981); affirmed 468 NYS2 391 (1983). The expert called was a graphoanalyst with certificate from the International Graphoanalysis Society (I.G.A.S.). "Though qualified by this court as an expert on the art and science of graphoanalysis . . . the weight to be given his testimony must be tempered by the fact that the witness is not forensic in his science or art."

Culbreath v. Johnson, 427 S2 705 (MS 1983). Marie B. Hill, graphoanalyst, testified as a handwriting expert. The court agreed with her conclusions and the appeal court upheld it.

Hooten v. State; murder conviction reversed and remanded, 427 S2 1388 (MS Sup Ct 1983); affirmed as modified, 437 S2 410; conviction reversed and remanded, 492 S2 948 (1986); rehearing denied. The trial court did not let Marie B. Hill, graphoanalyst, testify, which was reversible error. At 492 S2 948, pages 949–958, in the dissenting opinion, Justice Hawkins discusses Hill's supposed lack of expertise. However, Justice Hawkins must have had a recurring change of heart, because in *Culbreath* and *Henry* he concurred in all the findings, including that Ms. Hill was fully qualified.

Henry v. State, 484 S2 1012 (MS 1986). At page 1015 it is stated: "It is not necessary that one offering to testify as an expert be infallible or possess the highest degree of skill; it is sufficient if that person possess peculiar knowledge or information regarding the relevant subject matter which is not likely to be possessed by laymen."

Heckler v. State, 503 S2 269 (MS 1987). Trial court would not allow Marie Hill, graphoanalyst, to testify as an expert, but it would admit her as a skilled layman. Defense proffered what her expert opinion would be.

The Supreme Court cites *Hooten v. State* and *Henry v. State* where it upheld Ms. Hill's qualifications as a handwriting expert.

First Coppell Bank v. Smith, 742 SW2 454 (Ct Ap TX Dallas 1987). The court held that the testimony of the handwriting expert was properly admitted. The witness testified that he was experienced in graphoanalysis and had certificates from IGAS and a teaching certificate in forensic scripto-techniques from the Scriptology Institute in Colton, CA. The witness stated that he also had been a questioned document examiner for eighteen years and had testified in a number of courts

Moulton v. State, 486 SW2 234 (TX Cr 1971). It was held that a Graphoanalyst's opinion that two checks had been signed by the same person was sufficient to admit evidence of the second check in prosecution on the first.

Martinez et al. v. Martinez, et al., 123 NM 816, 945 P2 1034 (NM Ap 1997). At trial Plaintiffs called Judith Housley who said the disputed signature was forged and date altered, and she identified the writer. Ms. Housley, the leading document examiner in New Mexico, has a background in graphology. Speaking of Judith Housley's testimony, the Court of Appeal stated: "[T]he trial court expressly determined that Severo had submitted a fraudulent claim to the court and the fraud was established or substantiated by the testimony of an expert witness whom the trial court believed."

In re the Marriage of Ronald F. and Marie Richardson, Ronald J. Richardson, as Executor, etc., Respondent, v. Marie Richardson, Appellant, Fifth Appellate Division, California Court of Appeal, F032260 (2000). In an unpublished opinion, The Court of Appeal stated in reference to Marcel Matley's testimony at trial: "The trial court found, as do we, that Marie forged the letter. We have reviewed the testimony of the handwriting expert and find it credible and unimpeachable." Like Housley, Matley has a background in graphology.

EXCLUSION OF GRAPHOLOGICAL TESTIMONY

The following includes citations supporting nonadmissibility of graphological testimony per se, that is, testimony as to personality or character based on the peculiarities of handwriting. Some have misinterpreted these decisions as implying that one who has studied graphology may not be admitted as an expert in forensic document examination. Some case which have been so misrepresented have already been discussed.

People v. Williams et al., 96 CA Ap 2115, 273 P 1087 (1929). The court in a jury trial rightly refused to permit questions concerning character handwriting analysis to be asked of a forensic handwriting expert.

State v. Davis, 154 AZ 370, 742 P2 1356 (Ap Div 2 1987). A graphologist was not admitted as defendant expert to testify that handwriting showed defendant's insanity. There was no issue of questioned documents involved, although the case is sometimes cited as if there were.

Questions for Graphologists

We have seen how graphologists who have no training in document examination are not qualified to testify as forensic document examiners based upon their graphology training. Before hiring a graphologist to make determinations of authenticity or spuriousness, it is important to ascertain what training qualifies them to give opinions on questioned documents.

1. Have you taken any formalized courses in document examination?
2. What percentage of your work is graphological work?

3. What percentage of your work is document examination?
4. How did you become a questioned document examiner?
5. How much on the job training have you had, with whom and for what period?

ABUSE OF EXPERT WITNESS

Dannals v. Sylvania Township, 255 PA 156, 99 A 475 (1916).

At page 477 The Supreme Court of Pennsylvania stated:"The abuse of the witness by counsel was outrageous and the insulting language was without palliation or excuse.... Witnesses are entitled to the protection of the court. It was not enough for the trial judge to characterize the remarks as highly improper and to instruct the jury to disregard them."

EXAMINATION ON LEADING TREATISES

People v. Hooper, 51 P2 1131 (CA 1935). A document expert may be cross-examined on authoritative treatises which he recognizes or relied on in order to test his competency, but not on direct examination.

Ruth et al. v. Fenchel, 21 NJ 171, 121 A2 373, 60 ALR2 71 (1956). The ALR annotation, by W. A. Shipley, is titled: "Use of medical or other scientific treatises in cross-examination of expert witnesses."

Darling v. Charleston Community Memorial Hospital, 22 IL2 326, 211 NE2 253 (1965). At page 259 The Supreme Court of Illinois stated: "An individual becomes an expert by studying and absorbing a body of knowledge. To prevent cross-examination upon the relevant body of knowledge serves only to protect the ignorant or unscrupulous expert witness. In our opinion expert testimony will be a more effective tool in the attainment of justice if cross-examination is permitted as to the views of recognized authorities, expressed in treatises or periodicals written for professional colleagues. (Cf. Model Code of Evidence, Rule 529.) The author's competence as an expert is established if the judge takes judicial notice of it, or if it is established by a witness expert in the subject."

Ramirez v. State, 815 SW2 636 (Cr Ap TX 1991). An expert may be impeached by use of generally inadmissible hearsay evidence, such as a book, report, or other publication, in order to demonstrate a deficiency in the expert's knowledge.

ADMISSIBILITY OF EXPERT

Janopoulos v. Harvey L. Walner & Assoc. et al., 835 FS 459 (1993), 866 FS 1086 (1994), 1995 US Dist LEXIS 2751 (N.D. IL E.D). The opinions of James Hayes, the defense's document expert were admissible as based on generally accepted tests performed by a second expert, Robert Kuranz. These tests consisted of thin layer chromatography ink analysis and relative age solvent extraction comparison test. These ink tests meet Daubert standards for admissibility.

U.S. v. Acosta, 369 F2 41 (4 Cir. 1966); cert. denied 386 U.S. 921, 17 L Ed2 792, 87 Sup. Ct. 886 (1966). At 369 F2 41, 42, The Court of Appeal said: "On its face, the document examiner's opinion is a firm foundation for the finding of guilt. Handwriting identification can be as certain and dependable as another identification. While handwriting analysis may not be as scientifically accurate as fingerprint identification, it is, on the whole, probably no less reliable than eye witness identification which is often made after a quick glance at a human face."

OPPOSING EXPERTS

According to *U.S. v. Wainwright,* 413 F 2d 796 (1969), though adverse expert witness can be impeached by contrary testimony of another expert, it is improper to seek the opinion of one expert as to the credibility of another expert. While it is perfectly proper to impeach an adverse expert, it is improper to seek an opinion on the very matter which the jury alone must judge, which expert they wish to believe.

Sanchez v. Bay General Hospital, 116 CA App3 776, 172 CA Rpt 342 (1981). Trial court's curtailment of cross-examination on a witness' hospital privileges was proper. At 116 CA App3 776, 794, the court states: "Why Dr. Jeanes had did not have hospital privileges at other specific hospitals was a matter which could consume enormous amounts of time to no enlightenment on the key issues before the court." This might equally apply to inquiry why an expert does or does not belong to associations approved by the cross-examiner.

- An expert must be shown by the party calling him or her to have scientific, technical, or other specialized knowledge.
- A witness may be qualified as an expert by reason of knowledge, skill, experience, training, or education.
- There is no standard training program for document examiners.

PHOTOGRAPHS AS BEST EVIDENCE

Fenelon v. State 195 WI 416, 217 NW 711 (1928); rehearing denied, 195 WI 416, 218 NW 830. After the original document had been destroyed, the court allowed the introduction of photographs of the original to be admitted into evidence. The court opined that comparison with photographs "can as safely be made as with the originals themselves."

COURT CITATIONS RELATING TO HANDWRITING

There are numerous court citations that support the constitutionality of obtaining exemplars from suspects. Prior to 1913 only documents in evidence could be compared with questioned material. This handicapped document examiners since many cases did not have comparable material.

Citations Protecting Defendants

The following are three cases that give defendants protection under the Fourth or Fifth Amendment. The citations reversing these decisions are also included:

U.S. v. Harris, 325 FS 583, 453 F2 1317 (8 Cir. 1972); affirming *U.S. v. Long* sub nom.; cert. denied, 412 US 927, 93 Sup. Ct. 1909 (1972). Reversed by *U.S. v. McNeese*, 361 F2 1100 (E.D. OK 1973).

In re Riccardi, Grand Jury Impaneled November 4, 1970, 337 FS 253 (D.C. NJ 1972). The District Court denied a request for order for compelled handwriting exemplars since that would force the witness to provide evidence against self.

Mara v. U.S., 454 F2 580 (7 Cir. 1971); cert. granted (1972); reversed by *U.S. v. Mara*, 410 US 19, 93 S. Ct. 774, 35 L Ed2 99 (1973). Reversed in conjunction with *U.S. v. Dionisio*, 410 US 1, 93 Sup. Ct. 764 (1973).

CITATIONS SUPPORTING REQUEST WRITING

In 1967 several rulings were made that determined that request writing exemplars are identifying characteristics and are not protected by the Fourth or Fifth Amendment. *Gilbert v. California* covered the Fifth Amendment and *Katz v. U.S.* discussed the Fourth Amendment. The following are citations supporting the constitutionality of taking exemplars:

Gilbert v. California, 63 CA2 690, 47 CA Rptr 909, 408 P2 365; cert., 384 US 985, 16 L Ed2 1003, 86 S. Ct. 1902; remanded, 87 S. Ct. 1951, 18 L Ed 2 1178, 388 US 263 (1967).

Katz v. U.S., 389 US 347, 88 S. Ct. 507, 19 L Ed2 576 (1967). There is no constitutional protection for what a person routinely and knowingly exposes to the public.

Warden, Md. Penitentiary v. Hayden, 387 US 294, 87 S. Ct. 1642, 18 L Ed2 782 (1967). This case covers obtaining evidence from an incarcerated person.

U. S. v. Doe (Devlin), 405 F2 436 (2 Cir. 1968). A witness was found in contempt for refusing to provide handwriting exemplars.

U.S. v. Vignera, 307 FS 136 (S.D. NY 1969). This case involves taking handprinted samples as opposed to handwritten ones.

U.S. v. Doremus, 414 F2 252 (6 Cir. 1969). The defendant had an absolute right not to incriminate himself by testifying, but once he voluntarily took the stand, he had to answer all questions relevant to the issues.

U.S. v. Doe, 321 FS 10 (D.C. NY 1970). The defendant may be required to write at different writing speeds.

U.S. v. Rudy, 429 F2 993 (9 Cir. 1970). A page 994 the court stated: "We hold that handprinting is within the handwriting rule of *Gilbert*."

U.S. v. McGann and Pruitt, 431 F2 1104 (5 Cir. 1970); cert. denied, *Pruitt v. U.S.*, 401 US 919, 27 L Ed2 821, 91 S. Ct. 904. Requiring the accused to provide handwriting exemplars does not violate the privilege against self-incrimination.

In the Matter of the Grand Jury Impaneled March 1, 1971, 348 F S 1001 (C) (D.C. OH 1972). Requiring the accused to furnish handwriting exemplars does not violate the privilege against self-incrimination. Government reasonably showed connection between requiring handwriting exemplars and the purpose to be served, thus there is no violation of the Fourth Amendment.

U.S. v. Doe (Schwartz), 457 F2 895 (2 Cir. 1972); stay granted, 406 US 954 (1972); cert denied 410 US 941, 93 Sup. Ct. 1376 (1972). Exemplars are not testimonial. Request for literatim exemplars is proper.

U.S. v. Mara, certiorari granted, 406 US 956; 410 US 19, 93 S Ct 774, 35 L Ed2 99 (1973), reversing *Mara v. U.S.*, 454 F2 580 (7 Cir. 1971)."Handwriting, like speech, is repeatedly shown to the public—and there is no more expectation of privacy in the physical characteristics of a person's script than there is in the tone of his voice." See also *U.S. v. Dionisio.*

U.S. v. McNeese, 361 F2 1100 (E.D. OK 1973). *Harris v. U.S.* no longer has effect.

U.S. v. Dionisio, 410 US 1, 93 Sup. Ct. 764 (1973). In grand jury proceedings, compelled handwriting exemplars involve no violation of the Fourth or Fifth Amendments.

U.S. v. Hopkins, U.S. v. Jackson, 486 F2 360 (9 Cir. 1973). Requiring the accused to furnish handwriting exemplars does not violate the Fourth and Fifth Amendments.

U.S. v. Lincoln, 494 F2 833 (9 Cir. 1974). Requiring the accused to furnish handwriting exemplars does not violate the Fourth and Fifth Amendments.

In re Fernandez, In Proceedings Before a One-Man Grand Jury, 31 CT Sup 53, 321 A2 862 (1974). Requiring a witness to furnish handwriting exemplars does not violate either Fifth of Fourth Amendment privilege.

U.S. v. Hawkins, 501 F2 1029 (9 Cir. 1974); cert. denied, 107 L Ed2 141, 110 S. Ct. 186. A civil contempt citation for a second refusal to give court-ordered exemplars is not a violation of the privilege against double jeopardy.

U.S. et al. v. Campbell, a/k/a Holliday, 390 FS 711; 524 F2 604 (8 Cir. 1975). Handwriting exemplars are not testimonial or communicative but are physically identifying.

Paine v. McCarthy, 527 F2 173 (9 Cir. 1975). This federal decision upheld the state court decision in *People v. Paine*, that stated that handwriting exemplars do not violate federal constitutional rights.

U.S. v. Hayes et al., 388 FS 470 (W.C. PA 1975); affirmed without opinion, 521 F2 1399 (3 Cir.). No error occurred when the defendant was required to furnish handwriting exemplars by copying the text of incriminating letters alleged to have been written by him.

In re Palmer, Palmer v. U.S., 530 F2 787 (8 Cir. 1976). The Grand jury's request for exemplars from a witness was enforceable by the district court.

U.S. et al. v. Rosinsky, 547 F2 249 (4 Cir. 1977). Since exemplars do not violate Fourth or Fifth Amendment, "a witness under administrative summons may be compelled, subject to certain restrictions, to give handwriting exemplars." An IRS summons is like a grand jury summons and includes power to compel handwriting exemplars. For a contrary ruling, see *U.S. v. Brown*, 398 FS 444 (E.D. MI 1975); reversed in part and affirmed in part, 536 F2 117 (6 Cir 1976).

State v. Doe, 78 WI2 161, 254 NW2 210 (1977). The witness was found in contempt and sentenced to 60 days in county jail for his refusal to provide court ordered handwriting exemplars in John Doe proceeding. There was no violation under the Fourth or Fifth Amendments or under the state constitution or under what the Fourteenth Amendment imposes on the state.

Christian v. U.S., *Moody v. U.S.*, *Clark v. U.S.*, 394 A2 1 (DC Ap 1978). A grand jury may subpoena a suspect in order to secure his or her fingerprints and handwriting exemplars.

U.S. v. Euge, 587 F2 25 (8 Cir 1978); certiorari, 441 US 942, 99 S Ct 2159, 60 L Ed2 1044; reversed, 444 US 707, 100 S Ct 874, 63 L Ed2 141 (1980); reh. denied, 446 US 913, 100 S Ct 1845, 64 L Ed2 267. The compelling of handwriting exemplars by the IRS is not search or seizure under Fourth Amendment nor testimonial under the Fifth.

U.S. v. Cotner, 657 F2 1171 (10 Cir. 1981). Requiring the accused to furnish handwriting exemplars does not violate Fourth or Fifth Amendment privileges.

U.S. v. Waller, 581 F2 585 (6 Cir. 1978); cert. den. 439 US 1051, 99 S. Ct. 731, 58 L Ed2 711. Headnote 1 states: "Defendant's writings on yellow pad, seized after defendant took flight from trial, were not privileged communications, where writings were not intended as confidential communications between attorney and client and where writings were used only for comparison with signatures on checks after defendant had refused to provide police a sample of his handwriting."

U.S. v. Richardson, 755 F2 685 (8 Cir. 1985). Defendant's Fourth and Fifth Amendment rights were not violated by compelled backhand exemplars.

U.S. v. Hollins, 811 F2 384 (7 Cir. 1987). At page 387 the court stated: "A handwriting exemplar is neither a search nor seizure under the fourth amendment.... Nor is a handwriting exemplar testimonial evidence subject to the fifth amendment privilege against self-incrimination."

U.S. v. Jacobowitz, 877 F2 162 (2 Cir. 1989); cert. denied, 107 L Ed2 141, 110 S. Ct. 186. Headnote 5 summarizes: "Handwriting exemplars may be taken of possible aliases or other potentially incriminating names and defendant's refusal to comply may constitute circumstantial evidence of guilt."

U.S. v. McVeigh, 896 FS 1549 (W.D. OK 1995). The District Court rejected nine arguments by Defendant why the Government ought not be allowed to take handwriting exemplars from him. However, if he refused, not much could be done against him. Civil contempt would be futile and criminal contempt too costly; besides he was already in jail and had no money to pay any fines.

VALID GROUNDS FOR REFUSING TO PRODUCE EXEMPLARS

These citations offer some protection for witnesses and defendants.

U.S. v. Bailey, et al., 327 FS 802 (N.D. IL 1971), 332 FS 1351 (N.D. IL 1971). The grand jury needs reasonable grounds for obtaining exemplars.

U.S. v. Cassell, et al., 452 F2 533 (7 Cir. 1971). The defendant should have been given the Miranda warning first.

U.S. v. O'Kane, 439 FS 211 (S.D. FL 1977). A witness can refuse to give handwriting exemplars to a grand jury and can have a judge decide the issue.

U.S. v. Holland, 552 F2 667 (5 Cir. 1977). The District Court must have jurisdiction before it can order the defendant to provide exemplars.

Sanchez v. Attorney General, 93 NM 210, 598 P2 1170 (Ct Ap 1979). The District Court lacked the authority to require defendant to produce exemplars.

CONTEMPT OF COURT

The courts can hold defendants in contempt for refusing to comply with a court order to supply handwriting samples.

U.S. v. Askew a/k/a Kelley, 584 F2 960 (10 Cir. 1978); cert. denied, 59 L Ed2 94, 99 S. Ct. 1054.

U.S. v. Doe (Devlin), 405 F2 436 (2 Cir. 1968).

U.S. v. Rudy, 429 F2 993 (9 Cir. 1970).

U.S. v. Mara, 10 CR L 2235 (7 Cir. 1971), 410 U.S. 19, 93 S. Ct. 774, 35 L Ed2 99 (1973), reversing Mara v. U.S.

U.S. v. Roth, U. S. v. Kephard, 466 F2 1111 (9 Cir 1972); cert. denied 409 US 1048, 34 L Ed2 500, 93 S. Ct. 540 (1972). At 466 F2 1111, 1114, The Court of Appeal said: "After indictment, the government moved for an order compelling the execution of handwriting and handprinting exemplars by each defendant." The order was granted.

U.S. v. Stembridge and Stembridge, 477 F2 874 (5 Cir. 1973). Allowing a defendant to disguise handwriting samples is similar to permitting refusal.

U.S. v. Hawkins, 501 F2 1029 (9 Cir. 1974); cert. denied, 107 L Ed2 141, 110 S. Ct. 186. It was not double jeopardy to find the defendant guilty of contempt of court after the defendant refused to provide exemplars on two separate occasions.

INFERENCE OF GUILT

Various courts have stated that the refusal to comply with court-ordered exemplars can infer that the defendant is guilty. The following cases uphold the right of the prosecution to argue defendant's implied guilt.

U.S. v. Doe (Devlin), 405 F2 436 (2 Cir. 1968).

U.S. v. Campbell, 732 F2 1017 (1 Cir. 1984)).

U.S. v. Jackson, 886 F2 838, 28 Fed Rules Evi Serv 1141 (7 Cir. 1989).

U.S. v. Stone, 9 F3 934 (8 Cir. 1993).

U.S. v. Brown, 156 F3 813 (8 Cir. 1998).

EVIDENCE OF DISGUISE

The prosecution can also argue that a disguised exemplars by the defendant is an indication of guilt.

U.S. v. Wolfish, 525 F2 457 (2 Cir. 1975); cert denied, 96 S. Ct. 794 (1976).

U.S. v. Shively, 715 F2 260 (7 Cir. 1983); cert denied 79 L Ed2 233, 1104 S. Ct. 1001.

U.S. v. Jackson, 886 F2 838, 28 Fed Rules Evi Serv 1141 (7 Cir. 1989).

U.S. v. McDougal, 137 F3 547 (8 Cir. 1998).

U.S. v. Izzi, 427 F2 293 (2 Cir. NY 1970); cert denied 399 US 928, 26 L Ed2 794, 90 S. Ct. 224.

U.S. v. McGann and Pruitt, 431 F2 1104 (5 Cir. 1970); cert denied, Pruitt v. U.S., 401 US 919, 27 L Ed2 821, 91 S. Ct. 904).

Handwriting examiners are allowed to testify that handwriting is disguised. The following cases support the admissibility of such testimony.

U.S. v. Izzi, 427 F2 293 (2 Cir. NY 1970); cert denied 399 US 928, 26 L Ed2 794, 90 S. Ct. 224.

U.S. v. Wolfish, 525 F2 457 (2 Cir. 1975); cert denied, 96 S. Ct. 794 (1976).

U.S. v. Shively, 715 F2 260 (7 Cir. 1983); cert denied 79 L Ed2 233, 1104 S. Ct. 1001.

U.S. v. Hollins, 811 F2 384 (C) (7 Cir. 1987).

U.S. v. Blankey, 581 F2 1389 (10 Cir. 1978). The defendant can be cross-examined on his refusal to provide exemplars.

POST LITEM MOTAM

Writings made after a controversy arose may not be used by the party who wrote them to collaborate his testimony.

Hickory v. U.S., 151 US 303, 14 Sup Ct 334, 38 L Ed 170 (W Dis AR 1894); reversed and remanded, 160 US 408, — L Ed 474 (1896). Hickory had offered a writing he made at trial as evidence he did not make the questioned writing. The Supreme Court upheld the trial court's refusal to admit it. The Court quoted *King v. Donahue*, 110 Mass. 155: "A signature made for the occasion *post litem motam* and for use at the trial ought not be taken as a standard of genuineness." The reason is given in a quote from *Williams v. State*, 61 Ala. 33: "It would open wide a door for fraud if a witness was allowed to corroborate his own testimony by a preparation of specimens of his writing for the purpose of comparison."

U.S. v. Jones, 20 Blatch 235, 10 F 469 (Cir Ct S.D. NY 1882). The defendant was not permitted to introduce a writing made in the presence of the jury in order to prove that he had not written an incriminating letter.

OBSTRUCTION OF JUSTICE

Elliott v. U.S., 385 A2 183 (DC Ap 1978). A twin gave court ordered handwriting exemplars in place of his brother and was convicted of obstruction of justice. The conviction was upheld. His brother had agreed to go to the police station to provide exemplars, and in his own criminal trial he was proven to have signed documents relating to stolen credit cards.

U.S. v. Oberhellmann, 748 FS 1344; reversed, 946 F2 50 (7 Cir. 1991). A conviction of one attorney for forging another attorney's name to withdrawal from the case was reversed since it was not proved beyond a reasonable doubt that it had obstructed justice. However, the appeal court speaks sternly of both attorneys' behavior, as the one whose name was forged had improperly taken a file out of a law office from which he had been fired and then settled the case. The Court said the defendant might be prosecuted under other provisions of the law and sent the opinion to the state bar to take close look at both attorney's actions.

U.S. v. Valdez, et al., 16 F3 1324 (2 Cir. 1994). At page 1135 the court states: "There are few better examples of a classic obstruction of justice than a defendant who refuses to give handwriting samples when compelled by a subpoena. His disguise of his handwriting made difficult the comparison of his writing with that in the drug transactions notebook seized by the government, thus hindering the government in its investigation."

Appendix

RECOMMENDED READING

To learn more about the field of document examination, the following books are recommended:

Frank Abagnale, author of *Document Verificationand Currency TransactionsManual*, is a consultant to federal and local law enforcement agencies and financial institutions. This manual contains chapters on hot checks, forgeries, government checks, counterfeit money, traveler's checks/money orders/credit cards, driver's license and plate display, and armed robbery/short-change artist.

Russell and Ralph Bradford's *Introduction to Handwriting Examination and Identification* offers a good foundation in handwriting identification, that is particularly strong in areas not normally covered by other document examination books. The book covers the Bradford System, which is a simplified method of classifying and filing, searching and identifying check writers of nonsufficient checks, no account checks, and forged fictitious checks.

Wilson Harrison, author of *Suspect Documents,* was an English pioneer in the field of document examination. His book contains a wealth of information pertaining to the field of document examination. The book was written in 1958, and republished in 1981, but the information remains timely.

Scientific Examination of Questioned Documents, written by Ordway Hilton, covers a broad spectrum in the field of document examination. Ordway Hilton writes in his preface, "This book is a guide to all aspects of a questioned document for attorneys, investigators, document examiners, and others."

Roy A. Huber and A. M. Headrick have done meticulous research and quote extensively from their sources in *Handwriting Identification: Facts and Fundamentals.* The authors rely heavily on other writers' material, bringing together a rich comparison of ideas from respected leaders in the field and others not as well known.

DemonstrativeEvidence is a self-published book by Katherine Mainolfi Koppenhaver, which covers exhibit preparation for court or deposition in cases involving handwriting.

Red Flags on Forged Checks, Forgery Detection and Defense by Joe Lucas, discusses how to detect forged and fraudulent checks.

Marcel Matley's *QDE Index* lists published articles related to document examination since 1900. The book is well-organized, and contains over 2,650 entries. It also contains a section on court citations.

Marcel Matley also wrote *Reliability Testing of Expert Handwriting Opinions* which contains valuable information about testing the hypotheses of identification and elimination.

Albert Osborn is considered the father of document examination and his book, *QuestionedDocuments,* is considered the field's bible. This book was first written in 1910 and reprinted in 1929. The principles of document examination that were espoused by Albert Osborn are still the guiding principles for modern document examiners.

Edna W. Robertson authored the *Fundamentals of Document Examination.* This book is concise and easy to read.

The effects of various medication on handwriting are covered in *Drugs and Handwriting,* by Patricia Wellingham-Jones, R.N.

RESOURCES

DOCUMENT REPAIR
Northeast Document Conservation
Center, 100 Brickstone Square
Andover, MA 01810
(978) 470-1010
(978) 475-6021
www.nedcc.org

FORENSIC PHOTOGRAPHERS
David Leibman, CDE
981 S. Quail Street
Norfolk, VA 23515
E-mail: david1@Sybercom.net

Forensic Document Examiners
William Koppenhaver
403 Haslett Rd.
Joppa, MD 21085
(410) 679-8257
Fax (410) 538-8548
www.ForDocExam.com

FORENSIC IMAGING
Richard T. McEvoy, Jr.
P.O. Box 597
Victor, NY 14564-9998
(716) 924-9410
Fax (716) 924-8854
www.forensicimaging.com

HISTORICAL DOCUMENTS & RARE BOOKS
Kenneth W. Rendell
Box 9001
Wellesley, MA 01760
Phone (617) 431-1776
Fax: (617) 237-1492

INK EXPERTS
Speckin Laboratories
Eric Speckin, BA Chemistry
4121 Okenos Road
Okenos, MI 48864
(517) 349-3528
(888) 999-1009
www.4n6.com

LABORATORY SERVICES
McCrone Associates
850 Pasquinelli Drive
Westmont, IL 60559
(630) 887-7100
FAX: (630) 887-7417
www.mccrone.com

MAIL-ORDER BOOKS
Graphex
Dr. Ellen Bowers
P.O. Box 20175
Columbus, OH 43220-0175
(614) 457-9034
www.graphex-books.com

PAPER INSTITUTE
Institute of Paper Science and
Technology
500 10th St. N. W.
Atlanta, Georgia 30318-5749
1-800-558-6611
www.ipst.edu

RESEARCH MATERIAL
Handwriting Analysis Research
Library
(HARL) 41 Washington St.
Greenfield, MA 01301
(413) 774-4667
Curator: Bob Bachman

RESEARCH SERVICES
Marcel Matley, MA Library Science
P.O. Box 882401, 1846 39th Ave.
San Francisco, CA 94188
Phone (415) 753-2832
1-800-367-8403
MMatley@aol.com

WATERMARKS
Spencer Dandyroll Factory
P. O. Box 1430 Holyoke, MA 01041
78 North Canal St.
Holyoke, MA 01040
Ph: (413) 532-1525

DOCUMENT ORGANIZATIONS

ABFDE
American Board of Forensic
Document Examiners
Forensic Sciences Foundation,
Inc.7887 San Felipe #122
Houston, TX 77063
Members: 232

AFDE
Association of Forensic Document
Examiners
Members: 30

ASQDE
American Society of Questioned
Document Examiners
Members: 110

IAQDE
Independent Association of
Questioned Document Examiners
Members: 175

NADE
National Association of Document
Examiners
Katherine M. Koppenhaver, CDE,
President
P.O. Box 324
Joppa, Maryland 21085
NADE Toll-free # 1-866-569-0833
E-mail: PresidentNADE@aol.com
www.documentexaminers.org
Members: 140

NQDA
Patricia Johnson
3530 Forest Lane
Suite #155
Dallas, TX 75234
214-351-3668
Fax: 214-351-5412
1-800-960-1034
Members: 30

WADE
World Association of Document
Examiners
111 N. Canal St.
Chicago, IL 60606
312-930-9446
Members: 200

OTHER ORGANIZATIONS

ABFE, ACFE
American Board of Forensic
Examiners
American College of Forensic
Examiners
2750 E. Sunshine
Springfield, MO 65804
417-881-3818
Fax: 417-881-4702
Members: 12,000

NFC
The National Forensic Center
17 Temple Terrace
Lawrenceville, NJ 08648
Betty Lipscher
609-883-0550
800-526-5177
Members: 5000

EPIC
Evidence Photographers International
Council
600 Main Street
Honesdale, PA 18431
717-253-5450
Fax: 717-253-5011
1-800-356-3742
Members: 1000

Glossary

Abecedarium: the "a," "b," "c," names given to our alphabet.
Abrasion: method used to erase ink, graphite, or other markings from the writing surface.
Absorption: method by which paper soaks liquid ink into its fibers.
Accidental: abnormal stroke caused by the writer being jolted or bumped when writing or by a similarly occurring accident.
Adhesion: method of transferring material from a writing instrument onto paper.
Airstroke: traces of ink made when the pen is lifted slightly from the paper, which leaves a light trail of ink as the writer moves the pen to the next writing position.
Alignment: arrangement of writing on a page.
Allograph: writing or signature done by an individual for someone who is incapable of writing on his own.
Alphabet: system of writing using letters to represent sound.
Ambidextrous: able to write with both hands.
Ampersand: symbol used as an abbreviation for the word *and.*
Angle: an abrupt change of direction of the writing stroke.
Angle Value: measurement of the degrees of the angle of letters as they ascend from or descend to the baseline.
Annotations: notes in the margin of a manuscript.
Arcade: arch-like strokes in writing usually in the joining strokes.
Arch: a curved structure that spans an opening. In handwriting, this term refers to formations such as the letter *"m."*
Arm: a short horizontal or diagonal stroke on a letter originating from the stem.
Arrangement: the manner in which words are organized on documents such as checks, letters, and envelopes.
Ascenders: strokes of letters that ascend above the middle zone of the minuscule or lowercase letters ("b", "d", "f", "h", "k", "l", "t").
Autograph: from the terms "auto" meaning self and "graph" meaning write. To sign one's name or one's signature.
Bar: arm or limb of letters used in the construction of letters such as t-bars and cross-bars on "H" and "A."

Baseline: the ruled or imaginary line on which letters sit. It refers to all letters except those with lower loops.
Blob: refers to an ink spot as a result of the pen resting on the paper momentarily before continuing the writing act.
Block letters: handprinted capital letters.
Blunt stokes: untapered strokes as a result of the pen resting on paper before movement begins or when the writer stops writing.
Body of a letter: main part of the letter without lead-in, terminal strokes, or diacritics.
Buckle: indentation on downstroke of printed "R" and "B" and written "K."
Burr striations: marks made with a ballpoint pen creating gaps in the writing line.
CertifiedDocument Examiner: a forensic document examiner recognized by his peers as an expert in his field.
Chain of Custody: maintaining control and accountability for evidence. This term also can be referred to as chain of possession.
Chirographer: a writer.
Chirography: art of writing, or handwriting.
Class characteristics: handwriting characteristics common to a group of people, usually those who have been taught a particular system of penmanship.
Comparison Charts: charts containing side by side material to show similarities or differences of handwriting features.
Connecting strokes: strokes that join letters together in cursive writing, also known as ligatures.
Consciouslywritten: awareness of the act of writing on the part of the writer; paying close attention to the act of writing.
Cross mark: mark made by a person unable to write his signature.
Curriculum vitae: Latin term for life experiences. Summary of credentials supporting an area of expertise.
Cursive movements: connecting the letter forms.
Cut and paste: Refers to documents that have had material manipulated by excising and placing it in a different location, generally for the purpose of placing a genuine signature on a fraudulent document.
Demonstrative evidence: exhibits made from questioned documents, exemplars, and standards that support a witness' opinion.
Descenders: parts of letters that descend below the baseline ("f", "g", "j", "p", "q," and "y").
Desktop forgery: fraudulent documents produced on a personal computer system.
Desktop publishing: documents produced using a computer system that consists of a computer, scanner, and printer.
Deviations: in genuine writing, the normal variations in the writing of an individual. In forged writing, the differences from the known writing.
Dextrality: a preference for using the right hand.
Diacritic: mark used over letters such as an i-dot, or accent mark used in foreign alphabet systems to indicate a specific pronunciation of a letter, such as, acute, grave, circumflex, tilde, umlaut, breve, macron or cedilla.
Disguised writing: writing with an attempt to conceal the writer's identity by changing characteristics of writing.
Divergence: deviation from the copybook standards.

Document: any material on which a permanent or semipermanent message can be imprinted.
Elements: the constituent parts of letters and figures.
Embellishment: ornamentation that is not necessary to the design of letters of the alphabet.
Eradication: to erase or remove material from a document.
Escapement: the pitch or spacing of the letters in typewriting.
Exemplars: handwriting samples known to be the writing of an individual.
Exhibit books: booklets containing exhibits used as demonstrative evidence to support a witness' testimony; also called jury books.
Exhibits: documents produced and displayed during a trial or hearing to support the facts.
Expert witness: anyone who is qualified by experience or study which enables him to form definite opinions of his own representing a division of science, branch of art, or department of trade.
Extraneous material: unnecessary material that may clutter a document; also called background noise.
Eyelet: a small loop used in the formation of letters.
Facsimile machine: a machine that changes an image into electronic data that can be transmitted over the telephone wires and reconstructed.
Fax: abbreviation for facsimile. Refers to the document that has been transmitted over the telephone wires via a facsimile machine.
Familial characteristics: handwriting characteristics shared by members of a family.
Feathered strokes: serrated lines on letters.
Filiform script: cursive writing that trails into a line without distinguishable letter forms, resembling a thread or filament; also called thready writing.
Finger movement: using the fingers to manipulate the writing instrument.
First generation photocopies: photocopy made from an original document. Each succeeding generation is made from the previous copy.
Flourish: embellishment of letters by decorative strokes.
Flowback: result of one line of ink crossing another where the ink runs back over the line.
Fluency: or fluidity. Smooth flow of the writing line.
Foot: the part of the letter that rests on the baseline; also called the base of the letter.
Forensic: pertaining to the courts.
Forensic Document Examiner: handwriting analyst who makes determination about the authenticity of handwriting.
Forensic science: the application of scientific techniques to detect and prosecute crime.
Forgery: the fraudulent making or altering of a document.
Form: the shape of the letters.
Formal exemplars: request writing samples.
Freehand: writing without guidance. A freehand simulation is one in which the forger copies the letters without tracing them.
Fugitive ink: ink that appears on a document when it is altered or photocopied.
Garland: shallow u-strokes of writing used primarily to connect letters in a word.
Glob of ink: refers to an ink spot as a result of the pen resting on the paper; see blob.
Goop or gooping: phenomenon caused by ballpoint pens when they go around a curve in writing. The ink collects on the ball of the pen and is dispersed onto the paper in an excessive amount on the writing line.
Graphic maturity: level reached when all writing movement is made from the habituated neuromuscular patterns.

Graphoanalysis: registered trademark for a specific course on handwriting analysis.
Graphologist: anyone who studies handwriting; commonly used to describe an analyst who determines the personality of the writer from his handwriting.
Graphology: the study of handwriting; commonly used to describe the determination of personality from handwriting.
Graphonomics: the study of the science and technology of handwriting.
Grip pressure: amount of force used to hold the writing instrument.
Guided Hand: supporting and steadying an infirm writer's hand while writing.
Hand movement: using the hand to manipulate the writing instrument.
Handprinting: a system of printing letters by hand that are not connected. Also called manuscript writing and printscript.
Handwriting: the style of writing of an individual.
Handwriting analyst: a person who identifies handwriting.
Handwriting characteristics: the features or qualities found in handwriting such as slant, spacing, letter forms, size, proportions, and alignment.
Handwriting expert: another name for a document examiner.
Handwriting system: a copybook method of writing where penmanship system is taught.
Headline: the imaginary line the average tops of the letters reach.
Hiatus: spaces or breaks between letters in a word.
Hieroglyphics: word-syllabic writing system developed by the Egyptians consisting of pictographs or ideograms to represent words.
Holograph or hologram: handwritten document prepared entirely in the handwriting of the person who signed it.
Holographer: one who studies handwriting.
Holographic will: a will prepared entirely in the handwriting of the person whose signature it bears.
Holography: the science of handwriting analysis.
Hook: a spontaneous small curve made as part of a letter, usually at the beginning or end of the letter.
Horizontal alignment: the arrangement of letters in relation to the baseline of writing.
Horizontal bar: a stroke made parallel to the baseline as part of the letter ("A", "E", "F", "H", "T").
Ideographs: ways of expressing ideas using pictures.
Individual characteristics: characteristics in handwriting that deviate from the standard method of writing as taught in penmanship systems.
Informal exemplars: documents previously executed and known to be genuine.
Initial strokes of writing: the first or beginning strokes in a document.
Ink: the liquid used in pens to produce writing.
Ink eradicator: chemical used to bleach or remove ink.
Inscriptive movements: the movements used to create letter formations.
Intersection: the point where two lines cross each other.
Italic: writing based on Roman writing, usually written on an angle.
Junction: the meeting of two lines that do not cross.
Jury Book: a book of exhibits prepared to support a witness' testimony.
Kiting: "floating" checks and deposits between two or more accounts, to give false representation of funds.
Known signatures: signatures that are genuine samples of a person's writing.
Labored writing: writing produced with difficulty or strain.

Legible: writing that is capable of being read.
Letter of opinion: a letter stating the evaluation of questioned documents by an expert.
Ligatures: the connecting strokes between letters in cursive writing.
Limb: the lower part of a letter, also called the leg.
Line quality: the visible record of the line showing the skill level of the writer by its smoothness or irregularity.
Line value: also known as line quality, this term refers to the smoothness of the writing line.
Loop: two opposite curves united at one end in a turn and at the other end in an intersection. Letters are composed of upper loops and lower loops.
Lower loop: the loop of a letter that descends below the baseline and then returns to the baseline ("f", "g", "j", "p", "q", and "y").
Lower zone: the area below the baseline containing letters that descend below the baseline.
Macrophotography: the photographing of small objects at close range.
Majuscule: an uppercase or capital letter.
Manuscript writing: another term for handprinting.
Margins: the area between the edges of the paper and the written text.
Mark: an identifying sign made by someone who is illiterate.
Master pattern: all of the handwriting habits of a writer.
Medial letters: the letters located in the center of a word.
Metagraphy: symbols understood even though they have no conventional counterpart in speech. For example, footprints to illustrate walking or sawing wood for snoring. Punctuation marks are also metagraphic.
Micrographia: small writing.
Microphotography: photographs taken through a microscope.
Microscope: a precise optical instrument that magnifies images.
Middle zone: the area immediately above the baseline containing the lowercase letters that do not have ascenders; see minuscule.
Minuscule: lowercase letters ("a", "c", "e", "i", "m", "n", "o", "r", "s", "u", "v", "w", and "x")
Model signature: a genuine signature used to copy or trace a fraudulent signature.
Movement: a method in which the writing instrument is moved across the paper. Movement can include the finger, hand and wrist movement, or full-arm movement.
Mylar folder: a clear plastic folder used to protect documents from harm.
Opinion: the conclusion of an expert witness.
Opposite-hand writing: writing with the unaccustomed hand.
Original: the source document containing the actual handwriting and/or signature(s).
Oval: body of the small circle letters.
Paleography: methods of recording ancient languages on papyrus, paper, and wax; also the study of ancient writing.
Palimpsest: refers to legal, historic documents that contain writing over an erased manuscript.
Paragraphy: see *metagraphy.*
Paraph: another name for a rubric or underscore.
Patching: the retouching strokes of writing, usually by a forger who wants to improve the appearance of the writing.
Pen lifts: the unnatural places where the pen is lifted from the paper.
Pen position: the position the pen is held during the act of writing.

Pen pressure: the force with which the pen is in contact with the paper.
Penmanship: the art of teaching form, proportion, joining, and placing according to certain rules of the letters of the alphabet, words, and lines of handwriting.
Pictographs: symbols that represent objects.
Pictorial effect: the appearance of the writing.
Pixels: small individual dots that make up a picture in a computer image.
Pressure: the grip of the writer on the writing instrument and the force of the writer as he presses the writing instrument against the paper.
Pressure patterns: the patterns created when the writer varies the pressure of upstrokes and downstrokes.
Printscript: hand-printed letters that are not connected; see handprinting.
Proportion: the relationship in height and width of the letters in relation to each other particularly uppercase and lowercase and looped and non-looped letters.
Provenance: the history of a document.
Punctuation: the marks used in writing to separate ideas such as phrases and sentences. These include periods, dashes, brackets, parenthesis, colons, semi-colons, commas, hyphens, apostrophes, and quotation marks.
Questioned document: a document whose authenticity is being questioned; also called a suspect document.
Range of writing: the normal variations found in an individual's handwriting.
Request writing: handwriting samples made at the request and under the supervision of the police, document examiners, managers, or attorneys for comparison with questioned writing.
Retainer: an advance payment used to engage the services of a professional.
Reticles in optics: fine measuring lines in the focus of optional instruments. Some magnifiers and microscopes have them built in, others do not.
Rhythm: the even return to the baseline by a writer.
Rubric: a flourish under or after a name written as a signature. Ancient meaning was a red ornamental letter at the head of a division of a manuscript.
Safetypaper: specially designed paper containing features that reveal any alterations made to the document.
Sans serif: literally means "without lines," this is any typeface that doesn't have a serif.
Scanner: a device that inputs images into a computer.
Self-forgery: the deliberate attempt to disguise one's signature in order to deny it later.
Serif: additional lines at the bottom of a letter or at the end of curves on type styles that have nothing to do with the basic letter formations.
Sheet protectors: clear plastic sheets used to protect documents from damage.
Signature: the writing of a person's name by that person to enter into a contract or to identify the signer.
Similarities: resemblances between like letter forms.
Simplified letterforms: letter forms without ornamentation or extraneous strokes. Letters reduced to their most basic forms.
Sinistrality: a preference for using the left hand.
Skill level: the ability or competence of a writer to control strokes.
Skilled witness: a person who possesses special knowledge and experience in a technical field.
Slant: the angle of writing in relationship to the baseline; also known as slope.
Spacing: the distance between letters, words, and lines of writing.

Spoliation: the destruction or alteration of a document by a person not authorized to do so.
Spur: a short straight writing stroke in letters.
Spurious: something that is not genuine.
Staff: basic downstroke of a letter, also known as the shank or stem.
Standards: typewriter samples used for comparison with questioned typewritten samples.
Stem: the portion of a letter that consists of a vertical line such as the letter, “l”.
Stereoscopic microscope: a binocular microscope used for three-dimensional viewing.
Terminal spur: a hook at the end of a word.
Terminal stroke: the final or ending stroke of a letter or word.
Thready writing: see *filiform script.*
Tics or ticks: the short straight lines not consciously made that form an sharp angle with a letter but are not part of the form of the letter usually found at the beginning or end of the letter form.
Topline: The imaginary line to which the average tops of the looped letters reach.
Tops of letters: A curved top can be called a crown and an arch; also known as a crest, tip, or apex.
Trace: copying by following lines of a model.
Traced signature: a signature that is made by copying directly from a genuine signature.
Trash marks: the marks left on a photocopy as a result of a blemish from a photocopier.
Tremor: shaky or corrugated lines caused by slow writing either as a result of difficulty in writing or an attempt to forge.
Truncate: a banker’s term for not returning canceled checks to customers.
Tyvek: a tough, tear-resistant paper used primarily in envelopes, made by Dupont.
Uncial: manuscript writing that omits the joining of letters.
Upper extenders: the extensions on letters that arise above the middle zone of writing.
Upper zone: the area above the middle zone of writing that contains the extenders of upper zone letters. (“b”, “d”, “f”, “h”, “k”, “l”, “p”, “t”).
Variations: the natural changes in letter forms in a person’s writing.
Viscosity: ink having a high resistance to flow.
Watermark: an identifying mark placed on paper by a dandyroll during the manufacturing process.
Whole arm movement: the use of the entire arm to manipulate the writing instrument, usually seen on blackboard writing.
Wrist movement: the use of the wrist to manipulate the writing instrument.
Writing: the act of communicating through placing letters and words on paper in one’s own hand.
Writing environment: the circumstances under which writing is produced.
Zones of writing: the methods of distinguishing areas of writing. There are three zones: upper, middle, and lower zones.

Bibliography

Abagnale, Frank. *Document Verification and Currency Transactions Manual.* Washington, DC.: Abagnale and Associates, 1994.

Abagnale, Frank. "Twelve Ways to Detect Bogus Checks," *Real Estate Today*, Jan. 1983, pp. 29–32.

Baker, J. N. *Law of Disputed and Forged Documents.* Charlottesville, VA: The Mitchie Company, 1955.

Bradford, Russell R., and Ralph B. Bradford. *Introduction to Handwriting Examination and Identification.* Chicago: Nelson Hall, 1992.

Brunelle, Richard, and Robert Reed. *Forensic Examination of Ink and Paper.* Springfield, IL: Charles C. Thomas, 1984.

Conway, James. *Evidential Documents.* Springfield, IL: Charles C. Thomas, 1959.

Dyer, Harry ed. *1991 Lockwood-Post's Directory of the Pulp, Paper and Allied Trades.* San Francisco. Miller Freeman Publications, 1990.

Ellen, David. *The Scientific Examination of Documents.* Great Britain: Taylor and Francis, 1997.

Flynn, William J. "Paper Mate's New Erasable Ink Pen," *Journal of Police Science and Administration*, Vol. 7, No. 3, 1979, pp. 11–14.

"Forensic Science Foundation, Inc. 1979 Directory of Diplomates, Forensic Science Certification Program," Jan. 1979.

Gerhart, F. James. "Methods of Associating Typewriter Ribbons and Correcting Tapes with a Questioned Text," *Journal of Forensic Sciences*, Vol. 34, No. 5, Sept. 1989, pp. 1183–1195.

Gifis, Steven H. *Barron's Law Dictionary.* New York, NY: Barron's Educational Series, Inc., 3rd edition, 1991.

Hamilton, Charles. *Great Forgers and Famous Fakes.* New York, NY: Crown Books, 1980. (Out of print.)

Harrison, Wilson. *Suspect Documents.* Chicago, IL: Nelson Hall Publishers, 1981.

Hilton, Ordway. *Scientific Examination of Questioned Documents.* Boca Raton: CRC Press, 1982.

Huber, Roy A., and A. M. Headrick. *Handwriting Identification: Facts and Fundamentals*. Boca Raton: CRC Press, 1999.

Kelly, Jan Seaman. *Significant Dates of Modern Typing Methods*. Houston, TX: The American Board of Forensic Document Examiners, Inc., 1993.

Kilty, Lee A. "Numbers," *The NADE Journal*, Vol. 11, No. 3, Aug. 1990, pp. 12–28.

Koppenhaver, Katherine Mainolfi. *A Selection of International Penmanship Systems*. Joppa, MD: Forensic Publishers of Joppa, 1992.

Koppenhaver, Katherine Mainolfi. *The Business of Document Examination*. Joppa, MD: Forensic Publishers of Joppa, 1991.

Koppenhaver, Katherine Mainolfi. *Demonstrative Evidence*. Joppa, MD: Forensic Publishers of Joppa, 1996.

Koppenhaver, Katherine Mainolfi. *Evaluating Evidence*. Joppa, MD: Forensic Publishers of Joppa, 1991.

Koppenhaver, Katherine Mainolfi. *How To Be a Credible Witness*. Joppa, MD: Forensic Publishers of Joppa, 1992.

Koppenhaver, Katherine M. "Reducing Losses From Forged and Fraudulent Checks," *The NADE Journal*, Aug. 1991, Vol. 12, No. 3, 1–11

Lehman, Dorothy V. "Questioned Document Examination," *American Jurisprudence, Proof of Facts*, 3rd series, Vol. 15. Rochester, NY: Lawyers Cooperative Publishing, 1992, pp. 595–693.

Lucas, Joe. *Red Flags on Forged Checks, Forgery Detection and Defense*. Joppa, MD: Forensic Publishers of Joppa, 1995.

Marks, Lynn Wilson. "Forensic Identification of Handwriting,"*American Jurisprudence, Proof of Facts*, 3rd series, Vol. 27. Rochester, NY: Lawyers Cooperative Publishing, 1994, pp. 489–659.

Matley, Marcel. *QDE Index*. San Francisco, CA: Handwriting Services of California, 1990.

McAlexander, Thomas V. "Handwriting Opinion Terminology," presented at the 35th Annual Conference of the American Society of Questioned Document Examiners, 1977.

McAlexander, Thomas V., Jan Beck and Ronald M. Dick, "The Standardization of Handwriting Opinion Testimony," Presented at the 42nd Annual Meeting of the American Academy of Forensic Sciences, Cincinnati, Ohio, Feb. 19–24, 1990.

McCarthy, J. F. "Some Aspects of Normal Behavior: Their Use in Understanding Problems Encountered by Document Examiners," *Journal of Forensic Science*, Vol. 21, No. 1, Jan. 1976, pp. 201–207.

Mehta, M. K, *Identification of Handwriting and Cross-Examination of Experts*. S. Hackensack, NJ: Fred B. Rothmam and Co., 1970. (Out of print.)

Nickell, Joe. *Pen Ink and Evidence*. Lexington, KY: The University Press of Kentucky, 1990.

O'Hara, Charles E. *Fundamentals of Criminal Investigation*. 5th edition. Charles L. Thomas, Publishers, 1980.

Osborn, Albert S. *Questioned Documents*. 2nd edition. Chicago, IL: Nelson Hall Publishers, 1929. (Originally published 1910.)

Rapp, Burt. *Check Fraud Investigation*. Port Townsend, WA: Loompanics Unlimited, 1991.

Rendell, Kenneth. *Forging History*. Norman OK: University of Oklahoma, 1994.

Robertson, Edna, W. *Fundamentals of Document Examination.* Chicago, IL: Nelson-Hall Publishers, 1991.

Rychlak, Ronald J. *Real and Demonstrative Evidence, Applications, and Theory.* Charlottesville, VA: The Mitchie Company, 1995.

Saudek, Robert. *Experiments with Handwriting.* Sacramento, CA: Books for Professionals, 1978.

Sternitzky, Julius L. *Forgery and Fictitious Checks.* Springfield, IL: Charles C. Thomas, 1955.

"They Write Their Own Sentences." The FBI Handwriting Analysis Manual. Boulder, CO: Paladin Press, 1987.

Wellingham-Jones, Patricia. *Drugs and Handwriting.* Tehama, CA: PWJ Publishing, 1991.

Index

About the Author

KATHERINE M. KOPPENHAVER is a Certified Document Examiner and a Diplomate of the National Association of Document Examiners (NADE), of which she is currently president.